The New Hungarian Quarterly

VOLUME VI * NUMBER 20

WINTER 1965

NEW DEVELOPMENTS IN THE HUNGARIAN ECONOMY

I. TOWARDS A NEW SYSTEM OF GUIDANCE IN THE SOCIALIST ECONOMY

by

JÓZSEF BOGNÁR

I

Since the close of the post-war reconstruction period (1948), the Hungarian economy has completed a rapid process of growth which took place amidst radical structural changes. The momentum of this growth is indicated by the fact that per capita income has increased to 274 (1949 = 100), real wages to 170, foreign trade turnover per capita of the population to 271 dollars, and the contribution of industry to national income to 61.6 per cent (1949 = 49.9 per cent).

Agricultural production increased on an average to 124 (1949 = 100) during the five years from 1960 to 1964, and the ratio of the rural population to the total population fell below 30 per cent (1949 = 50.1 per cent).

At the start of industrialization, Hungary lacked capital and raw materials, and had a labour surplus both in the cities and the countryside. Hence, the increase in production had to be assured first through increasing the number of those employed. This type of industrialization and economic development is known as extensive.

The factors that have marked the industrialization period can only be understood under the special conditions imposed by the cold war, the American economic blockade and embargo. Industrialization had to assume an import-replacing character. Before 1953 this was true of developments in the national economy; after 1953, it was valid only if applied to the Comecon, the economic community of the European socialist countries.

Where you have extensive, import-replacing industrialization, production costs are relatively high (the labour force is still inexperienced, and it is necessary to introduce the manufacture of certain goods which cannot yet be mass-produced), technical development does not keep pace with demand, and the rapidly developing internal market immediately absorbs everything produced. Another characteristic of the period of extensive development is the neglect of auxiliary, complementary and secondary investments. This has an unfavourable influence on productivity. Our present problems will be eliminated through replacing extensive with intensive development. Instead of economizing on imports the emphasis is now on increasing economically produced exports.

The change in the type of development has been necessitated by the exhaustion of labour reserves. Further increase of production must be accomplished primarily by increasing efficiency. The question of economically produced exports has become significant because Hungary is an import-sensitive country. This means that its imports, due to the lack of raw materials, rise faster than its national income. Between 1959 and 1964, each 1 per cent increase of national income was accompanied by a 1.5 per cent increase of imports. Assuming that the balance of payments is in equilibrium, a 5 per cent per annum increase of national income (which may be considered desirable and realistic in Hungary), requires an 8 to 9 per cent increase in exports. The share of exports in the national income is already 34 per cent today, and according to reliable estimates this will increase to between 40 and 41 per cent by 1970. Under such circumstances, wastefully produced exports reduce the distributable portion of the national income, and this can lead to a decrease in investments or a fall in the standard of living.

If there is an essential change in the proportion of the sources of production increase to one another as well as in the normal position of the national economy in its relation to the world economy, we can speak of a new tactical period of economic growth. In the new tactical period, the very planning methods, value relationships, economic motives, and incentive factors which fostered economic growth in the previous period, now hamper it and slow it down. In the new tactical period, we can certainly base ourselves on the technological and infra-structural achievements of the past, but we must make thoroughgoing changes in the field of management and economic administration.

2

In central planning, consideration must be given to the requirements of both the domestic and the foreign market. In order to achieve economic growth and assure equilibrium, the plan must foresee developments which will occur independent of it (e.g., demand on the world market, the introduction of new technological principles in production, population increase etc.). It must take into consideration the internal movement of the sectors and economic units that play a part in the national economy, stimulate the economic units to act in accordance with the interests and objectives of society, and distribute the bulk of the investments in accordance with up-to-date demands; but it is not realistic to prescribe in detail the functioning of the various economic units, i.e., production processes, purchases and sales.

The administration of the economy must limit itself primarily to basic questions. Otherwise management loses its effectiveness in over-departmentalization.

In today's economy the number of interdependent factors is so large and the indirect, collateral, and derivative consequences of economic decisions so complex that even an administration that thinks in the broadest categories can scarcely hope to anticipate them all.

The increased complexity of the economy is caused by the multiplicity of industrial production, the establishment of a whole series of new branches of industry, and at the same time an increase in the number of enterprises. Obviously, it is extremely difficult to get an all-over picture of the investments, purchases, sales, technological premises, wage relations and financial connections of so many enterprises. In a simple economy there is seldom more than one method of attaining an objective. In a developed economy similar objectives may be attained in various ways.

In a complex economy, the number of influences, reciprocal effects and collateral and derivative consequences stemming from central economic decisions are multiplied. To keep pace accurately with these processes in an economy whose branches are increasingly interdependent, we would have to extend the planning apparatus six to eightfold within a decade.

Finally, in this many-echeloned system of economic administration, it takes a long time for information to reach the top; the pressure of time then limits the capacity of management to make decisions, and time is again lost before the decisions reach the enterprises. As a result, by the time the decision is carried out, the conditions which obtained when the information was first imparted and the decision was taken, have already changed (i.e., deteriorated).

It is obvious that even a central administration that functions as well as possible cannot make allowances for all the immediate reactions of its economic units (the enterprises) to market impulses. At this point, however, the impulses that affect an enterprise do not reflect the objective economic processes operating in the market, because:

a) the enterprise is acting in a "conditioned environment" (with prices divorced from value—an out-dated method of measuring the functions of enterprises, the formal character of plan indices, etc.),

b) numerous economic organizations, bureaux, and administrative boards come between the market and the productive enterprises.

In consequence, those market impulses which do make themselves felt are transmitted through so many agencies that an immediate and accurate reaction is scarcely possible.

The impulses of which we speak here come from such processes as supply and demand, changes in demand, changes of price on the world market, competition in the world market, etc.

The enterprise may react to these impulses accurately if :

a) the impulses that reach the enterprise reflect objective economic processes in the market,

b) reaction to the impulse brings the enterprise profit and ignoring it brings loss,

c) the enterprise has the freedom, the means, and the flexibility to adapt itself to a changing situation.

(Might I remark parenthetically that in the very fast changing economic conditions of our times, flexibility is one of the chief criteria of the proper functioning of an enterprise.)

It is obvious that each enterprise should be granted enough independence to be able to react directly and correctly to market impulses.

The central bureaux, on the other hand, must restrict themselves to deciding basic questions (grand strategy in developing the economy, integration of economic and non-economic factors, economic structure and investments, broad concepts of technological development, optimum solutions in coordinating with the international division of labour, etc.), with a view to long-term (15 to 20 years) or shorter-term (3 to 7 years) planning.

3

Most of the ideas put forward by both the Soviet economist Liberman and the Czechoslovak economist Sík have my support. Both concepts testify to considerable intellectual courage, for it is always harder to drop one's native dogmas than those of other social systems, epochs, or distant countries.

The ideas of Professor Ota Sík and his collaborators cover more ground; they lay down a new coordinated system for the planned direction of national economy.

I also hold that in a centrally directed economy it is not enough to try to solve problems of individual enterprises or their individual incentive systems; for basic economic policy decisions are taken by the leaders of party and state.

There is no doubt that the concepts and way of thinking of the leaders (in a certain sense one may apply the term leading stratum) as expressed in institutions, principles of operation and personal conduct, play a large part in determining the spheres of economic activity.

After the assumption of power and the great achievements of the reconstruction years, this stratum displayed practically unqualified optimism. In other words, they overestimated the quantitative results which could be attained within a certain period through their own measures, while underestimating the objective difficulties of economic growth. They often expressed the opinion that the obstacles in development could be removed simply through their direct, continuous, personal intervention.

This was a period in which the personal direction of the economy prevailed, rather than guidance through coordination.

This period is over. The leaders' way of thinking, perspective and style have developed considerably, especially in the higher and medium echelons.

The fact that the new system of guidance involves a thorough decentralization of the central spheres of authority seems to me a very important factor.

I might point out in this connection that in the case of widespread decentralization, the indirect power of the central organs is not reduced but increased.

The question of power cannot be separated from the results attained in carrying out the main objectives of a system. If the central administrative organs hold great power of decision in their hands and yet economic growth is unsatisfactory, then—in an economic sense—we can speak only of bureaucratic but not of actual power.

The actual power of the central administrative organs will increase in proportion to the more effective preparation of decisions—through the involvement of a wide scientific apparatus—and in proportion to the more thorough discussion of the problems—through involvement of the whole population.

4

In the socialist economy, the enterprises are relatively self-supporting, collective economic units which produce merchandise and mutually exchange the results of their production processes. They are also the basic units of the social division of labour, which satisfy through use values (definite products) the requirements of other enterprises and the demands of the population. When the sphere of authority of the enterprises is extended in such a way that they are enabled to react directly to market impulses, all direct and indirect methods of economic management are affected. The ability to react directly to market impulses greatly increases the responsibility of the enterprise and its management. Elements of risk are involved in every decision of the management, and if a series of incorrect decisions is made and it manoeuvres itself into an untenable position, reorganization of the enterprise must be undertaken.

This additional responsibility requires raising the standard of management (more selectiveness in staffing, continuous training of management executives, salaries scaled to the success of the enterprise), and extending democracy within the plant. These two objectives must be achieved step by step and parallel with one another.

At the same time the public has to be educated on the economic situation, to ensure a cooperative attitude as their part. This must be done consistently and in respect to various problems, including that of foreign trade; the workers are more likely to assume responsibilities when they understand not only their own tasks but the larger picture as well.

The principle of socialist democracy must be put into effect not only in the political and social life of the country but in the national economy as well.

Socialist democracy in national economy demands that :

a) every citizen should receive regular information on the economic situation of the country, on the results achieved and on the difficulties to be coped with,

b) every worker, in his capacity as member of some economic unit (an enterprise, a producers' cooperative) should be enabled regularly to express his views about the plans, projects and working methods of his economic unit, its relationship to other economic units, and the fulfilment of its basic tasks (satisfaction of consumer demands).

It can be seen from the foregoing that we would like the Hungarian economy to be directed and managed more expertly, on the basis of a more informed scientific approach, and more democratically, through broader cooperation from the people.

We are convinced that know-how and democracy are by no means mutually exclusive in a socialist society. On the contrary, they are mutually indispensable.

II. REFORM OF THE ECONOMIC MECHANISM

An interview with REZSŐ NYERS,
Secretary of the Central Committee of the
Hungarian Socialist Workers' Party*

Q: What are the factors that have necessitated a reform of the system of economic administration and what does this concept actually imply?

A.: The system of economic administration—or, to use a more current term, the economic mechanism—is an interrelated system of the means, methods and institutions of planned economy that serves to realize the aims of economic policy. It comprises economic planning, price control, financing, credits, investments, inter-firm relations and contracts, wages and material incentives; supervision of the firms' activities, division of jurisdictions and regulation of the right to dispose of the means of production as between firms and supervisory bodies; collective participation in the management of the economy.

The methods, means and institutions listed above are intricately interrelated in their functioning. The essential requirement is that they should be in harmony with the basic features of socialist production relations as well as with the stage of development of the means of production, and that they should best serve to realize the current socio-economic targets. These preconditions make it clear that the economic mechanism is undergoing —and must undergo—constant change. Although these changes are taking place continuously, from time to time requirements accumulate that call for comprehensive and concerted reforms. Such a stage has now been reached in Hungary.

Our system of economic administration is thus not regarded as a category independent of time and place but as one that must at times be adjusted to meet the tasks deriving from the economic situation. It was the recognition of this fact that prompted us already in 1957 considerably to modify the then existing mechanism. Planning methods were rendered more

* From the April 25, 1965, number of *Népszabadság*, daily of the Hungarian Socialist Workers' Party.

flexible, compulsory delivery of agricultural produce was abolished, the system of profit sharing introduced. The changes proved to have been in the right direction. Ever since, we have in effect continued to modify various administrative forms that had become ripe for change. A few facts will illustrate the continuous character of this work. In 1959 a general adjustment of producers' prices was carried out and a system of price cuts and clearance sales was introduced in domestic trade; in 1959 and 1961 a basic system of technical development was established in industry; in 1962 and 1963 large industrial combines were brought into being; 1964 saw the introduction of interest charges on capital. All these reforms have had a positive effect. An adherence to outdated methods was avoided. On the basis of the experiences hitherto gained we must now prepare for more important and comprehensive steps.

What is it that has necessitated the comprehensive reform now begun? Briefly, the following:

The reserves for extensive development in our national economy are rapidly decreasing and a more accelerated transition to intensive development has become inevitable. For a long time the main source of increase in national income was the increase of the available labour force; from now on this role must be taken over by technical development. Both the "economic gauge" and the system of incentives must, accordingly, be revised.

The scientific and technical revolution which is taking place all over the world is bringing about speedy changes in the productive forces of society. Demand too is growing and changing at a swift rate both in external and internal markets. Considerably greater flexibility will therefore be needed in production and trade alike.

Now that socialist production relations prevail in all branches of the national economy, greater flexibility in the economic mechanism has become possible. To complete the building of socialism, on the other hand, a large-scale increase in economic efficiency is required, and this, in turn, imposes increasing demands on economic administration.

Development of the productive forces thus necessitates a reform of the economic mechanism because, as a consequence of the changed situation, the two have to a certain extent come into conflict with each other. The fruitful debates which have been taking place in Hungary as well as in other People's Democracies on various problems of economic administration and of socialist political economy have also greatly contributed to recognition of the need for change.

Q.: To our knowledge, preparatory work is already in full swing. Who are those participating and how are they proceeding?

A.: Some time ago already we undertook to clarify certain fundamental questions of principle. Here, a major role fell and still falls to the Study Group on Economic Theory, working under the direction of the Central Committee of the Hungarian Socialist Workers' Party. Within this study group, questions pertaining to closer cooperation between science and production, the formation of prices and the appropriate price types, the more accurate measurement of national income, the role and measurement of costs in agriculture, interest on capital, and several other important subjects were thoroughly discussed. These debates provided a suitable basis for the work now in progress by generalizing the practical experiences and passing them through the theoretical "sieve."

Extensive and concrete preparatory work got under way after the December resolution of the Central Committee. With the participation of some 130 economists, engineers, jurists, industrial and commercial experts, and research workers, eleven work teams have been set up to investigate the various problems of economic administration. The work teams will also request the assistance of outside experts for the study of individual problems. The circle of those participating is thus comparatively wide already at this initial stage, and will further widen as the work proceeds.

The work teams are to deal with the following subjects:

Economic planning and role of the plan in economic administration;

methods of management of industrial, building and commercial enterprises, transport services, and state farms, including studies on how to integrate them more effectively into the national economy and what their relations should be with the state organs and with one another;

better coordination of planned economy, autonomy and internal democracy in the farmers' cooperatives;

improvement of methods of planning and financing in foreign trade; increased influence of foreign-trade considerations on the activities of productive and commercial enterprises;

development of domestic trade and, in general, problems pertaining to the supply of the population with goods and services;

the price system and price control in all branches and sectors of the national economy; the role of prices and the most effective methods of price formation;

wages and labour relations; increased material incentives;

problems concerning the determination, preparation and realization of investments, together with the principal questions connected with the management of fixed capital;

increased influence of the economic mechanism in raising the technical level of production;

   activities of the local councils in the sphere of economic administration and their material interest in the sound functioning of the
enterprises;

   methods of increasing the participation of the labouring masses in
economic administration.

The problems listed above show that the tasks facing the individual work
teams are closely interrelated, even overlapping. This overlapping ensures a
study of each set of problems under several aspects and in several contexts,
thereby facilitating the ultimate emergence of a coherent system of proposals.

The work teams will now proceed to an elaboration of the proposals,
based on the preceding critical analyses and on the experiences gained in
other socialist countries, to the extent that they are applicable to Hungarian conditions. The proposals worked out by a number of eminent
scientists and economic experts upon the request of the Party will be
equally helpful. The work teams will also pay attention to papers and
articles on the subject published in the press, whose number is likely to
increase in the future.

The results of experiments being carried out by several enterprises will
also be used. From what has been said it must be clear that already in
the preparatory stage the work was based on collective experience. As the
work proceeds, those affected and interested will be given ample opportunity
to discuss the more important details of the proposals to be worked out.

Q.: When are the proposals likely to be adopted and the measures
put into operation?

A.: The guiding principles of the reform of the economic mechanism will
probably be submitted early next year to the Central Committee of the
Party. To the extent that they are approved by this body, they will be
presented to the competent state organs as the proposals of the Party.
Before this stage is reached, however, a great deal of work remains to be
done. A whole range of possible variants will have to be subjected to many-
sided analysis. The work carried out so far has already proved that it would
be most unrealistic to expect a complete and comprehensive system of
proposals ready for acceptance and implementation to spring from the
heads of a few experts in the way Pallas Athena is said to have sprung from
the head of Zeus. It often happens that the solution of one problem gives
rise to new ones in some other domain. We were, therefore, compelled to
adopt a more painful but more expedient method: that of many-sided

analysis, exploratory and expert debate and constructive summing-up. It is to be hoped that before the end of this year the proposals concurred in by most of the experts will have taken shape. These will then be ready for more extensive discussion.

The proposals are expected to give a clear outline of an economic mechanism that will lend itself to a more successful implementation of our economic policies, at the same time furnishing the basic ideas concerning the period of transition, during which the mechanism will be gradually introduced. All that can be said at present is that the proposals to be worked out will be put into practice step by step within the next few years. Among the proposals already put forward some can naturally be realized without comprehensive reform of the existing mechanism since they evidently conform to the trends of development we envisage. There is no reason to delay their implementation.

It is impossible to exaggerate the importance of the reforms now in preparation. At the same time, our interest should not be excessively concentrated on them at the present juncture. They are meant to serve the future—a not too distant future, it is true—and cannot be considered a substitute for present-day economic efficiency. "Critical analyses" and "proposed reforms," important though they are, cannot take the place of material goods, or of income—whether at the level of the enterprise or at the national level. Neither criticism nor reforms can be distributed according to an annual plan, or sold over the counter instead of goods. Yet in 1965 and 1966 already, the country will need more goods, a greater volume of foreign trade and an increased national income. Better work organization and more efficient utilization of available means of production constitute urgent targets that cannot be replaced by anything else.

Q.: You mentioned that upon the request of the Party proposals have been submitted by scientists and economic experts, and that experiences gained in other People's Democracies and utilizable in this country will also be taken into consideration. What are the principal trends in these proposals and experiences?

A.: As regards the main trends, our own ideas are largely in harmony with the experiences gained abroad, though inevitably there will be divergent opinions as regards practical application. The principal trend of the reforms may be summed up as follows: like most of the socialist countries, we too are striving to achieve a more effective correlation between central planning on the one hand and the commodity-money relationship on the other. To approach the optimum of economic development it will be necessary to restrict the scope of the direct (authoritative and administrative) regulation of economic processes and to ensure a broader application of commercial methods and of the socialist interpretation of the commodity-money relationship.

It is undoubtedly necessary to strengthen the directing role of the national economic plan by divesting it of the task of minute regulation and enabling it to concentrate on the most important aspects of the national economy. The individual enterprises must, moreover, be made increasingly independent, with a concomitant increase of their responsibilities. Nor is the former conceivable without the latter.

Such a more flexible system of management will considerably facilitate the fulfilment of the yearly targets of the current plans. It will at the same time enable the central administration to concentrate to a higher degree than before on elaborating and designating the concepts of long-term development and to give greater emphasis to long-term planning.

The solutions to be sought must be such as to make the further development of the planned economy instrumental in bringing about a differentiation in the management methods of the individual industrial sectors and enterprises. It is inadmissible to subject industry as a whole to the same rules. Already now methods that are expedient in one of the industrial sectors prove unworkable or outright harmful in another.

What we have in mind is not just the reform of economic methods and the issuing of regulations—it is equally import nt that these measures should find a favourable response among the workers and employees. The fate of even the most constructive proposals and resolutions depends on the extent to which the workers realize that their efforts on behalf of society also serve their individual welfare.

No panacea can, of course, be invented for all our ills—nor are we trying to invent one. We are well aware that only disciplined work and a spirit of initiative can bring good results and that, in the future no less than in the past, higher living standards can only derive from work. We expect the reform of economic administration to lead to a quickened realization of the Party's economico-political aims and to improved conditions for more fruitful work.

III. NEW ASPECTS OF THE PROFIT INCENTIVE

ECONOMIC MODEL AND MATERIAL INCENTIVES

by

BÉLA CSIKÓS NAGY

One of the most widely debated and yet insufficiently clarified problems of socialist economy is that of material incentives. In what organizational framework do people work according to their best ability in a socialist economy? What preconditions must be realized in order that people will find themselves in circumstances that will stimulate them to contribute toward planned development on the basis both of their socialist consciousness and their material incentives? These are complicated questions, to which we have often given erroneous answers that were based on wrong hypotheses. From time to time, we sharply criticized existing forms of incentive and placed all our hopes on new forms just suggested.

Once again the mechanism of material incentives is being re-examined. Are we not again faced with the danger of exaggeration in both directions? Such a possibility is not excluded. But this time the approach to the problem is more fortunate and acceptable to scientific thinking. We are now in a position to deal with the question of material incentives comprehensively, in the general context of the socialist economic mechanism.

In earlier years, when the question was asked in what direction material incentives should operate in a socialist economy, many (including the author of this study) gave the following answer: towards the fulfilment and over-fulfilment of the State economic plan. This answer was based on the hypothesis that the socialist economy is free of problems and that planning has a ready solution for everything. Once we have the plan, all we have to do is to set to work to realize it.

It was on this basis that we confronted capitalist market economy with socialist planned economy, instinctiveness with consciousness, anarchy with purposefulness. Today we know that socialist planned economy is a kind of commodity economy to which the relations of commodity exchange apply. We also know that planning and other current methods of regulating the economy often disregard the conclusions that have to be drawn from this fact. There is therefore no justification for limiting the concept of socialist planned economy to the mechanisms already existing in socialist countries. In principle, we have to recognize that when society abolishes private property in the means of production, it has the possibility of choosing between a variety of economic measures and institutions.

The criteria of the model variants of the socialist economy may be formulated in several ways. Years are still needed before this question can be satisfactorily clarified through scientific discussion. It is usual to distinguish between the centralized and the market model. But the experiences gathered during a critical analysis of the economic mechanism indicate that it would perhaps be more correct to take as the two opposing basic models of socialist planned economy that of natural economy and that of commodity economy. By natural economy we mean an economy where—in its classical form—products are exchanged directly against products, that is to say, without the intermediary of money. Our present economic mechanism may be described as one which is still burdened with numerous elements of natural economy although in our economic system we use the categories of market economy (money, trade, price, credit); however, this tendency is hidden, which makes it difficult to fight it.

Let us again put the question as to the aim of the workers' material incentives? After what has been said, the answers are bound to be divergent. The aim of material incentives obviously depends on the nature of the economic model. The material incentives have to serve a different economic purpose in a system of natural economy than in a system of commodity production.

In a system of natural economy (direct exchange of products) it is supposed that the regulation of production according to needs can only be realized through central socialist State planning, preferably down to the minutest detail. Under such conditions, material incentives have to induce:

workers at the bench to work at a satisfactory intensity and rhythm,

managers to fulfil the plan at maximum efficiency.

The incentives corresponding to these requirements are those which concentrate on piece-rate wages, as well as premiums for the fulfilment of production plans and of plans for the reduction of costs.

However, if the socialist planned economy is to be realized through a real commodity economy, it is presumed that central State planning is confined to fixing the principal proportions of reproduction on an enlarged scale and the principal outlines of the economy, whereas the detailed regulation of production may only take place operatively, through the system of commodity and pecuniary relationships between the enterprises. In this case the incentives must serve to interest the workers in achieving maximum efficiency in their own plant by way of adjustment to the market relationships of supply and demand.

The incentives corresponding to this requirement are those which concentrate on securing a maximum profit for the enterprise.

It is necessary to emphasize that in the last resort it is the method of the regulation of production and not the form of the material incentives that decides whether the socialist planned economy has the character of a natural economy or of a commodity economy. A change in the form of the material incentives does not in itself affect the character of the mechanism. On the contrary, if its character is that of a natural economy, and the material incentives are those of a commodity economy, then the contradiction between planning methods and incentive will result in more disadvantages than advantages. For in such a case the material incentives would bring about tendencies towards commodity production in the absence of an actual background of commodity exchange. Our present economic problems arise in part from the fact that the inner harmony of the economic model has not been satisfactorily assured.

GROSS INCOME AND PROFIT INCENTIVE

The debate on the economic mechanism now going on in the socialist countries includes a discussion of the concrete form to be given to incentives based on income in a planned economy based on fuller application of commodity and money relationships. Two prototypes of such an incentive have come to the fore—one based on gross income, the other on the principle of encouraging maximum profit in each enterprise.

Gross income incentive arises when the State taxes the gross income and the enterprises dispose of the income left after taxation in accordance with the relevent regulations. The workers' wages, the social and cultural expenses, and the investments are thus paid from gross income.

Profit incentive, on the other hand, arises when the wage fund is set aside separately within the gross income, and profits remain, in whole or in part, at the disposal of the enterprises. Workers' rewards and premiums, social-cultural expenses and investments are financed from profits in line with the relevant regulations.

The principal features of incentives based on gross income are:

1) Wages are proportionate to accomplishment, and the amount due per unit of accomplishment depends on the gross income of the enterprise.

2) The organic connection between the wages of the workers and the economic results achieved by the enterprise permits a reduction of individual incomes from one year to the other, and in principle this is inevitable whenever the economic results deteriorate.

3) If personal income depends on the gross income of the enterprise, then the same work is of necessity differently rewarded in the various enterprises.

The profit incentive shows the following fundamentally different features:

1) The wages paid for the total product are independent of the total value of the commodities produced. The work carried out according to technological prescriptions—in line with quantitative, qualitative and time factors—is paid for on the basis of predetermined wage rates. In the case of this type of incentive, a deterioration in economic efficiency does not reduce the gross income but the profits, and may even put the enterprise in the red.

2) Income is regulated through two independent systems, that of wage regulation and that of profit regulation.

Both these forms of material incentive, or at least certain elements of each, are present in the Hungarian economic mechanism today. The material incentive of the cooperative farms is based on gross income, while workers in State-owned industry share in the profits of their enterprise.

The material incentives applied in the cooperative farms are based on cooperative ownership and the peculiarities of agriculture. Cooperative ownership is group ownership. Therefore, the personal income of the members of the cooperative farms cannot be regulated by the State's wage policy. But apart from this, in agriculture personal income was always organically connected with the results of production. In the long run the crops are influenced by natural factors, and this is reflected in income relationships. In itself this is not considered as something bad by the peasantry, as is shown by the fact that they often prefer wages in kind, a form of sharecropping. The unequal distribution of incomes is also in accord with the traditional income relationships in agriculture, resulting historically from differences in the quality of land and proximity to the market and the extensiveness or intensiveness of farming. The State, through its taxation policy, has so far been able to influence this only to a very small extent.

In agriculture, the dual character of the small producer of commodities (owner-labourer) united in one and the same person responsibility for labour fulfilment and for risk. In large scale industry these two were separated from the very beginning. Already under capitalism, the line dividing the mechanism of wages and that of capitalist profit was clearly drawn. Nobody found it strange therefore that, when we established our socialist economy, we maintained in State-owned industry the categories, developed under capitalism, of wages and of economic calculations (production costs, production budgets, profitability). In 1957 we introduced profit-sharing by the workers as a new incentive. Still, it cannot be asserted that in the State-owned industry material incentives are centred on profits. On an average, only 4 to 5 per cent of workers' income comes from profit sharing. The managers and leading employees of the enterprises also receive a premium which may in certain cases reach 40 per cent of the basic income. But the present system of premiums is frequently built on a multiplicity of indices, on a broad system of compulsory prescriptions, on the realization of specific tasks.

Coordination of material incentives with the requirements of a commodity-producing economy undoubtedly calls for a change in the system of premiums in industry. The managers of the enterprises must have a substantially free hand in judging who among their workers should be rewarded, and on what basis. And the premium of the managers must not contradict, or even deviate from, the essential form of the material incentives. The only question is whether this harmony should be brought about on the basis of gross income or of profits.

In judging this question, one may assume that it is not absolutely necessary to apply the same incentives to the entire economy. The fact that in cooperative farms the incentive is related to gross income, while in State-owned industry it is related to profits, does not cause any problems. On the contrary, this difference expresses the divergent characteristics of the two domains of material production, and they should be left intact, especially in a commodity-producing economy.

In the cooperative farms the endeavour to achieve a maximum gross income is based on objective social and economic facts.* This effort also has a powerful influence on the peasantry's views regarding profitability. For the cooperative farms a given amount of land is available and cannot be changed. The amount of the population to be maintained on it may also be considered as fixed. Under these circumstances, the farmers have an objective interest in achieving a higher annual gross income through more intensive utilization of the available land and more rational utilization of the labour force. Various investigations show that the cooperative farms (and even the

* See Gyula Varga: A Cooperative Village, The New Hungarian Quarterly, Vol. 6, No. 19, Autumn 1965.

small private holdings) determine crop rotation and develop the structure of production on the basis of achieving the largest possible gross income. Their material interest in this end leads the peasantry to judge various agricultural products according to the degree to which these maintain a given population (assured employment) on a given area. The State's price policy has to take this into account if it wants to exercise an effective influence on the decisions of the cooperative farms.

In industry, the situation is different. The processing activities of Hungarian industry depend to a considerable extent on the importation of raw materials. Our foreign exchange is largely the result of industrial exports. It is therefore especially important that we should measure labour efficiency in terms of the complicated inter-connections of the modern industrial structure. For this we need modern forms of economic cost accounting. Every category of value here should serve to advance economic foresight. This calls for harmony between State regulation of income and the workers' material incentives. This harmony can most favourably be brought about through the profit incentive.

PROFIT INCENTIVE AND ECONOMIC MECHANISM

Almost a decade ago a group of Hungarian economists advocated a link between economic incentives and the index of profits in State-owned industry, because this index was a synthetic reflection of all the partial indices of the plan. They pointed out at the same time that the index of profits (profitability) may not always unequivocally express the quality of the work done in a way suitable for comparison, because of shortcomings in the price system. To harmonize the general interests of society and of the individual enterprise through the profit incentive, thus became one of the main objects of price reform. Almost simultaneously the concepts of indifferent price and of equilibrium price were set up as against the concept of cost price, then in general use.

Should prices serve to regulate production? Those who proposed an indifferent price, replied: prices should only serve to stimulate the enterprise to fulfil the tasks prescribed in the plan with the least possible labour input, but should have no effect on the composition of the products of the enterprise. This is why they linked the principle of profit incentive with that of equal profitability for each product. Those who proposed an equilibrium price regarded it as essential that prices should have the function of regulating production. In their opinion, sound price ratios should contribute towards balancing demand and supply. They sought to replace profits adjusted to production costs by profits adjusted to the satisfaction of demand.

Cost price, indifferent price and equilibrium price, each with a different economic background, thus competed for recognition.

1) The cost price, as opposed to the subsidized price system, was developed as a means of offering—within the narrow confines of its regulatory functions—a sounder basis for economic costing under the slogan: "cover every cost as far as possible where it arises."

2) The indifferent price was to ensure that once the workers were interested in profits, prices should not have a negative effect on planning but should provide the foundation for correct judgment.

3) The equilibrium price was formulated from the start with a reform of the economic mechanism in mind.

The discussion soon made it clear that, when prices are fixed by the authorities, set forth in a pricelist and left unchanged through a long period, it is quite unrealistic to demand that the profits included in the prices of the products should be proportionate either to production costs or to the satisfaction of demand. The first cannot be achieved because costs and the second because market conditions are always changing. This also explains why the debate over prices steadily broadened. Ten years ago the discussion started with the aim of defining the correct type of price. It centred on accurately expressing the socially necessary input of labour in terms of money. The price debate later changed into a debate on the mechanism. Attention first centred on bringing about an elastic price mechanism. Price type, price mechanism, economic mechanism have a definite relationship to the concrete mechanism of profit incentives. Let us investigate this relationship.

PRODUCTION PRICES AND MAXIMUM PROFITS

The concrete forms of the profit incentive may differ. Profit sharing as introduced in Hungary in 1957 was a further development of the method of rewarding fulfilment of the cost reduction plan, and its concrete form corresponded to the requirements of a system of fixed cost prices. In the first years this system was based on the assumption that the enterprises should annually increase the profit ratio—i.e., the percentage of profitability—in line with price returns. In the course of the annual regulation of profit sharing, a basic level of profits was fixed, and only if this basic rentability was surpassed could the employees share in the profits. In later years, this mechanism was somewhat modified through the introduction of profit sharing as a reward for "maintaining the level." The workers and employees were accordingly entitled to a share in the profits if and when the enterprise maintained the level of profits achieved in the previous year.

What should the concrete form of the profit incentive be in the future? To answer this question, we should first know how the price system and mechanism will be shaped. The debate on the price type provides several points of reference in this direction. On the one hand, we wish to transform our price system into a production price type. On the other hand, the production price should function within an elastic price mechanism and be adjusted to the actual nature of commodity and money relations between the enterprises.

In the new price mechanism, authority to fix and change prices will presumably fall to those whose economic decisions, including those affecting prices, will be based on the profit incentive.

It is not the production price in its classical interpretation, what is known as the multi-channel type of price, that we have in mind. In the sphere of industrial production, we propose that one third of the net income reflected in the prices should represent labour costs and two thirds the value of the means of production. One part of the net income thus realized would be in the form of tax, and the other in that of profits. This is essential: every price structure must reveal production costs and profits (losses). Indeed, an undisturbed functioning of independent costing on the part of the enterprises calls for a relatively large profit share. There must therefore be an increased emphasis on the necessity of regulating profits in harmony with the requirements of the production price. This is precisely what has to be realized through the profit incentive.

The principle of a basic profit level, and especially that of measuring profitability in terms of a ratio between produced value (income of the enterprise) and production costs, does not correspond to the production price type. A yardstick is needed which ensures an optimum incentive at the point where gross income coincides with the centre of prices. This may be assured, if tax-free gross profits, which are at the disposal of the enterprise and are proportionate to the wages and the value of the means of production, contain precisely that part of the net income which the State does not skim off in the shape of pay-roll tax or capital charges (interest).

Let us assume that the centre of prices is calculated by adding 10 per cent for capital charges and 30 per cent for wages, whereas the actual capital charges are only 5 per cent and the pay roll tax is 25 per cent. In this case, the tax-free profit (the tax threshold of profits) has to agree with the sum of the missing 5 per cent for capital charges and 5 per cent for wages. This does not mean that profits exceeding the tax-free profits should be completely drawn off through a profit tax, thereby limiting the full utilization of production capacities. The profit incentive has to be based on the principle of achieving the largest possible profit. Therefore, only a portion of profits in excess of the "threshold" should be drawn off, while leaving part of the taxable gross profits to the enterprise with a view to establishing a maximum profit incentive. To sum up:

from profitability measured in terms of production value, we should go over to the principle of profitability measured in proportion to the means engaged in production;

from an interest in the profit ratio we should go over to an interest in the amount of the profit;

for the purpose of extending production capacities and reconstructing existing enterprises, the necessary sums should be made available in the form of credits;

the centralized share of the profits of the enterprise should be drawn off in the shape of a profits tax. In determining the tax-free threshold in harmony with the price type, wages and capital charges should be taken into account.

PRICE FIXING AND PROGRESSIVE PROFIT TAX

What new situation may production prices—functioning in an elastic price mechanism and linked with the profit incentive—create in the management of the enterprises? According to the theory of the equilibrium price as construed in Hungary, one would have to suppose that:

given a "perfect" market equilibrium, i.e., when the market is proportionately supplied with various products, each price embodies a proportionate profit;

given an "imperfect" market equilibrium, the profit realized in the prices of various products is dissipated depending on the market supply of these products.

This description of the price mechanism presupposes that any change in market conditions or input is followed by a corresponding price movement, because otherwise the enterprises would reduce or even stop the production of unprofitable goods or goods bringing in a less-than-average profit. Such an "on again off again" automatism would be harmful as regards both price stability and rational organization of production.

In what respect is the idea of the competitive price wrong? It is perhaps because of the exaggeratedly centralized functional direction of the economy that our thinking has for a long time been excessively concentrated on the product as such. The product has gained a sort of autonomy and become detached from the rational system of complex company management. This is harmful because it dismembers the plant and breaks up the organized character which was already brought into being by capitalism and which should be raised, in the socialist economy, to a national level. In our planning technique this harmful point of view is regrettably in evidence even where it is a question of determining labour efficiency and its qualitative rather than its quantitative characteristics. This finds expression mainly in the planned production costs of selected products and in the prescribed reduction of costs of comparable production. Such concentration on the product is strengthened by the present form of price fixing. The theory of the equilibrium price, though critical of the bureaucratic price mechanism, is still based on this erroneous point of view.

Now, what will happen when the enterprises are given greater independence? It is almost certain that the issue of the profit-making aspect of company management will arise in all its complexity. This tendency will be strengthened by the production price (an enterprise and not a product category) and by the corresponding profit incentive. Here too, a reduction of production costs is an objective, but it will be subject to a different approach and different preconditions. The interconnections of production costs, the relativity (based on the commodity structure) of all priorities of profitability, are obvious to the enterprises. Therefore, in industrial branches which produce a great variety of products, the economic calculations serving to orientate the enterprise give preference to such formulae as restrict prime costs to the narrower sphere of variable costs; or examine the capacity of products to carry overhead costs; or analyse marginal costs, calculate optimum prices and capacities, etc.

Once the profit incentive gets a bigger role in company management, the attitude of the management will obviously vary from branch to branch. We may, however, get some pointers from the organizational forms which exist today. Assuming the existence of a balanced economy, the company will strive to achieve:

a maximum utilization of its production capacities in such a way that the income derived from goods whose sale is most unfavourable will still somewhat exceed the variable costs connected with their production;

a production structure in which both production capacities and profits are as high as possible.

The management of the company will consequently take the different profit ratios of the various products into account. In a modern industrial commodity structure these differences are not simply caused by the degree to which demand is met, but by those peculiarities of the price system which follow from a rich selection of goods, a fast turnover and wide-scale replaceability of products. The management of the company takes account of the life cycle of the products and the price movements connected with it. The company knows that it can work economically only if it produces certain predetermined and regularly increasing quantities. In its organizational work it regards optimal utilization of production capacity as one of the most important regulators. In industrial branches that produce a great variety of products, the company thinks in terms of quantities and commodity structures; it thinks of individual products only in this context. The reality of the equilibrium price thus does not present itself to the company in plant costing but in the commodity nexus, since in price bargaining it is the quantitative relationship of supply and demand that is the determining factor.

These considerations may convince us that the effort of the companies to achieve maximum profits through an elastic price mechanism can lead to a sound organization of the economy, provided the money remains stable and there is no inflationary process. Any inflation injures the interests of socialist society on the one hand; on the other hand it puts a premium on price speculation as against technological and organizational measures in company management.

Stability of the price level has to be assured through a planned equilibrium and through the price mechanism. Elasticity of the price system may not lead to liquidation of price fixing from above. The forms of fixed price, maximum price and free price will have to be applied in a concerted way after giving due consideration to the situation of the economy and the peculiarities of the various branches. We must, of course, realize that the behaviour of the enterprise depends on whether, within the elastic price mechanism, the prices of the materials it purchases and of the products itself are fixed from above or whether they result from bargaining and whether such bargaining is limited by rules or left free. In this connection the advisability of variations in the mechanism of profit incentives needs to be studied.

The interest of society in price-level stability is so great that the profit incentive must not become a factor operating against it. It is therefore desirable to tax gross profits progressively as they increase. This must be achieved in such manner as not to put a brake on the desirable tendency to reduce production costs.

Economic Efficiency and Profit Making Capacity

The profit incentive is closely connected with the purpose for which the enterprise may use the profits left to it. At first glance it may appear that the incentive is sufficiently assured through the profit-sharing of the workers and through its coordination with the premium of the managers. Individual material incentives are undoubtedly an extremely important element of this mechanism, but in themselves they only create an interest in the biggest possible profits.

But maximum profits should be realized in harmony with the interests of society. This is subject to further conditions, which are connected with economic planning.

Harmony between the economy on the national level and profitability on the company level is hardly imaginable if the managers think only in terms of the present and if today's results have no influence in guiding future development. The faster the development of the economy, the more important it is to make sure that the static equilibrium should provide optimal conditions for enabling the new equilibrium variants of the expanding economy to be realized. This cannot be achieved without the cooperation of those who organize the market processes in the system of commodity and pecuniary relationships.

Social cooperation in the State's economic planning is assured even today. In his own way each of us participates in preparing the plan and in formulating investment policies. The real trouble arises from the sharp line which, in industry, divides the organization of investment activities from the costing mechanism. What happens, in practice, is that the trend towards a static view becomes strengthened precisely in the sphere where, as a result of material incentives, social cooperation is most active.

Whenever there is a genuine interest in regulating gross profits, it is desirable, within certain limits, to dissolve the sharp separation of simple reproduction and reproduction on an enlarged scale, of production regulation and investment regulation. Maximum profits cannot be achieved efficiently, if more decentralized forms of production regulation are applied parallel with the present centralized methods of investment regulation.

The development of the economy naturally has to be carried out in a purposeful way, in accordance with the State investment plan. The "law of the average profit rate" and planned economy are mutually exclusive. But self-financing by the enterprises can be coordinated with planned expansion. This increasingly applies in agriculture and is being already successfully applied in State-owned industry in the domain of technological development. It is therefore desirable that in the various industrial branches planned expansion should be increasingly financed from the profits of the enterprises. This is desirable even if the investment plan and its coverage from profits do not always meet at the enterprise level and if part of the company profits consequently have to be re-distributed within the industrial branch.

The introduction of profit sharing was a very important step. If we make the enterprises strong enough financially to carry the risks which are inherent in the new price mechanism, and if self-financing is realized as one of the means of extending production, more favourable conditions than those prevalent today may develop for efficient company management.

CHANGES IN THE SOCIAL AND ECONOMIC STATUS OF HUNGARY'S PEASANTRY

by

GYULA VARGA

Changes in the number and social stratification of the agricultural population

The ratio of the agricultural population to the total population is continually decreasing. This symptom can be observed—with the exception of the developing countries—in nearly every country throughout the world. The rapid development of technology and the separation of the processing industry from agricultural production (now almost entirely restricted to the output of raw produce) brings about, at a certain stage of economic development, an absolute reduction in the size of the agrarian population. This phenomenon can be observed in Hungary since the 1950's. The changes that have occurred for the last thirty years—a decrease in the ratio of the agricultural population in the first phase, and its absolute decrease in the second phase—may be illustrated by the following data :*

	Agricultural population		Agricultural workers	
	Number in millions	Percentage of entire population	Number in millions	Percentage of all workers
1930	4.50	51.8	2.03	50.7
1941	4.57	49.1	2.16	48.0
1949	4.52	49.1	2.19	48.9
1960	3.54	35.5	1.82	34.6

* The data given in this study are taken from the various publications of the Central Statistical Office, and from a volume entitled *"Studies on the Village of Today"* by Csizmadia, Erdei et al., Kossuth Publishers, Budapest, 1964.

Although the decrease has been very considerable in the last ten years (the number of our present-day agricultural population does not even reach the 1880 figure), the ratio of the agrarian population in the developed West European countries is still much lower. This can partly be ascribed to the greater importance of agriculture in Hungary within the national economy and partly to its lower productivity.

Simultaneously with the stagnation and the decrease of the size of the agricultural population profound changes have also occurred in the class relations of society, as evidenced by the data of three distinct years. Those for 1930 show the property relations of capitalist Hungary, those for 1949 the property structure of small peasants who received land, and those for 1963 the structure of the population in agriculture, which in the meantime had changed into intensive, large-scale socialist farming.

The stratification of the agricultural population in 1930 was as follows:

	Wage-earners in thousands	per cent	Wage-earners and dependents in thousands	per cent
Middle and big landowners (lessees) with landed property (lease) above 57 hectares*	10.8	0.5	25.1	0.6
Big farmers with landed property (lease) of 11.5–57 hectares	144.2	7.1	286.3	6.3
Middle peasants with landed property (lease) of 2.9–11.5 hectares	530.3	26.1	1065.5	23.7
Dwarf holders (lessees) up to 2.9 hectares	517.8	25.5	1145.7	25.4
Independent sharecroppers, gardeners, shepherds, etc.	59.2	2.9	151.9	3.4
Farm-hands	215.9	10.6	597.5	13.3
Workers, day-labourers	553.3	27.3	1,227.4	27.3
Total	2,031.5	100.0	4,499.4	100.0

* The figures for land units are not round, as a result of the conversion of the Hungarian land measures into the decimal system. One Hungarian cadastral yoke equals 0.57 hectares.

The greatest political and socio-economic event of the post-liberation years was, no doubt, the Land Reform, which affected 35 per cent of Hungary's arable area, i.e., over 3 million hectares, about 75,000 holdings.

The half-million hectares of land belonging to the "biggest landowner," the Church, and the landed estate of the Esterházy family, about 230,000 hectares, were thus distributed. One-third of Hungary's lands had been owned by a thousand families, and when the big estates were carved up, 640,000 people received plots, among them 260,000 agricultural workers, 110,000 farm-hands and 215,000 dwarf holders, while 800,000 hectares of forest were nationalized, model and experimental state farms set up, public pastures designated and house-sites distributed. These new property relations were marked in 1949 by the following figures of social stratification (in thousands of the agricultural population):

Independent farmers with farms of less than 14 hectares	3,850
Independent farmers with farms of more than 14 hectares	170
Cooperative farm members	30
Agricultural workers and day-labourers	470
Total	4,520

Between 1949 and 1962 new changes occurred in the property relations of agriculture—changes that in their importance could be compared only with the Land Reform. It was then that the framework and dimensions of the two main forms of socialist property—cooperative farms and large state farms—were formed. The following percentage figures of the distribution of arable land according to social sectors also indicate that the cooperative "sector" was not free from slowdowns, even set-backs:

	1949	1953	1958	1961
State sector	1.2	15.8	13.6	13.3
Cooperative sector	0.8	26.0	13.0	79.5
Individual and auxiliary farms	98.0	58.2	73.4	7.2
Total	100.0	100.0	100.0	100.0

The social structure of the agricultural population between 1961 and 1964, based on these property relations, can be indicated only with limited exactness, as compared with the data for 1930 and 1949, because the decrease in the size of the agricultural population resulted from a considerable fall in the number of pronouncedly agricultural families, with the greater part of those who abandoned agriculture continuing to live with their families. A clear picture of the property relations of this period can therefore only be obtained by presenting the stratification of agricultural wage-earners (1961) rather than that of the total population.

	In thousands	Percentage
Agricultural workers	321.0	17.7
Agricultural employees	36.0	2.0
Cooperative members	1,123.2	61.8
Assisting dependents of cooperative members	113.2	6.2
Individual farmers (with their assistants)	224.1	12.3
Total	1,817.7	100.0

A comparison—of limited accuracy—with the data of previous years shows that a fundamentally new social structure has materialized, which can best be characterized by the fact that over four-fifths of the agricultural bread-winners work on big cooperative farms, while the number of individually farming peasants scarcely reaches one-tenth.

Development of agricultural production

From the point of view of the development of the income and socio-economic importance of the agricultural population, the development of agricultural production plays a fundamental role in itself and also as compared with other branches of the national economy. The changes in gross agricultural production are indicated by the following indexes:

1934–1938	100
1949–1952	94
1953–1956	104
1957–1962	120
1963	130

Despite the increased production of the last ten years, the role played by agriculture in social production is decreasing. The ratio of the participation of agriculture in the volume of social production is shown by the following percentages:

	Social product	National income
1938	55	53
1949–1952	29	34
1953–1956	23	30
1957–1962	19	24
1963	17	19

Although these indexes are unfavourably influenced by the low price level of agricultural produce as compared with that of industrial articles, and though the contribution of agriculture to social production is actually greater, the decrease in its ratio is unequivocal. The indexes clearly reveal the declining importance of agriculture.

Profound changes have also occurred during the last few decades in the structure of agricultural production. The most essential of these are: an increased quota of horticulture (fruit, wine and vegetable growing), cereal fodder, pig and poultry breeding, and a decrease in bread crops.

Together with the growth of agricultural production and the change in its trend, agricultural exports have also increased. Of particular importance is the fact that for the last twelve months there has been an increase in the exportation of products of the tinned food industry (particularly tinned vegetables, fruits and meat). The general perspective is favourable in this sphere too. The main endeavour also in agriculture—besides meeting domestic demands—is therefore to step up production mainly of the raw products of the food industry and of articles that can be sold fresh, like fruit, vegetables and grapes. This means at the same time that the job opportunities in agriculture will grow, thus counteracting the tendency of mechanization and chemization to reduce the labour force.

It would be unwise to forget, when judging the development of agricultural production, that the increases in production of the last fifteen years have taken place simultaneously with a major decrease in the number of people employed in agriculture. In 1949–1952 one agricultural labourer produced some 13 per cent less and in 1957–1962 about 35 per cent more than he did in 1938.

The recent increase in per capita income of the peasantry has resulted largely from the quantitative growth of production and the drop in the peasant population, but the abolition in 1956 of the system of compulsory deliveries and the concomitant adjustment of producers' prices has also had a considerable influence in bringing about this increase.

Income of the peasantry

The trend of the personal income of the peasantry* is shown by two indexes.

The first index shows per capita annual income,** the second per capita annual consumption.*** To distinguish between the two is important when examining the personal income of the agricultural population, since the peasantry may increase its consumption—in the case of an unsatisfactory trend of income—to the detriment of production funds, or may to some extent make it independent of the income trend. The following data (in forints) reveal the trend of the two indexes between 1960 and 1963:

	Per capita		Per capita	
	personal	total	personal	total
	income		consumption	
1960	8,632	9.890	9.102	10.360
1961	8.955	10.317	8.874	10.236
1962	9.556	11.067	9.222	10.733
1963	10.216	11.891	9.503	11.178

The 1960 data show that, at the time of the large-scale organization of cooperative farms, the peasantry decreased its reserves and endeavoured to consume more than the income earned. This fact and the consumption in 1961, which scarcely differed from the income attained, indicate that the peasantry then judged the situation rather precarious, and as a result did not save but, on the contrary, overspent. At the same time, the savings in 1963

* In this part it should be borne in mind that—because of the statistical records—the agricultural population does not include workers and employees on state farms. The number of the latter is 180,000, about 5 per cent of the total agricultural population.
** Total value of assets available for personal consumption and overhead costs, acquired by the peasantry in one year.
*** Total value of goods consumed by the peasantry in one year.

3

(about 7 per cent) from income indicate that the sitation of the peasantry was by then essentially consolidated.

From this viewpoint it is of interest to compare the volume of the peasantry's personal income and consumption and their mutual ratio during the last fifteen years:

| | Per capita personal | | Consumption in percentages of income |
| | income | consumption | |
	(Index of real value, 1949 = 100)		
1949	100	100	85
1950	102	110	94
1951	118	119	86
1952	66	107	138
1953	107	101	80
1954	110	111	86
1955	118	125	90
1956	114	131	99
1957	132	137	88
1958	121	137	96
1959	134	153	97
1960	133	162	104
1961	138	157	98
1962	147	164	96
1963	157	169	93

The data of the third column follow like a seizmograph the peasantry's assessment of their situation. Of particular interest is the fact that the ratio of consumption to income in 1963 is favourable even at the hitherto highest level of consumption.

The source of the income and consumption of the peasantry is more and more shifting towards pecuniary incomes. Natural husbandry is disappearing more and more. Unfortunately, it is very difficult to compare the scanty pre-liberation data with the present situation, so we shall abstain from comparing the levels of real income, so fundamentally important in shaping the standard of living, though we shall provide a few data designed to give an idea of the basic changes that have occurred in the form of the income. The following figures show the annual income of farm-hands working "for fixed wages," between 1925 and 1930, on a countrywide average of the large estates.*

* Lajos Ecsery: "The Labour of the Hungarian Agrarian Population", Szentes, 1930.

Money	Equivalent of 1 quintal of wheat
Grain	21 q
Salt	28 kg
Bacon	40 kg
Milk	1 litre a day
Footwear	1 pair of high boots
Use of plot free of charge	0.5 hectares

Prior to 1945 only a small fraction of the small-peasant farms produced for the market. With the setting up of the cooperative farms, the income of small-peasant agriculture—which, even after liberation, had produced for the market only secondarily—underwent a fundamental change. Within a few years a considerable change occurred in the ratio of cash incomes to incomes in kind, and today the proportion of cash income (and consumption of commodities bought for money) is further increasing as compared with income in kind. This is revealed by the following data. Annual income per capita (in forints):

	1962	1963
Net income in cash	5,564	5,961
In kind	4,369	4,245
Total personal income*	9,556	10,216
Change in assets*	minus 377	plus 10
Social allotments*	1,511	1,675
Total real income	11,067	11,891

* Three componentes of the above income data require explanation:
 a) Personal income means at the free disposal of the individual.
 b) Change in assets represents a change in the peasantry's production funds and stocks in the period examined.
 c) Social allotments include health, cultural and other social benefits, free of charge or at reduced charges.
 b) and c) also apply to the consumption indexes.

Annual per capita consumption (in forints):

	1962	1963
Consumption in kind	4,625	4,537
Consumption through purchase	4,597	4,966
Total personal consumption	9,222	9,503
Social allotments	1,511	1,675
Total consumption	10,733	11,178

3*

The analysis of the Hungarian peasantry's income would, however, be misleading, if we failed to point out that the income of other social groups is higher than that of the peasantry—a world-wide symptom. In 1963 the peasantry made up 31 per cent of the total population and had 27 per cent of total personal incomes.

The income and consumption quota of the peasantry compared with workers and employees is indicated by the following figures:

	The peasantry's per capita	
	real income	consumption
	(in percentages of corresponding data for workers and employees)	
1960	77.2	84.2
1961	80.1	82.3
1962	83.1	83.6
1963	82.7	82.6

The almost 20 per cent difference in income is considerable and can scarcely be left out of consideration. An examination of how this difference arose during the last fifteen years reveals that the level of the real income of workers, employees and peasants was about the same up to the mid-fifties. In 1957–58 a marked difference arose, which has not essentially changed since.

Today a considerable part of workers', employees' and peasant families hardly deserve this designation any longer, as their incomes derive from several sources. The existence of a population with a dual income virtually amounts to an intermediate stage of the agricultural population's turning into workers and employees. It is the result partly of attachment to traditions, partly of economic causes—the desire to make use of an additional source of income—and of the geographical confinement of the village population. In the statistical data those with a dual income are classed among the worker-employee or peasant population depending on the main source of their income.

Separate data concerning incomes of workers' or employees' families, on the one hand, and of peasant families, on the other, are available only for 1960. Though the following figures have since considerably changed, they reflect the comparative indexes of annual per capita consumption:

Per capita consumption of	In forints	In per cent of average incomes	In per cent of wage incomes
Families with income only from wages	11,430	111	100
Families with only a peasant income	8,470	82	74
Families with dual income	9,590	93	84

The income of the purely agrarian population is thus the lowest, and not even those with a dual income reach the level of the wage-earners. The reason for the smaller income of the agrarian population is to be found in the level of agricultural production and in the still prevailing relationship between producers' and consumers' prices. The agricultural yields, measured in West-European terms, are low, while production inputs in agriculture are high. Moreover, one should not underestimate the role played by seasonal limitations in agriculture, i.e., the fact that those engaged in farming are not always able to work the year round.

A further cause of the divergence in incomes is the relative senescence of the peasantry and the consequent decline in work performance. The age distribution of active bread-winners in agriculture and in other spheres of the national economy changed as follows between 1930 and 1960 (in percentages):

Age groups	Agriculture		Other spheres	
	1930	1960	1930	1960
14	3.6	0.9	1.3	0.6
15–39	56.8	41.2	67.0	62.3
40–59	25.0	37.0	25.8	32.1
60 and above	14.6	20.9	5.9	5.0
Total	100.0	100.0	100.0	100.0

The decline in working capacity is expressed in performance and, consequently, in the size of incomes. But there is another important factor affecting incomes—that of professional qualifications. Higher qualifications are naturally reflected in higher incomes everywhere. But—as can be seen from the data below—here too there are basic differences between agriculture, industry, and the national economy as a whole. This is one of the reasons for the lower level of agricultural production and may, to a minor extent, account also for the lower per capita income of the agricultural population. The school qualifications of active bread-winners in 1960 were as follows (in per cent):

Among all bread-winners	In agriculture	In industry	On a country-wide scale
Less than 8 school classes were completed by	77.8	46.3	53.7
At least 8 classes were completed by	19.2	53.1	44.7
G. E. C. was obtained by	2.0	11.2	12.1
University degrees were obtained by	0.6	2.0	3.4

Income of cooperative farm peasantry

A separate survey of the income and consumption levels prevailing on cooperative farms is justified for two reasons. First, this stratum of the peasantry has become the most numerous, and more detailed data are at our disposal regarding it, mainly in respect to differentiation of incomes and the factors motivating it. Secondly, the living conditions of the cooperative peasantry are of particular interest, bearing in mind that not only abroad but in Hungary itself the income situation of the cooperative farmers is least known, a circumstance which gave and still may give rise to many misunderstandings and wrong conclusions.

The income of the cooperative peasantry has two main sources. The first is the cooperative farm: the members share in the farm's gross income according to the quantity and quality of the work performed as well as to the economic value of the land they have contributed to the common property. The second source of income is the household plot (cultivated within set limits), which is designed to meet the personal requirements of the cooperative farm families and to supplement personal incomes. It is the total income derived from the cooperative farm and the household plot that has raised the income level of the peasantry far above that of pre-liberation days and made it possible for the social status of the peasantry to undergo a fundamental change.

In addition, the income deriving from other labour relations—outside the cooperative farm—as well as the old-age annuities and pensions of aged cooperative members are, naturally, also considerable.

These incomes are complemented by other benefits—of great importance from the viewpoint of subsistence—such as health service free of charge or at reduced prices, free education, adult education, etc. We shall abstain from examining the personal incomes derived from sources other than the cooperative farm and the household plots, partly for lack of adequate data and partly because the size of social allotments depends on needs.

The per capita income of the cooperative peasantry received in the form of pension, annuity and family allowance was from 1,300 to 1,400 forints in the past few years, while total social allotments amounted to from 1,500 to 1,600 forints per capita.

In the past several years the annual income of cooperative families (the average family in 1963 had 3.2 members) derived from the cooperative farm and the household plots was the following (in forints):

	Cooperative farm	Household plot	Together
1958	11,870	9,000	20,870
1959	11,400	9,200	20,600
1960	8,400	8,600	17,000
1961	7,800	9,300	17,100
1962	9,000	9,600	18,600
1963	10,000	10,100	20,100

This means that the cooperative farm, from the viewpoint of insuring personal incomes, is equivalent to the household plot. In reality, its role is far more important; indeed, it is no exaggeration to say that it is decisive. The fact is that members working on the cooperative farm are paid partly in kind, which, besides serving personal consumption, also provides the household plot with the necessary agricultural products, such as fodder, porkers, breed animals, etc.

The composition of the average share in incomes of the cooperative families shows that the allotted produce in kind meets part of a family's food requirements and also assures a fair quantity of fodder for the livestock of the household plot:

		Annual share per family	
		1962	1963
Bread-grain	kg	569	427
Barley, oats	kg	220	215
Maize	kg	362	365
Potatoes	kg	177	201
Vegetables, fruit	kg	87	82
Rough fodder (hay)	kg	218	282
Sugar	kg	13	13
Rice	kg	1	1
Wine	litres	9	9
Fodder beets	kg	50	67
Other produce in kind	ft	381	426
Cash	ft	5,504	6,620

Another important circumstance is that the cooperative members may buy a certain quantity of agricultural produce from the cooperative farm at reduced prices, partly for personal consumption, partly for use on the household plot.

Naturally, the above figures change considerably according to regions and cooperatives, depending on the character of agricultural production (e.g., in wine-growing regions the members get more wine but there is no rice or sugar allotment), and partly on the general customs prevalent on some cooperative farms. Of much greater significance than this is the divergence in the absolute amount of incomes derived from the cooperative. It is primarily this divergence which defines the differences in the standards of living of the cooperative peasantry. Before going into details on this question, it must be pointed out that an increase in income derived from the cooperative does not necessarily mean a decrease in income derived from the household plots; on the contrary, there is a positive—if weak—connection between the two. The natural inference is that the differences in the incomes deriving from the cooperative farm are fairly indicative also of the differences in the total incomes of the cooperative peasantry.

The differences in the incomes derived from the cooperative farm are unhealthily great and can only partly be motivated.

The following table illustrates the differentiation of cooperative members according to the incomes derived from work on the farm (in percentages):

	1961	1962	1963
Income under 4,000 ft	34.4	29.7	23.9
Income of 4,000 to 15,000 ft	55.7	56.5	54.1
Income above 15,000 ft	9.9	13.8	22.0

These three years indicate an important change in a favourable direction. However, the differences in income of cooperative farm families may show even greater extremes, inasmuch as a single family may include one or more working members. These are by no means new symptoms and have nothing to do with the setting up of the cooperative system. To prove this, suffice it to compare the percentage distribution of incomes among peasant families living on private farms on the one hand, and among those belonging to co-operative farms on the other:

Per capita agricultural income (ft)	Private farm families* (1957)	Cooperative farm families* (1960)
Under 6,000	11.4	9.1
6,000 to 10,000	18.9	15.6
10,000 to 15,000	19.2	21.8
15,000 to 20,000	15.3	19.1
20,000 to 25,000	10.7	14.3
25,000 to 30,000	8.7	9.1
Over 30,000	15.8	11.0
Total	100.0	100.0

* Based on a survey made by the Central Statistical Office, in 1957 and 1960, of the incomes of peasant families. The 1957 data concern 12,000 private peasant families, the 1960 data 26,000 co-operative families. A comparison between the two surveys is admissible despite the passage of three years, because the incomes differ by only 6 per cent—and that in favour of the private peasant families. In the case of per capita incomes, the difference does not even amount to 2 per cent.

Among cooperative members the ratio of incomes below and above the average is smaller than among peasants on private farms; the income of cooperative members is thus more balanced and less differentiated. If we compare the above data with the earlier table relating to 1961–1963, we may assert that the divergences in the peasants' income have decreased with the setting up of the cooperatives and that this process will continue as the collectives consolidate.

Factors causing divergence in incomes of cooperative farmers

Cooperative farms are classed in statistical records in three groups, according to the value of their production per unit of area. There are good, fair and weak cooperative farms. Since the members of the cooperative farms do not work for fixed wages but share in the annual income of the farm according to the work performed, their pay necessarily differs depending on the farm they work on. This has its positive side in that the members feel the production results of their farm "on their own skin," as it were, and are collectively interested in improving their farming. The negative side is that the same industrious and conscientious work is differently paid for on the various cooperative farms. It should be remarked in this context that a collective interest in work can be a good incentive only if coupled with an adequate individual interest.

The classification of the cooperative farms into good, fair or weak depends on several factors: natural endowments (quality and situation of the lands), level and structure of production, economic conditions, leadership, and finally the members themselves. The good or poor work of the members may improve or worsen the possibilities determined by the other circumstances. Unfortunately, the last factor cannot be expressed in figures, and this circumstance should be taken into consideration in assessing the data which follow. On the other hand, good or poor work, the enthusiasm or passivity of the cooperative members, are not inexplicable phenomena; nor are they the result of purely subjective causes. There are evident objective reasons, though economic and sociological research still owes us an investigation of these symptoms. Suffice it to mention here the strong influence which management, production conditions and anticipated wage levels exert on the members' work and their ambition to work. After these preliminaries let us now look at per capita income deriving from work on the cooperative farm, classified according to the quality of the farm in question and presented in percentages of the general average of farm incomes.

		1962	1963
Good		143.4	138.1
Fair		107.3	102.9
Weak		70.9	68.6
	General average	100.0	100.0

However, it is not only the members' personal income that depends on the efficiency of the cooperative farm, but also the extent of accumulation and technical development, which in turn decisively influences production. This self-intensifying process that automatically increases polarization would, if left to itself, before long lead to unpleasant economic consequences; moreover, a relative economic decline of part of the peasantry is inadmissible from the political and social point of view. That is why the state takes special measures to support the weak cooperative farms. This support, however, has not yet reached the proportions desired, though well-founded economic analysis shows that investments made in weak cooperative farms can be more quickly recovered and result in a more favourable effect than in the case of those made in average or above-the-average farms.

The other factor that affects the income of the cooperative farm peasantry is the extent to which it takes part in the common work. This circumstance serves to differentiate the members no less than does the economic strength of the cooperative farm itself. Since these two main income determinants exert their influence together, the results also tend towards extremes. The hard-working member of a good cooperative farm thus has a particularly large income while the poorly working member of a bad cooperative farm earns disproportionately little.

The average figures given in the preceding table do not adequately show the differences that exist among the members as to the size of their income. To correct this, let us examine the following table which divides the members into income groups (in percentages) within the good, fair and weak cooperative farms (1963 data):

	All cooperative farms	Good	Fair	Weak
Earning under 6,000 ft	40.6	22.3	36.7	59.1
Earning from 6,001 to 10,000 ft	21.8	21.4	23.1	20.9
Earning from 10,000 to 15,000 ft	18.2	21.1	20.4	13.2
Earning over 15,000 ft	19.4	35.2	19.8	6.8
Total	100.0	100.0	100.0	100.0

As already mentioned, the farming level of a cooperative farm does not depend on the decision and activity of one man. Does this mean that the extent of participation in farm work is also independent of individual decision? Of course not—at least, not entirely. Within a cooperative collective it depends partly on individual decision whether a member chooses this or that particular job. However, the number of jobs is fairly strictly defined in harmony with the character and dimensions of production. This does not apply to plant-growing. Here, however, the seasonal character of production limits work to a period of from six to eight months, and even this is not steady but subject to interruptions or, if required, to a prolonged daily working-time. The employment of the members is consequently determined primarily by production and by the circumstances of work. Part of the members can find work the year round, but the balance can work on the cooperative farm only for six to eight months.

The extent and type of employment are naturally influenced also by the sex and the age of the participants. Women and elderly men can shoulder only tasks that do not involve excessive physical labour. Mothers with several children—because of the still inadequate number of day nurseries and crèches—can scarcely undertake steady work.

The following table, compiled by Ferenc Erdei for the third quarter of 1961, indicates the employment status of cooperative farm members and the division into spheres of work:

	1,000 persons	Per cent
Pensioners taking no part in common work	175.9	15.7
Non-pensioners taking no part in common work	83.3	7.4
Pensioners undertaking a certain amount of work	47.4	4.2
Total of those not or only irregularly taking part in common work	306.6	27.3
Members working in professional management and administration	30.5	2.7
Members working on building constructions and at auxiliary plants	73.0	6.5
Members engaged in livestock breeding	94.0	8.4
Members engaged in horticulture	78.7	7.0
Total of persons working at steady jobs	276.2	24.6
Members engaged in plant-growing	540.4	48.1
Total number of cooperative farm members	1,123.2	100.0

The figures reveal that about one-quarter of the cooperative farm members do not work at all, or very little, almost half the members work for six months, and about one-quarter can work the entire year on the collective farm.

Naturally, with the rise in the technical level and intensity of production the ratio of those working all the year round will increase. This can already be observed on the better mechanized farms. However, we cannot reckon with a decrease in the number of non-workers, because, due to the senescence of the population already referred to, the proportion of members of pension age will not decrease during the next ten to fifteen years, but will rather stagnate or even increase. Through the extension to cooperative farms of pension rights and of increasing social assistance, as well as through the allotment of household plots to aged members, the problem of care for the aged on cooperative farms can be regarded as solved in the main.

The one-quarter of the members who can work throughout the year rely fully on the joint work of the cooperative farms. Their daily life is closely linked with the life of the cooperative farm, and their relationship to work differs basically from the earlier labour relations of the peasantry. True, the peasantry of the past and the cooperative farmers still share many common features in their living conditions. Among the reasons for this we may mention habit, the more or less unchanged village dwellings and mostly, perhaps, the nature of the work performed. One-time peasant labourers now doing work of an industrial character on the cooperative farms or holding leading positions there have changed—also in their way of life—much more than those engaged in livestock breeding or horticulture, where labour conditions have scarcely changed. The desirable change, which has already begun in many places, may be expected, also in this field, primarily as a result of the technical revolution.

Members working only for half a year represent, from a social standpoint, the biggest problem. About half of them are women, mostly mothers of families. Though it would be desirable to provide these latter with steady work, possibly on a part-time basis, it is more important to improve the situation of those men and single women who are unable to apply their full working capacity on the cooperative farm. There are already solutions, or rather part-solutions for this problem. These include the extension of share-cultivation*, household plots which can take up part of the surplus working-time, and efforts on the part of those concerned to find jobs outside agriculture. However, in general, the number of these outside work opportunities is insignificant compared with the number of those seeking them; or they involve a change of residence, which few people would undertake.

* Share-cultivation means that in those branches of plant-growing which require much and careful labour, the workers undertake to perform all the work needed on an agricultural area of a given size, for which they receive a certain number of work-units, or fixed wages, plus a share in the crops raised. The advantage of this system is twofold: first, within the period set for this kind of work, the labourers themselves can decide when to carry out the task entrusted to them (that is, they themselves organize their time); secondly, they have an interest in producing as much as possible, will therefore work more carefully and industriously.

The picture here drawn applies notably to cooperative farms that are not situated in industrial areas and where technical equipment is at a low level.

The question presents itself differently on well-mechanized cooperative farms without superfluous manpower. In plant-growing—especially in horticulture—manual labour is still partly indispensable. So even the well-mechanized cooperative farms need a certain number of seasonal workers, mainly at harvest time. These farms, therefore, try to lighten the domestic tasks of the women (establishment of common canteens, nurseries, kindergartens, day-time homes) and to draw them into seasonal work.

Another solution is sought by those cooperative farms that have a plentiful labour supply and where there is no chance for working outside the farm, as a result of which the excess of labour power can be felt even with full use of the household plots and application of share-cultivation. These farms concentrate on branches of cultivation that demand plenty of manual labour. Unfortunately, it may also happen that manual labour is used also in branches where mechanization has long been applied on the farm in question. Under these circumstances, the income available for distribution among the members of the farm in question will naturally not increase, even though such distribution becomes more just, that is, polarization of the incomes lessens.

A full solution of this problem will inevitably come about in the next few years, because the ageing of the cooperative farm members will greatly reduce the number of members with full labour capacity. Shortage of labour power, on the other hand, can be counter-balanced only by mechanization, which means a prolongation of the period of employment. The seasonal labour force required in the coming years will be obtained by relieving members of household chores, by the seasonal employment of persons not engaged in agriculture (students, soldiers), until a rising technical level will render it possible greatly to level off labour peaks. Even so, we shall always have to reckon with considerable fluctuation in the daily working hours during the various stages of plant cultivation.

A few more words about the role played by the income derived from the household plots. As to its amount, the data previously cited have shown it to be largely identical with the income derived from the cooperative farm. An increase in the income from the cooperative farm does not involve a decrease in the production of the household plots or in the resulting income, though it does reduce its relative share of the total income. Since differences in the size and in the production levels of the household plots are smaller, the household plot can be regarded, to some extent, as a balancing factor in the differentiation of the peasantry's income. This role is of particular significance in the case of poorly functioning cooperative farms.

THE WRITER AND HIS AUDIENCE*

by

ARTHUR MILLER

Among the other revolutions we are living through is a revolution in the relationships between the writer and his audience. This subject is as complicated as society itself and since I believe in short speeches more readily than long ones, I will not attempt to exhaust you or the subject, but merely to make some comments on it.

However much we tend to romanticise the writers of the past—especially their roles as prophets of the people, spiritual leaders, and so on—the fact is that the number of people who could read a book was extremely small. For the most part literature has been the property of an elite, statistically speaking. But no technological society can exist without mass education, and whatever its political system, the same basic phenomenon is occurring in every place where the machine is predominant—the masses of the people have become the consumers of culture.

Aside from the fact that intellectuals are the first to call for social change, and the last to accept it, a certain uneasiness exists as to the quality of the present revolution. I have heard it said that if tens of thousands more people buy classical records in the United States, they do not listen to them. And if they do they can hardly understand them. The same is true of the flood of paperback books being sold, including many titles which until recently no one but specialists bothered to read. In Russia, recently, I expressed surprise at the enormous audience for poetry readings, but even there some people told me that for many, perhaps even the majority, this had little to do with poetry and was more of a show, or a chance to emotionalize in public.

I am not here to announce that we are entering an age of philosophy,

---

* This is the text of Arthur Miller's contribution on the subject of "The Writer and Contemporary Society" at the thirty-third International P.E.N. Congress in Bled (Yugoslavia), where Mr. Miller was elected International President.

and that the mass distribution of culture means that a renaissance is at hand. I do believe, though, that we will not evaluate the present situation with attitudes which are hangovers from the very recent past. In a word, I think literature is on the verge of becoming public property instead of the preserve of the relative few, and that the techniques of promotion and publicity, unless their nature is understood, will tend to alienate writers either from their own standards of value or from the very conception of a popular and at the same time a good literature.

There is, of course, an objection toward this new mass market based on snobbism. Having spent so many years getting a degree and formulating one's opinions about poems, novels, and plays, it is disconcerting to think that anybody at all has the right to accept or reject our hard-won views, even without a degree or any specialized interest in literature. It is even worse, perhaps, to face the fact that ideas which one had always thought beyond the sensibilities of most people have become popular with them.

But snobbism aside, there is a real question as to whether the mass consumption of the arts is actually a consumption of the values of the arts themselves or of the publicity surrounding them, or even a passing fad which will pass away.

Years ago I knew a seaman on a freighter. At every port he would rush off and go to the railroad station, the bus depot, the various institutions of the port and come back with armloads of magazines, books, pamphlets... anything printed. There were movie magazines, religious magazines, a carpentry manual, Oliver Twist, a pamphlet on the evils of alcohol, something from the Salvation Army, the poems of William Cullen Bryant, a broken-off section of the Sears Roebuck Catalogue. Once I tried to find out the basis of his selection, and he said it was all "Readin' matter." At night, there being no place to store the masses of paper he had collected, it would all lie beside him on his sheets, and he would wake in the morning covered with paper, the poems and the carpentry manual, Oliver Twist and the department store catalogue—it was all there keeping him warm, one book melted into the other. At the next port he would cart it all off, a mass of paper he had somehow consumed. I ought to add that he also collected stuffed animals, deer horns, and the hoofs of animals. He liked these because he had never had a home and imagined that one day he would cover his walls, when he had walls, with his trophies. It was like his reading—a kind of longing. When I asked him about what he had read, his replies always veered away from books altogether. It was the act of reading that pleased him, not the content of what he was reading. It was also the labour of collecting and at the next port getting rid of what he had collected.

I think of him sometimes, when I pick up one of the many book reviews and literary magazines, or when I walk along Broadway past the theatres, or glance down the listings of television shows, or stop at a newsstand on any corner of Europe. This torrent of words and pictures pouring out of high-speed presses every day, every night; the paper-back bookstores bursting with masterpieces. And customers for everything. Is it all a kind of universal masochism, or a mass urge, like smoking cigarettes, to simply do something of our own will instead of being compelled to do it—or are we moving into an age of philosophy? For along with the trash that fills the stores and stands are fine books and these also sell. Not infrequently to the same buyer, in fact.

It seems to me that the day of the clique audience is closing. The good book now is advertized and sold in quite the same way as what was once called the popular book. And the retiring solitary author now finds his picture, full-page, in national magazines, his biography is part of the public imagination almost like a politician's or a screen star's. In short, because the audience is there and is so vast, everything has turned into "Readin' matter."

The consequences are not without irony. A famous avant-garde playwright, who had spent most of his life writing for small theatre groups and had lived anonymously and neglected, has suddenly discovered that his rebellious works, whose message mocks all social and political if not human presumptions, are the most popular stage works of the age. It depressed him, he said, made him uneasy. By the nature of the thing, how can one be far ahead of one's time and still be so damned acceptable?

But this is, I believe, implicit in the situation. Due to mass communication, high-speed publicity and promotional methods undreamed of a decade ago, the important thing becomes not what the nature of the work is, but the sheer fact of its existence as matter for publicity. I hope the following story is not too inappropriate. A few years ago I had received a medal from the Institute of Arts and Letters, and after the ceremony a famous poetess, now well along in years, came up to me and said how happy she was to meet me, how much she had enjoyed "Death of a Salesman" and "The Crucible." I was flattered by the compliment from so great a writer and told her so. "Oh yes," she went on, "and 'The Glass Menagerie,' that was marvellous. And 'Winterset.'"

I changed the subject before she confused me not with two other writers but with half a dozen, but the thing is understandable. A few weeks ago a young Negro boy came running up to me on the street to tell me how much he admired my work. I was especially pleased to think that my stuff

4

had meant something to a boy of eighteen until he said, "You done the best music I ever heard." He had confused me with a band leader named Glen Miller. And I cannot help adding that some years ago two of my plays were taken off the stage in, I believe it was Rumania, because Miller was a writer obsessed with sex and a pornographer.

Not too long ago the complaint was that, at least in America, the writer or artist was almost totally ignored by the public. This was taken to be a mark of the materialism of our culture. We are rapidly approaching the time, I think, when the writer will join the other public entertainers, like the politicans and the actors, as a figure equally amorphous, equally well-known, and epually at the mercy of the whims of mass publicity. And two equally depressing alternatives stem from this condition.

Allen Ginsberg, a writer crying out against the mores and the values of his society, is nevertheless reported in the press whenever he appears some-where to deliver his rebellious opinions. Presumably this publicity causes more people to pay attention to his work. Painters who overthrow every rule and value of previous art find themselves not barred from galleries and gatherings of serious people, but sought after and celebrated—institutional-ized before their paint dries. The essential quality of the mass culture is its tendency to absorb everything without differentiation, and at a rate unheard of before. "Peyton Place" becomes a movie but so does Kafka's "The Trial," so does Mary McCarthy, Nabokov and Saul Bellow. And what is the object of the movie but to interest the maximum number of people? My point is that it is not only those who write for fame, for money, for easy popularity who will find themselves smack in the middle of the new literary stardom, but those who for one reason or another are public movers.

On the crudest level, culture pays today when it did not before; it has mass consumers, mass distribution, mass publicity just like automobiles and bathing suits. Years ago to say you were a writer was not the highest recom-mendation to your landlord. Today he at least hesitates before he refuses to rent you the apartment—for all he knows you may be rich. A poet's opinions on politics were not much listened-to a short while ago. Today, a Robert Lowell condemns American foreign policy, and the very heart of government contracts. And I emphasize that it is unlikely one percent of those contracting hearts had ever been exposed to Mr. Lowell's poetry, let alone the newspaper readers who read the reports of his criticism on the front pages.

There cannot be more than twenty-five thousand people who really know anything about Lowell's poetry, yet obviously a certain political power has accrued to him. In his particular case part of it may be due to the aura surrounding his family, which has provided poets, educators and distinguished men for generations. But this is nevertheless incidental. During the Spanish Civil War, for example, many very famous authors condemned governmental policy towards Spain, but I cannot recall any such stir resulting. The fact, I think, is that communication today, especially television, reach down into the mass of people as never before, so that people who formerly were known only to a relatively specialized group are now injected into public consciousness on every level, and in that way become, potentially at least, elements of political and social power.

But again, it is not necessarily the literary value of the writer's work which decides whether he shall have such power. Rather, it is the communication itself of his importance—perhaps only of his existence—and its confirmation by the organs of communication. What has not been reported has not happened. What is reported exists. And this applies not merely to the naive and uneducated mind but to all in one degree or another. I daresay that if the authors' names were removed from every new book and play and poem in the next six months, and critics had to evaluate them intrinsically, blindly, there would be a chaos which would take years to sort out. For suddenly we would be confronted with the works themselves rather than the mythology surrounding authors and their lives, and reputations, a mythology in very large part created by reportage.

I think that what is wrong with the situation is the inevitable tendency of mass communications to seize upon whatever is journalistically startling, unusual, or newsworthy about a work rather than what is intrinsic to it. There is an atmosphere of suppressed hysteria in which truth must surely suffer. It is the hysteria of the reporter, the critic, the television producer who must fill space. Because it is his job to keep the machine fed. I can testify that time after time reporters have asked me for an interview; I have declined on the ground that I had nothing I especially wished to say that day. The answer, subtly or crudely put, has always been: well, say anything. I have read interviews I allegedly gave to reporters I have never met or heard of in my life, I have read remarks of mine, witty or otherwise, which I never made. It all reminds me of a theory which an anthropologist I know has evolved, a theory of institutions. A hospital, he says, is not there to cure the sick, it is there to continue being a hospital. A library is not there to dispense books, it is there to continue being a library. Mass communications, in a very great part, do not exist to communicate anything, but to go on blackening white space and keeping the television tube from going blank.

It is, or is becoming, an age of entertainment, an age of organized dis-

4*

traction. The process of mass communication is converting all its subjects into actors. From the head of government to the lowly poet, the makeup man is always waiting with his rouge and talcum powder, and his advice as to how to face the camera as best you can to deliver your sermon on the mount.

What can be the writer's reaction to all this. A Salinger flees to the woods and sees nobody. A Hemingway confides in columnists and guides his own biography. But at both extremes one must see the distorting power of reportage.

For myself, I do not see how it can be controlled, or very materially changed. Mass communications are voracious; each week, each day a thundering new masterpiece must be heralded, and each succeeding day a new one found to supplant the last. Fashions which formerly took years to mature and fade away now appear, dominate, and collapse in months or even weeks; the avant-garde is overtaken and institutionalized before it has had an hour of neglect to prove its purity.

All of which suggests that nothing essential has changed. The whole business cannot finally matter to any man who is truly moved in his heart to speak.

In the great periods—in classical Greece and Elizabethan England—the audience too was broad and encompassed the whole of society. The theatre at Epidaurus seated fourteen thousand people; one may assume that the majority was somewhat less refined than Sophocles might have wished; that it was difficult to draw them into thoughts and feelings more sublime than vulgar, or to hold their attention once it was aroused. A mass audience may intimidate the artist; but it can also challenge him to speak in a more living language and to share more profoundly the common life of his time.

WHAT I BROUGHT HOME FROM A WRITERS' CONGRESS

by

GYULA ILLYÉS

At international writers' meetings, it is not the exchange of ideas that matters. It is, much rather, the exchange of feelings. I believe this holds good for all international meetings of any profession. The advance of astronomy and medicine, for instance, would be greatly hampered, if astronomers and physicians had no other way of transmitting experiences than through journeys such as ours and not through an exchange of printed words. What, after all, can a surgeon communicate to another surgeon between a good lunch and a pleasant afternoon excursion? Perhaps a trick of the trade—or, mainly, the fact of his being pleased to meet his opposite number, particularly if he has known him before by repute.

Hence, such gatherings of artists or scholars can be deemed satisfactory or successful merely to the extent that its participants enjoyed it, that is, by the measure of the warmth and cordiality of handshakes exchanged, by the atmosphere, not so much of the conference hall but of conversations in the lobby, the cafeteria, the pub where they have a drink before retiring.

Last not least, success depends on the hospitable town, and on the country which affords the opportunity for meeting.

*

Considered from this aspect, the Pen meeting at Bled was a real success. Everybody knows the kind of handshake that is not a contact of palms, when two men facing each other get hold of their elbows, press them and shake them, looking at each other with eyes somewhat dimmed, in a sort of preliminary hug. This is how the writer from the Danube banks and the Italian Silone greeted each other. Hardly had that long-overdue meeting begun when both repeated these gestures almost precisely, saluting the Croatian Krleža who suddenly appeared and joined them.

The so-called masters of the word, the craftsmen of the art of the language are particularly affected by scenes in which words fail them, voices falter. How closely these three men were to follow the same route, thirty years ago. How much there was to be explained, twenty or ten years ago . . . And how much there is to tell each other now, judiciously re-considering problems, discussing the immediate future.

By mere chance, this scene took place in front of the conference hall of the Congress. It was equally by chance that, at the same moment, the doors at top of the high and broad stairs opened up, and the writers of five continents, relieved to be able to step out into the open air after a whole morning's consultation, began to stream downwards, smiling and blinking in the harsh noon sun.

On the other hand, it was certainly not chance that determined which of these writers came up to our little group, repeating the same half-hug, half hand-shake. The tiny nucleus grew and widened. We all felt that the sun, suddenly emerging after long rainy days, although still breaking through a drift of clouds, "will consolidate its rule not only there, above the snowy peaks, but also over the hearts." That is how the French Follain, screening his eyes against the sun, put it, as he addressed the blinking Croatian Popa, asking him to transmit his words to the Russian Surkov, who had just joined them. Surely Popa would know how to translate the French into Russian.

*

As it happened, for some time my journeys abroad have not been made on my own initiative, nor at my own expense. Neither were they paid for by the Hungarian people: I was the guest of foreign literary associations and cultural bodies. Thus, it was Her Majesty the Queen of the United Kingdom who graciously invited me to make a tour through the native country of the Scotsman Burns, my favourite peasant poet, a journey which was highly instructive to me; and my visit to the native town of Rousseau, another commoner I greatly admire, was arranged by the Municipality of Geneva. All these visits left me with the impression that the world at large is a generous and hospitable place, full of open doors and inviting tables. That is how I feel once more, here in Yugoslavia. Accompanied by my wife, I enjoy a twofold hospitality. Actually, it was the London Presidium of the Pen Club that tendered this invitation to me for its yearly round-table conference, this time in Slovenia, but all the "natives" I met here held out a cordial right hand to shake mine while, almost invariably, they put their left hands on my shoulder, with the beaming smile of model hosts. Whether

they were Slovenes, Serbians, Croatians, Macedonians or Montenegrines
(I still call them so), they welcomed me with equal friendliness and warmth,
often even in Hungarian.

I pride myself in the belief that this was not meant for my particular
person. Krleža, for example, speaks French better than I do. Whenever we
met in the last twenty years, in Budapest or in Tihany, that was the intermediary language we used. Now, I am touched by his delicacy and obviously
conscious courtesy in speaking to me only in Hungarian—here in his home
country—even when we are in company where many languages are being
spoken. Whenever he manages to make his point in Hungarian, his doubly
triumphant smile indicates his pleasure at being able to use the idiom of a
poet he loves, the Hungarian Ady.

*

"Is literature more, or less important today than in the past? Has the
writer's role in Society expanded or declined?"

Nothing is easier—or more comfortable—than to launch a problem of this
order for debate. But five or six such questions are already characteristic of
him who asks them, even impose a certain obligation on him. One might
even say that to ask ten questions in an appropriate context amounts to some
sort of answer as well.

This is how the questions of the first day ran:

"Does Society still turn to the writer for its own definition, for its view
of the world, or has this traditional task shifted to other hands?"

And, if the answer is no:

"In what way does the writer of today affect reality? Is he, indeed, under
any obligation to reflect contemporary reality? And is he necessarily isolated
if he does not?"

These questions, if asked one by one, may be replied to in various ways.
They may be shrugged off, or you can simply say "yes" or "no," but you can
also answer by a bulky volume. Taken separately, however, the questions
sound trivial.

Yet, when it became inevitable for me to step onto the enormous rostrum,
or rather to the speaker's chair, complete with multi-language transmitters,
as a participant of the debate, my opening phrase was one of praise for the
manner of assembling these questions. The new context in which these often-
uttered phrases were spoken, testified to no small amount of acumen and,
especially in view of their birthplace, to considerable familiarity with the
situation. You cannot catch a fish with a yard of bare rope. But a thousand yards,

if made into an elaborate net—and placed properly crosswise—will catch all the fish of a brook.

The ideas launched for debate achieved meaning—and thus originality—through the way they were composed. Hence, they became not only clearly intelligible but relevant to all the participants, to the East as well as the West. Blacks and whites, believers and non-believers could discuss them to the benefit of all—conveying their connotations and their own experiences, occasionally stirring up emotions and passions. All this, of course, became clear only after the gigantic net had been extracted, after the preconceived great speeches had been heard, and after following the debates in major and minor committee meetings, lasting several days. And still more so, as I sum up things retrospectively, after my arrival home.

*

"Is there such a thing as a recognizable public taste, and can literature, should literature conform to it?"

"What attitude should literature have towards mass communications? Are the two in opposition or in concord? And what effect does the growth of leisure time and the multiplication of the means of diversion available have on the writer and on literature?"

It was, however, not in the great conference hall, nor in the pleasantly arranged round-table conferences that the real debates, the muscle-tending, bonecracking mental combats took place. As I said, it was during occasional strolls, in the street or by the lake that "single combats" suddenly arose. Polemics and arguments started during smoking breaks, or in conversations like the one born out of the accidental meeting of Silone and Krleža.

Let me quote some more of the ensuing questions, those which I could not resist commenting upon, though in small committee only:

"Is there any essential difference between the literature of a highly-developed country and that of an underdeveloped country?"

A stab to the heart, to a writer's heart.

"Or between that of a country with direct linguistic access to the wide world and one with a limited access?"

Another stab in the heart.

Then, lastly, a thrust that went home:

"Is it possible to 'understand' another literature? One for which one lacks the context? Is translation a satisfactory solution?"

Clearly, no.

Yes. All the same, yes.

Why ?

Again, one could write volumes in support of either statement—but these volumes ought to be up-to-date, untold. The earlier comments on the subject would already fill libraries.

What we consider as beneficial food for the mind is, strangely enough, that which turns us inside out, which robs us of our sleep, which emaciates us. And that, precisely, is the kind of food I took along from Bled. Yet I came home full of hope, in good cheer. Because, as a recreation, I and some fellow writers, also concerned with momentous problems like the ones treated, were invited by re-discovered friends to a journey covering half of Yugoslavia.

FROM OUR NEXT NUMBERS

(Continued from p. 27)

BEFORE AND AFTER GRADUATION
Attila Kristóf — Judith Elek

IMPRESSION OF HUNGARIAN BUILDING
Nikolaus Pevsner

REMBRANDT IN BUDAPEST
Teréz Gerszi

MODERN ENGLISH AND FRENCH DRAMA
Péter Nagy

LÁSZLÓ NÉMETH'S NEW NOVEL
Anna Földes

"NON-ARISTOTELIAN" MUSICAL AESTHETICS?
Dénes Zoltai

THURSDAY, DAY OF SUPERSTITIONS
(poem)
Ferenc Juhász

RAGS AND RICHES
György Moldova

(Continued on p. 103)

THE EXCOMMUNICATOR

(Passage of a new novel)

by

TIBOR DÉRY

Every street, some say, is littered with literary themes waiting to be picked up. Others think they multiply by fission in library rooms. In my opinion, no matter where the author takes his themes from, they invariably furnish him—intolerable gossip that he is—with an excuse to start talking about himself and his relation to the outside world. I have always been surprised at writers in search of "themes." Could they possibly have lost their own selves?

At one time, when I was in the happy position of being able, as translator and editor, to maltreat other authors instead of having to compromise myself, I came across the character of St. Ambrose of Milan in a biography of Masolino. From a distance of fifteen centuries, all I knew about him was that during his beneficial tenure of office he excommunicated a Roman emperor and that his memory is preserved by a church in Milan which is named after him and where his bones are preserved. From a remark in that biography I also learned that a bond more enduring than his bones links him with our time: he took a stand against private property and commerce (and the Church canonized him nevertheless). Here was a good theme, here the "street" and I found common ground.

When some years afterwards I got down to writing this book, I began by reading —or rather re-reading—Gibbon's standard work on the Roman Empire. I also read F. Homes Dudden's outstanding two-volume biography of St. Ambrose and some two dozen other pertinent books, all with the same result: they confirmed my original mistrust of historical studies, but I did find relaxation in them. I stuck to my long-standing belief that the most arid historical datum has as much poetic force as a good poem and that it all hinges on the interpreter's ability to bring it out. From the point of view of authenticity, I see little difference between St. Paulinus' biography of St. Ambrose and Churchill's memoirs: both authors are inspired by an equally estimable and high-minded partisanship, although Churchill undoubtedly writes in a better style.

I have therefore written—in close adherenae to the historical facts and, here and there, to available records—my own legend of the great Father of the Church, the distinguished theologian and propagandist, poet, composer and silver-tongued orator, and one of the greatest politicians of the early Middle Ages. As trustworthy sources tell us that he performed numerous miracles, I have included them among the historical data. I have, of course, done this throughout in the naive belief that my knowledge of people is more reliable than the poetic visions other interpreters have extracted from Ambrose's figure. I have a suspicion, alas, that, had they been able to read my book, my two principal inspirers—Gibbon and F. Homes Dudden—would have raised their eyebrows.

T. D.

THE GUILEFUL COUNCIL OF AQUILEIA*

Having thus satisfied himself, more or less, that the Almighty had withdrawn the heavy cloud of His wrath from above his head, the holy bishop addressed himself with renewed energy to the task of carrying out his plans for the final annihilation of the Arian heretics. For he who aspires to power—be it in the name and on behalf of the Lord—must first set his own house in order.

Since this self-sacrificing work called for helping hands of great power and efficiency, the holy bishop scrutinized a hundred thousand hands which on either side of his path were idling, resting or waiting, or were pointing and even stretching towards him; and from their vast, swirling multitude, which at times darkened the horizon and thronged his sleepless nights with flourishing forefingers—long or short, straight or gnarled, horny, smooth—or broken-nailed, stubby, lean or swollen—he selected an imperial hand on his right and an imperial hand on his left, believing that their support would enable him to perform his urgent mission fruitfully. For in his guileless simplicity, he held the view that it could do no harm if, in addition to the support of the heavenly powers, you had some influential secular friends who could be of help to you in your sundry affairs and disputes.

One imperial hand, which, as we know, he had already clutched for some time, was the finely articulated, attractive hand of the immortal Gratianus, the young head of the Western Roman Empire. The holy bishop, after mature consideration of his plans, again clasped this hand with sudden vigour by sending the emperor the manuscript collection of his most celebrated sermons, entitled *De Fide*, so that the imperial hand might profitably thumb them, especially the inspiring leaves on the accursed Arian heretics. The other imperial hand—the muscular, soldierly, stubby-fingered hand of the immortal Theodosius, the recently elected ruler of the Eastern Roman

* Chapter Three of the novel. [Ed.]

Empire and co-emperor with the immortal Gratianus—was placed, without his own initiative, in the holy bishop's tender white hand by God Himself. Secure in such bilateral support, the humble servant of the Lord thought he could now safely set out on the rough and cloddy road ahead of him.

And lo! no sooner had the holy bishop lifted his spidery leg and set his foot on the chosen road than the clods crumbled into dust. Less than half a year had elapsed since the sequestration of Portiana's Church, and already his Imperial Highness, the Emperor Gratianus voluntarily, of his own accord and free will—returned that finest of all the Lord's sanctuaries and its lofty tower dripping with honey to the Catholics, that is, to Ambrose. True, in his letters to the august Caesar—published later in volume I of *Epistolae*—the holy bishop surmised that it may have been the Holy Ghost who inspired His august disciple to this noble and beneficial decision. This prolonged and energetic inspiration presumably also gave birth to the Caesar's decision to revoke his edict of tolerance issued earlier at Sirmium (Mitrovica), and to issue a decree ordering heresies of all kinds and complexions to be suppressed and extinguished forthwith.

The first victory! The first partial victory along the rugged road that was leading—whither? A great victory! For at Sirmium, the most gracious Caesar, moved by his kind heart, and acting in the spirit of his predecessor, the immortal Valentinianus I—and no doubt prompted by the Empress Mother, the distractingly beautiful Justina—had granted full freedom of worship to every sect except the Manichaeans, the Photinians and Eunomians (who were indeed visitant devils from hell); and now, with one stroke, the Holy Ghost had put an end to that intolerable tolerance and liberalism. By favour of the Holy Ghost, therefore, order would now at last be restored in the Western Empire!

Just as it was being restored in the Eastern Empire as well! More and more clods were crumbling into dust.

The immortal Theodosius, the recently elected Caesar, was a strapping figure of a man with a healthy complexion; the movement of his limbs was at once so determined and stately that it was impossible to imagine him without the imperial purple. The public orator was no doubt speaking the mind of an appreciative populace when in his welcoming address he spread this Homeric quotation before the Emperor's august feet:

"Never have my eyes seen as pleasing and stately a figure."

And if we add that he was outspoken and informal, a good-humoured though irascible man, generous and fond of splendour; that he would with soldierly discipline watch over his physical fitness, his diet, the condition of his stomach, digestion and muscles; and that, above all, he clung to the only true dogmas of the Church of Christ with a fanatical devotion that was in accordance with his Spanish extraction and upbringing—then if he had not forgotten Ambrose's lapse (possessing as he did a remarkably—indeed quite exceptionally—long memory), he had finally, or at least for the time being, forgiven him.

Following his election, the new Caesar set up temporary headquarters in Thessalonica, the capital of Macedonia, whence he waged a successful guerilla campaign against the blood-sucking Visigoths. And, as in other matters, he carried on his work with shrewd caution and with much common sense, although even now his quick temper would occasionally get the better of his moderation.—On these occasions, he was so frightful that even his wife and children dared not show their faces; he would then conceive preposterous schemes, orders and decisions such as might have become fatal for the whole Roman Empire as a whole, had not his common sense eventually prevailed and led his self-critical hand to erase and cancel the pernicious decrees. Proceeding along his bumpy road, the holy bishop was to gain much heartening experience in this respect.

It was soon after taking his first imperial steps—he had just temporarily restrained the sanguinary barbarians in Macedonia and the neighbouring provinces and entered Byzantium (Constantinople), the Eastern capital of the empire, in a triumphal procession—that the great and admirable Theodosius, with unwitting suddenness, grasped the holy bishop's small white hand held out to him in supplication and, just as unwittingly, pressed it in a soldierly manner as a token of his friendship. For although—as is usual with emperors and wordly potentates—his sanguine and impetuous temper drew sustenance from his pleasing and stately figure, compounded of earth, air, fire and water, it would in the long run submit to his immortal soul, which, as we know, is the antithesis of the body, both in structure and in essence, although strongly attracted by one of its fleshy parts. Already two days after entering Byzantium (Constantinople)—on November 26th, 380—the great and admirable Theodosius ordered all the churches of the city to be taken away from the accursed Arian heretics and turned over to the good Catholics. Shortly after this had been accomplished, he issued his celebrated edict forbidding the heretics to air their unrepenting, obdurate madness before the people by holding divine services in public places of worship, or even to approach the threshold of any sacred church with their illegal doctrines. The Council of Constantinople, convened soon after, solemnly and emphatically reaffirmed the articles of the true Catholic faith and expelled and excommunicated from the Church every accursed faction, whatever its degree of colour.

Victory! Victory! Clutching the two august hands on right and left, the holy bishop boldly advanced along the road he had chosen for himself. A great victory! One of his missions—the crushing and annihilation of heresy—had been virtually achieved. All that remained to be done was to crush and annihilate the heretics themselves; that is, to translate theory into practice. Nothing could be easier! The holy bishop, therefore, burying his face in his hands and heaving a heavy sigh, got down to making suitable preparations for the famous guileful Council of Aquileia. The heretics who, though suppressed, were still infesting Nothern Italy and the Danubian provinces in large numbers would have to be dealt such a heavy blow that, in practice too, they would sink through the floor, that is, into hell.

In the small hours of a spring morning, long before sunrise, the holy bishop—who, as usual, was up and about at daybreak—knocked on the door of one of the guest rooms in the episcopal palace, occupied by a colleague of his, Valerianus, Bishop of Aquileia, who had arrived in Milan the previous evening to attend the talks preparatory to the Council. Having succeeded with much difficulty in rousing the visitor out of his heavy snoring, he took him for a stroll in the spacious, portico-enclosed courtyard, in the middle of whose stone pavement a small quadrangle of carefully clipped and watered greensward symbolized nature as conquered, tamed and perfected by man, in harmony with the holy bishop's judicious taste.

"Father and Colleague," Ambrose said to his burly visitor, who, though taller than his host by two heads, and broader-shouldered by two spans was scarcely able to keep level with the brisk little Bishop of Milan. "When you have cleared your throat and rubbed the sleep out of your eyes, I should like you to set forth your opinion and stratagem concerning the time-table of the Council that is to meet shortly."

"The Oecumenical—that is to say, universal and plenary—Council," replied the Bishop of Aquileia, weighing his words, "has been convened by the immortal Emperor Gratianus, at the request of the bishops Palladius and Secundianus, for the purpose of discussing some unsettled questions of dogma."

"Palladius and Secundianus, dear colleague, are Arian heretics, both of them," Ambrose said; "and I do not wish to enter into discussions or disputes with them. Besides, there are no unsettled questions of dogma, anyway—you realize that, I hope."

"Why, of course I know, Father," the powerfully built, hard-breathing visitor replied in haste, eagerly nodding his head. "Nevertheless, the immortal Emperor Gratianus has convoked the Oecumenical Council for the express purpose of enabling the two Danubian bishops to expound their doubts before that assembly of ecclesiastics and to discuss them thoroughly with them."

"I am telling you I won't have any argument with Arians," Ambrose cried impatiently. "You misunderstand the situation completely, my sleepy colleague. What Gratianus thinks and imagines is his business, ours is to wipe out the last vestiges of heresy and all kinds of factionalism in our provinces."

At this moment, the sun rose over the roof of the episcopal palace, and in its golden rays the gentle sward in the middle of the courtyard burst into a glistening green. The holy bishop paused for a moment to admire nature, tamed and trim; then he opened his arms and raised them towards the sky.

"We shall wipe them out—to the greater glory of God!" he cried enthusiastically in his sweet, ringing voice.

"As for convening a universal and plenary Council," he went on, resuming his short, quick steps through the recurring shaded circles of the colonnades, "that's out of the question! Oecumenical Council, forsooth! To see Master Palladius and his friends receive support from their absolutely unreliable comrades-in-spirit from Asia Minor, Syria, Mesopotamia and Cappadocia! And have them vote us down in the end! Not if I can help it! We'll have no truck with heretics!"

"What'll we do?" asked the visitor, panting. He found it utterly impossible to keep abreast of his quick-moving, quick-thinking host, who continually outpaced him by two or three steps and out-thought him by as many thoughts. "What'll we do?"

"We'll destroy them," Ambrose shouted over his shoulder. "We'll have a majority at the Council."

"I hope we shall," said the burly Valerianus, and from his towering height cast a pensive eye on the crown and nape of the little bishop striding in front of him. "All the same, I ask myself, Father, how can we make sure, beyond any shadow of doubt, that we do have a majority if the unreliable Eastern fathers respond to the immortal Caesar's decree by attending the universal and plenary Council?"

At this point, Ambrose took a sudden turn and made his way towards the gate of the episcopal palace. "Let's take a stroll through the town!" he suggested. "I love to watch the early stir and bustle of the awakening city, reminiscent in its innocence of the delightful twittering of birds. The Eastern fathers will not come. We will explain and make it clear to Gratianus what a pity it would be to take the Asian fathers away from their highly responsible duties and subject them to the strains of a long and tiresome journey—to say nothing of the considerable travelling expenses—

just for the sake of the insignificant complaints ot two Arians. The issues before us can well be decided by a smaller number."

"It can, undoubtedly," said the Bishop of Aquileia. "But if the Asian fathers stay away in a body, what right shall we have to call the council oecumenical, that is to say, universal and plenary?"

"Oh, sleepy Father," said the little Bishop of Milan, speaking upwards over his shoulder, "your massive wisdom will see to it that one or two reliable and devout adherents and friends of ours, representing the Eastern fathers, turn up at your episcopal see."

As he reached the end of this sentence, Ambrose halted abruptly and spun round, enabling the visitor to observe at some length the exaltation radiating through the skin of his host's pallid, narrow face and the ethereal devotion in his red-rimmed eyes. "That means," the burly, slow visitor said after a while, reflectingly and with eyes down-cast, "we shall gather, not in a universal and plenary—or oecumenical—Council where the articles of our sacred faith will be discussed, but at a trial where the accused heretics are to be convicted and excommunicated from our Church?"

"Ah, you've woken up," said Ambrose.

Meanwhile the two pious bishops had got to the densely inhabited popular quarters of the town. Here, in narrow lanes, windows were being flung open one after the other; black-haired, pale-checked Milanese women, while gathering in shirts, sheets and pillow-cases that had been hung out to dry, sent their sonorous morning thoughts—accompanied by an occasional hearty yawn—humming along the clotheslines stretched across the street to all the neighbouring women; old men seated themselves in the doorways, while children drove their wooden balls along the cobbled pavement, shouting merrily or wailing; and the menfolk—cobblers and dyers, tailors and chandlers, butchers and orange-vendors, blacksmiths and wainwrights— to say nothing of the stout, copper-nosed wine-merchants—entered their small ground-floor shops and workshops and set sprucely about their daily work with an occasional exchange of views across the street.

The holy bishop halted at a crossing, where from four sides, and even from the upstairs windows, he was met by cheerfully shouted matutinal greetings, which he acknowledged by briskly waving his hand and nodding his narrow Gothic head.

"Should we not protect these people?" he said, his eyes filling with tears as he looked about the street.

"From whom? From what?" enquired the visitor, astonished.

"Why, from the heretics," replied the bishop.

"Oh, I see," said the visitor from Aquileia.

The holy bishop set out once more between the waving hands and greeting mouths that lined the street, now and then stroking a child's tousled head that bumped into his stomach and deftly avoiding the heavy wooden balls that rolled towards his feet. At the next street corner he again stopped to permit the hefty visitor faltering behind to catch up with him.

"We must protect them from our very selves," he said in a strong voice. "From the spirit of dissension, strife and hatred, which always conceals itself behind a thesis and grabs at every pretext to show its fangs, destroy and kill."

"You mean, Father," said the visitor in his slow, thick voice, "that in every man there lives an undeveloped, rudimentary heretic? How large a part of a human being would you say the heretic takes up, Father?"

"Quite a large part, Father," Ambrose said, and once again his large, melancholic eyes filled with tears. "Although Man is the flower of creation and the most accomplished work of God, if we do not drain the stagnant morass within him, he will gradually become fetid from top to toe and, one by one, taint every fellow-creature, creating hell on earth. And you cannot drain the morass and heal Man unless we direct his every thought and action towards God."

"That can be undertaken and fulfilled by the only true Mother Church alone, of course," the visitor from Aquileia said meditatively after a while.

"Why?" cried the holy bishop. "Why should it be the only true Mother Church alone that could undertake and fulfil this end? Anyone should be able to do that who would drive our unhappy sheep into one fold. Anyone who could persuade the soul, which craves for the kisses of this world, to become united with its Divine Lover; to heed nought but His words, sweeter than honey; and, rejecting every other pleasure, desire and fear, to secure the key of Matrimony and become united with Him. Why should the Mother Church alone be able to accomplish this?"

"Forgive me my sins, O Lord!" the slow-moving visitor said, this time after a somewhat shorter pause, and crossed himself with his fat hands in alarm.

The holy bishop broke into laughter.

"Anyone could achieve it," he cried, "who, having stamped out idle and pernicious curiosity in the human soul for good, were to drive the sheep into one fold. For is there anything more idle and more pernicious than inquisitive thirst for knowledge, unless it is aimed at God? Are there pleasures more dangerous than the pleasures of the intellect, is there passion more stupid than the passion of research, which breeds strife, rivalry and hatred? What is knowledge but an endless, evil fabric of deceitful obscurities? Is there anything more preposterous than to discourse on astronomy and geometry and express the firmament and the earth in figures? And can there be a greater folly, a more perverse propensity than to meditate independently after the manner of the ancient philosophers, instead of seeking the soul's salvation in the Scriptures?"

The two bishops had now reached the nearby town gate, and after passing through it, found themselves beside an encampment of Illyrian emigrants travelling by waggon. The smoke of kitchen fires and stew-pots rose towards the spring sky, accompanied by the cheerful sound of women singing. Peering over the fence, the holy bishop saw the lustily yawning women in the act of folding freshly laundered shirts, bed-sheets and pillow-cases; he saw the old men sitting in the sun in front of their tents and the scampering, squealing children kicking wooden balls between the waggons; he saw the men attending to their masculine labours with more or less unwrinkled brows.

"Are these people, heretics though they be, more unhappy than my own good sheep?" asked the holy bishop, raising his voice. "And especially now that the stench of suffering has mostly gone from them?"

"God have mercy on me," Valerianus, the burly Bishop of Aquileia, repeated, and crossed himself again.

"Man, as we know, is a free agent," the holy bishop continued, striding along the fence. "Otherwise, there would be neither virtue nor sin upon earth. He is free to choose between the two—between Christ and the Devil, grace and damnation. Yet precisely because he has a free choice—not a day passes, alas, without his sinning. That is why, O, Father and colleague, we drive them into the one fold of the Lord—my own meek sheep and the heretic and heathen wolves alike—so that with the help and by the grace of God, they may be saved from themselves through swallowing the body of Christ and assimilating His example."

"But aren't the heretics more unhappy, after all, since they are a bit farther removed from the person and example of Christ?" the visitor asked, resolutely standing still to recover his breath.

"Apparently not... apparently not," said the holy bishop, and with his outstretched white finger he pointed at the encampment of waggons.

"How trifling is the difference, O, father and colleague, between lesser and greater happiness!" he exclaimed, suddenly starting off again on his nimble feet in the direction of the green olive grove stretching behind the camp, as though in a hurry to escape the vicinity of those unhappy creatures into the clutches of an unequivocally ruthless Nature. "The world is a sad, dark place. I keep telling them that life is of no value, and that

death is nothing to be afraid of, for to die is more advantageous and useful
—since it puts an end not only to the sufferings of the body but also to the
torments of the soul and above all to sin. Death is the only possible peace
for men. To call death the end and termination of life is an untruth; for the
soul, released from the body's prison of clay, lives on."

"Yet it shies away from this release," said the visitor, panting as he tried
to keep up with Ambrose.

"Experience shows us, however, that we are all mortal," the holy bishop
cried excitedly. "Why, then, should we fear what we know to be inevitable? We should love death. Even the Apostle John died and so did Our
Lord Jesus Christ, and only Moses, Enoch and the prophet Elijah are
exceptions to this rule. And as for Job and David, Solomon and Simeon,
far from fearing death, they yearned for it . . . Just as I yearn for it, too—
although I cannot compete with them in wisdom," he added, lowering his
voice to keep the Bishop of Aquileia from hearing these words.

"What did you say, Father?" the latter asked.

"That you shall take the chair at the Council," Ambrose said.

"I? Why I, of all people?" the visitor exclaimed in alarm. "Oh, Father,
I have no wish to be in the chair at this universal and plenary Council
from which the Asian fathers will, presumably, be absent. The chairman
is bound to be gravely attacked for this."

"You have no wish to take the chair? Your modesty, Father, stirs the
heart," said Ambrose. "So does your truly Christian humility which will,
if need be, enable you to endure the heavy attacks. If need be, I say, for
I have the feeling that there will hardly be any need for you to flaunt your
humility, since we shall be between ourselves, you will not be exposed to
attack."

"All the same," the visitor repeated, with a sweeping gesture of refusal,
"I do not wish to be chairman!"

"Nevertheless, it is you that shall take the chair," the holy bishop said,
quietly continuing his way through the lovely olive grove. "And now let
us get down to the responsible and most delicate task of selecting and
screening those who will be invited to attend—a task for which I solicit
and entreat your help."

"No, I do not wish to be chairman," the good Bishop of Aquileia repeated
a second time, albeit somewhat more faint-heartedly.

"Our colleagues from Northern Italy," Ambrose said, "I think we may
in good conscience invite to attend the Council. They will, with your
concurrence defend themselves zealously and strike the foaming jaws of
those two complaining heretic hounds with even greater zeal—an action

5*

which you, in your capacity of impartial chairman, will, I'm afraid, have to forgo. The same applies, I should think, to the good shepherds of the dioceses of Pannonia, whom we shall deploy to a man at the Council. You agree, father?"

"I do, indeed!" said the visitor with a resigned gesture.

"My secretary will draw up a list of these brethren and hand it over to you, Father," Ambrose said. "All right. Let us proceed. We shall invite the Bishop of Rome, of course, the great Pope Damasus, who is recognized by us. We shall not, of course, invite the scheming Antipope Ursinus, although it is to be feared that this or that adherent of his will stealthily introduce his spirit of plotting into our meeting."

"To be sure," said the visitor. "And we shall invite the holy fathers of the provinces of Southern Italy, too."

"Yes. We shall do so, in more or less cordial words," said the holy bishop.

"We'll invite the Bishops of Capua, Tarentum, Neapolis, Arpi, Croton, Syracusa, Agrigentum," said the visitor, "as well as the fathers of the minor bishoprics, whom, for the sake of brevity, I shall refrain from enumerating."

"The Bishop of Neapolis, dear colleague, you should omit from the list," Ambrose said. "From what I heard, he recently wrote a long letter to Antipope Ursinus, whom we cannot abide. You should also omit from the list the Bishop of Agrigentum, whose sister lives at Empress Justina's court."

"Why not?" asked the slow visitor.

"I wish, dear colleague, you wouldn't always lag behind by three steps and as many thoughts!" said the holy bishop irritably. "I tell you that the maiden is becoming contaminated at the heretical court of a heretical Empress Mother."

"Whom shall we invite from Gaul?" the visiting bishop asked, after some meditation. "The Bishop of Trever?"

"Right," Ambrose said.

"Brigantium?"

"Right," said Ambrose.

"Lutetia?"

"Right," said Ambrose.

"Massilia?"

"With pleasure," said Ambrose.

"Tolosa?"

"Better drop Tolosa," Ambrose said. "The father and grandfather of that colleague were of the Arian faith. He himself only abjured his heresy ten years ago. We'd better drop Tolosa!"

"Drop Tolosa?" the visitor murmured. "I don't know what to say."

"Don't say anything," replied the holy bishop. "From Spain we shall be most happy to receive everyone at the Oecumenical Council."

"Most happy! Saguntum, Valentia, Tarraco," said the visitor, slipping the euphonious names one by one on to his thick fingers. "Nova Carthago, Ebore..."

"Everyone of them, I tell you," cried the holy bishop. "From Spain, everyone of them! Come on! Now to Africa."

"I would recommend Alexandria, Cyrene, Berenice..."

"Right." the holy bishop said.

"Caesarea, Carthago, Tingis, Utica..."

"Utica you should also omit from the list," the holy bishop said.

"Utica!" the visitor exclaimed. "Why should I omit the good Bishop of Utica, one of the most valiant athletes of Christ?"

"He may be one of the most valiant athletes of Christ," the holy bishop said; "but who can stand the sight of his clumsy bearing and vulgar, unpolished gesticulation? It makes me nervous even to hear his voice."

The two bishops, acting in pious harmony, thus discussed at great length the eligible fathers to whom invitations should be sent and, after careful consideration of every detail, drew up a list of names—from which even the Britannic fathers were not omitted—although it looked doubtful whether these would have the strength and the cash for the crossing and long journey. Finally, after mature consideration, the fathers agreed upon the wording of the letter in which they would advise the Asian fathers, in the most general and harmonious terms, of the holding of the Oecumenical Council, and cordially invite them in a body to come to Aquileia, in the hope—so the letter would conclude—that, despite the relatively insignificant agenda, the esteemed and beloved fathers (or at least a few of the younger ones among them) would not be deterred by the strains of the extremely long and expensive voyage.

"I wonder how many of them, after reading this letter, will come," said the visitor, puzzled and shaking his head.

"Not many," said the holy bishop. "As far as it is humanly possible to foretell, very few." Nor is there any need of them. You should time the invitations so that our beloved Eastern brethren would be allowed little time for meditation and consultation, should they, contrary to all expectations, desire to attend the Council."

By now the sun had reached its zenith and infused the surrounding countryside with its friendly warmth, and the two fathers laid themselves down in the scanty shadow of an olive tree. The burly visitor from Aquileia felt hungry, and concluded from the position of the sun that it was meal-time;

however, he did not, for the moment, dare to communicate this observation aloud, for the holy bishop sitting beside him was evidently deeply engrossed in contemplating nature.

"Behold this olive-tree," he said, speaking into the air and to himself, as it were. "Behold its twisted and cracked branches, gray with age, and the smooth young leaves upon them, fluttering like silver-winged butterflies! What an eye-gladdening, edifying spectacle! At the end of my meditation I shall compare it to the human soul that has been pruned and disciplined by the hand of the Lord. What useful—because lovely—and what lovely—because useful—things trees are! What splendid beams are hewn of cedar! And cypress yields durable planks for roofing, while children are taught to read and write with the aid of alphabets carved of boxwood. How closely, on the other hand, Nature illustrates the Almighty's majestic design of the universe! The dog symbolizes loyalty; the bear, paternal care; the king-fisher, hope; the crane, charity; and, lastly, Man himself is symbolized by the fishes that play and splash in the Ocean—that is to say, the Church. How mighty is the Lord!"

"Amen," said the visitor from Aquileia.

"Let us follow Nature," the holy bishop went on; "for Nature has been created by God, and created with purpose. Nature is beautiful and right-eous; whatever derives from Nature teaches us modesty, search for the truth, abstemiousness, conjugal fidelity and selflessness. It is contrary to the laws of nature to deprive our fellow-men of our assistance. We are created such that our limbs must be in mutual harmony and assist one another, and if the hands were to gouge out the eyes or injure the feet, the whole body would suffer harm. And it is a graver sin by far to injure a whole human being than a mere limb. For if the crippling of one limb injures the whole body, the injury of a single human being will surely entail the disintegration of the entire human community, defile the nature of the human race and violate the unity of the Church, bound together by the ties of faith and charity. How mighty is the Lord!"

"Amen," said the visitor. "I see, Father, that you have been studying the pagan philosophers to advantage."

"The Lord, however, is mightier and more perfect even than Nature," the holy bishop continued. "No wonder, considering that He created it with His own hands. The laws of nature do not apply to Him, since they too are His work and through them He governs Nature. Man's knowledge is advancing slowly, step by step. The Lord, on the other hand, is, by His nature, omniscient; His knowledge, perfect from the beginning, cannot be increased, and, unlike man, He knows not only the past and present but the future as well. For what is the future but His plan, His intent and deed? How mighty is the Lord!"

"Amen," the visitor said, somewhat belatedly; by now he was listening not so much to his colleague's words as to the rumbling of his hungry stomach, which was, at times, so vociferous that it would drown his companion's praise of the Lord. However, the holy bishop's ears, eyes and nose were filled with the devotion of his soul to such an extent that he failed to hear those rumblings. "So mighty is the Lord," he went on, riveting his red-rimmed eyes on the olive-tree, "that He is capable of changing the laws of nature at will. He can reverse the course of rivers so they will flow backwards, and the sea will recede at His command. If it suited Him, He could change all of Creation and make new laws of nature. Christ spoke, and something that was not was begotten of nothing. Why, then, should not something that is be changed into something that, as yet, is not?"

"Alas!" sighed the visitor, giving voice to a plaintive thought at the back of his mind.

"Take the Blessed Virgin Mary," continued Ambrose, blind and deaf. "According to the laws of nature, a woman can give birth only after having had congress with a man. It is clear, therefore, that the Blessed Virgin, in giving birth to our Lord Jesus, successfully defied the laws of nature. This was because Her body was God's temple, and she partook of the flesh of God and quenched her thirst on the blood of God. Defying Nature and its laws, she remained a virgin when she conceived through the Holy Ghost, and she remained a virgin even after giving birth to our Lord Jesus. The heretic Heldevedianus' doctrine—which he adopted from the impudent Photinians—alleging that the Blessed Virgin, after giving birth to the Saviour, bore several other children begotten of Joseph is idle talk and sheer lies."

"It is, indeed," said the visitor. "How mighty is the Lord!"

"Verily He is!" Ambrose cried, raising his eyes towards the sky. "All of Creation is groaning and suffering in the sweat of its brow, not only the human soul imprisoned in the body, but the angels themselves, whose celestial peace the Lord again and again interrupts by sending them down to earth to avenge and punish. And all are looking hopefully toward their ultimate physical annihilation, when, redeemed, they will finally become united in the Lord."

"Amen," said the visitor from Aquileia. "Behold, the sun is setting," he added, also lifting his eyes towards the sky. "Like the Arians' glory, which is on the wane."

"That selfsame sun will rise again to-morrow morning, Father," Ambrose said. "Let us be cautious in the use of metaphors!"

"Perhaps we might go home," suggested the visitor, pressing his hands on his stomach to stifle its rumbling, which was jarring upon the ear. However, receiving no reply from the holy bishop, he cast down his eyes in shame. "About half-way through our talk," he went on after a while, "you promised, Father, that you would compare this olive tree with its pruned and disciplined branches—whose shadow is now lengthening rapidly—to the human soul. I am waiting hungrily and thirstily for you parable."

"I have no mind to tell parables now," Ambrose said. "Your hunger shall remain unappeased. I think, after all, you had better omit the Bishop of Saragossa from the Spaniards on the list. I am advised that last year he received an invitation to the court of the Empress Justina. True, he did not go, yet why was he invited?"

With these words the holy bishop suddenly took leave of his visitor and, scrambling to his feet from the grass, quickly struck out in a direction away from town as though, tired of human company, he meant to mingle and become united for good with the world of trees and birds. And although his return to his palace late in the evening, revealed that his supposed scheme had failed and that he remained stuck in his authentic earthly form, the holy bishop for a good many days became more taciturn than was his custom and spent more time than usual at his prie-dieu.

After Easter, which fell on March 28th and 29th that year, and during April, the bishops slowly began to gather in Aquileia. First to arrive were those from northern Italy; they were followed, successively, by the bishops of the Danubian provinces, those from southern Italy, and the zealous African fathers. Those from Gaul trickled in more slowly, no doubt on account of the greater distances and the uncertain political situation—the pious fathers had been terrified, presumably, by the recurring incursions and raids made by the various tribes of Barbarians, especially the unruly Germanic Alemanni (or Svevi, as they called themselves).

In the beginning, while waiting for the late-comers, the holy fathers would only engage in preliminary or preparatory negotiations and conversations with Palladius and Secundianus, the two Arian bishops at whose request the immortal Emperor Gratianus had convoked the universal and plenary Council (which, according to all indications, promised to be neither universal nor plenary). As these lobby conversations were not placed on record and, consequently, only interloping long-eared spies were to be feared (against whom the Lord Himself can provide not protection) the fathers could debate and develop the multicoloured fabric of their opinions more freely during these informal exchanges. Thus, the Western fathers used the occasion vigorously to question the need for the immortal Caesar's burdening his august hands and mind with trivial causes which, in fact, came under the exclusive jurisdiction of, and were settled within, the Church itself. For their part, the two complainant Arian bishops, secure in the absence of official records and heedless of spies, shamelessly aired their sacrilegious views. To put an end to such useless and ridiculous private debates, Ambrose—who scarcely ever took part in them—a few weeks later, proposed to the executive committee that they should officially convene the meeting and get down to the real issues at hand.

The Council was opened in the first week of May, the time of year when even the sparrows upon the housetops chirrup in praise of the Lord, when field and forest ring with the sweet warbling of blackbirds and blue titmice and the trees, their branches stretching upward like so many organ-pipes, breathe their verdant songs of happiness towards the sky. Men and beasts, flowers and bushes are now filled with hope, and even the low grasses believe they will live on for ever. The whole of Creation is one great cry of exultation and every creature is singing, in its own humble idiom, its alleluia to the Almighty, Who, cupping his palm behind His ear and smiling with satisfaction, is listening to the gentle murmur of the living.

The Council met in the sacristy of the Cathedral, and its confined space proved spacious enough to hold the participants. The Bishop of Aquileia was elected chairman, of course—by unanimous vote, of course, and the same unanimity was displayed in electing the recording secretaries, shorthand writers and other officials. The chairman opened the meeting at daybreak, at 4 a.m. On entering the sacristy, the Arian Palladius greeted those present with the words, "We have come as Christians to Christians." The holy fathers murmured in reply.

The armchairs, upholstered in red silk brocade, were arranged in a semi-circle in the sacristy, facing a throne on which the Scriptures were placed, but St. Paul's letters and other necessary ecclesiastical writings were also available, in case anyone wanted to brush up or complement his knowledge with their aid. The first meeting was attended by thirty-two reverend fathers—no doubt the most brilliant diamonds and sparkling rubies of the Church—who, seated round the enthroned Word, like a glittering Crown of Knowledge and of Faith, infused the whole sacristy with the beauty of their pious light. Yet, not one ruby or diamond had come from Rome or from Spain, or from Britain—to say nothing of the provinces of the East; on the other hand, each of the thirty-two bishops attending—with the exception of Palladius and Secundianus, the two complainants—stood with the broad soles of his manly feet firmly planted on the foundation-stone of the only true orthodox doctrines. From which Ambrose, the holy bishop, drew the pious conclusion that the Lord looked with gracious benevolence upon his tireless activity in this field. His case was as good as won.

The elections having been held, the recording secretary of the meeting, the deacon of Capua, standing in front of his armchair, solemnly read out an ordinance from the most gracious and immortal Caesar Gratianus to the imperial Proconsul of Italy, in which His Majesty convoked the Oecumenical—or universal and plenary—Council. Thereafter Ambrose, Bishop of Milan, requested leave to speak. To pay due respect to the assembled brilliant diamonds and sparkling rubies, he too rose from his seat. Only during the later proceedings of the meeting did he remain seated while speaking—the short and delicate dimensions of his figure were less conspicuous in this posture than if he had always assumed a standing position when facing that sturdy, hulking big dog of a heretic, Palladius and that other impudent heretic, Secundianus, who was even taller by a head; either of them could have removed the holy bishop from the council chamber with a flourish of his mighty beard or a flick of his fingers.

"As a Christian among Christians," said that tiny servant of the Lord, after greeting the assembled diamonds and rubies with appropriate humility and thanking them for having come from distant lands and even crossed the seas, sparing neither money nor the effort, and brought their brilliance to pious Aquileia, "and with Christian humility, I should like to suggest that, before we enter upon the merits of the issues before us, we commune with ourselves and examine, on the one hand, whether we have provided ourselves with the forbearance and love required for the performance of our task, and whether our judicial sight is not dimmed by unfair bias and partiality; and, on the other, whether we are ready to sacrifice even this our Christian forbearance and brotherly love—the greatest of all our treasures—in the defence of the Lord, should the necessity arise."

At the sound of these words the sacristy, which was already wonderfully illuminated by the collective knowledge of the holy fathers, suddenly became infused with an even brighter light. Ambrose, the holy bishop, quickly seated his graceful figure in his armchair and continued his address in this posture. "After this examination," he said in his sweetly ringing, melodious voice, "which will no doubt take place in our minds in less than a minute, I should suggest with due modesty that, for our instruction, we listen to the letter, heinous beyond belief, which the heretic Arius wrote to Alexander of Alexandria about half a century ago, a year before his death—that is, his descent to hell. This unbelievably heinous letter—whose contents, by the way, are common knowledge—luckily survives whole and intact, a deterrent that makes our cheeks blush."

"Why blush if we can help it?" one holy father presumably inquired.

"Why pollute our ears with it?" another presumably said.

"Seeing that it's common knowledge, anyway?" said a third, presumably.

"Dear Fathers," said Ambrose, the eminent statesman and holy bishop, "as this letter, heinous beyond belief, sets forth, one by one, all the articles of faith held by the heretic Arius, we shall provide our colleagues Palladius and Secundianus a welcome opportunity to refute them, one by one, and thereby brilliantly clear themselves of the charge and suspicion of heresy.

What greater satisfaction could we give them? And what more eloquent proof could we supply of our Christian forbearance and brotherly love?"

"As I can hear the concurrent murmur of my fellow ecclesiastics," the chairman presumably said, "I order the letter to be read out."

The full text of the letter having been read, as evidenced by the minutes of the council—while several particularly pious fathers concealed their blushing cheeks behind their hands—the rays of the rising sun reached the orange-painted eastern windows of the sacristy, bathing the delegates to the Council in a shining, nay, dazzling golden light and eluding only the two Arian bishops, Fathers Palladius and Secundianus, who were both seated in the contemptuous shadow of one and the same column. However, even that condemnatory shadow failed to shake the towering, long-bearded Palladius in his determination to rise and speak.

"Honoured and devout Congregation," he said in his somewhat hollow voice, stretching his elongated body. "His Majesty, the immortal Caesar Gratianus, as evidenced by his gracious ordinance, has convoked an Oecumenical—that is to say, universal and plenary—Council to listen to and pass judgement on our grievances. Yet I am amazed to observe although I am somewhat short-sighted that not only does this devout assemblage lack the presence of the Head of the Church Bishop Damasus of Rome, His Holiness the Pope, not to mention the newly sprouted head of the Church, the Antipope Ursinus—but it is deprived of the presence of such columns and pillars of the Faith in the western provinces as the Bishops of Spain and Britain, without whose firm support no council can be raised to appropriate heights, and covered with the roof of reassuring determination. Worse yet . . . . . Where are the delegates of the Asian provinces, of Mesopotamia, Syria, Cilicia, Cappadocia, Bithynia, Lycaonia, Paphlagonia and other Eastern dioceses? Where is the Bishop of Byzantium? Not one of those fathers can

I see though I admit I am a little short-sighted. If, for all that my finding should be correct and there are no more than thirty pious and learned fathers to illuminate this inadequately lighted chamber . . ."

"Thirty-two" one father, presumably, interposed.

"I have counted those present myself," Palladius replied. "Naturally, I did not include the two of us, since we two are virtually absent. . . If therefore, I have counted well, and of the many hundred learned luminaries of the world-wide Church not more than thirty are assembled here, in these inadequately lighted premises, to transilluminate our case and our grievance, then the immortal Gratianus' ordinance that our questions and answers be discussed under the umbrella of an universal and plenary Council has, in my respectful view, been violated. On looking around carefully I see although, of course, I am very short-sighted—that this is an assembly of only the North Italian and Illyrian sections of the Church, their ranks interspersed by one sympathising luminary, respectively, from Africa, southern Italy and Gaul."

"And what conclusion would you draw from that?" one father, presumably, asked at this point.

"Just a minute!" exclaimed Ambrose, the holy Bishop of Milan, maintaining his sitting posture. "Ere Palladius draws short-sighted conclusions from his findings we should remind him of the fact that the dioceses and districts of the East do not as a rule take part in the Councils of the West."

"Except the universal and plenary ones," Palladius replied.

"So far as we know," said Eusebius of Bologna, a friend and adherent of Ambrose's, eminent advocate and apostle of monastic life, who, for the first time in Italy, had had a nunnery built and furnished for high-born virgins, "so far as we know, the Eastern fathers have been dulyin vited to attend this Council."

"Therefore it has rested with them to come or stay away," said another holy father presumably.

"According to information received by us," Palladius answered, stretching his very long waist, "though they did receive the invitations, it was not made clear to them with due emphasis that in accordance with the most gracious imperial ordinance a universal and plenary Council was to be held at Aquileia."

"What is Palladius' wish?" Ambrose demanded.

"He does not wish to give evidence," another father presumably said.

"I do wish to give evidence and make a statement," Palladius said, "in due form and with Christian humility, before my only competent court —

the universal and plenary Council. I do not, however, consider this brilliant assemblage of luminaries and gems in itself competent to judge our grave concerns and thoughts. I hereby protest."

"Aha," said Ambrose from his seat.

"I therefore ask you beloved brethren," Palladius continued in his hollow voice, which—this was the decided opinion in the chamber—was at perfect odds with his strapping physique and huge bearded head, "I ask you, beloved fellow ecclesiastics, to postpone my hearing and interrogation till the next Oecumenical Council is convened. Then and there I shall answer every question, put to me, whether thorny or thornless, with my customary candour."

"Aha," Ambrose said for the second time.

"He's taking to his heels," one father presumably exclaimed.

"He's trying to find a loophole of escape, evade the issue," presumably said another.

"The cloven hoof is showing," presumably cried a third.

"I wish you would stop insinuating, O, beloved brethren and fellow ecclesiasts," Palladius said, while irritably agitating his long beard. "It stands to reason, that I am reluctant to lay my case and plaint before an assembly which has been hand-picked with statesmanlike care—not to say guile—so that it would like a corner-stone and rock, be of one faith and one conviction, rejecting and excluding in advance every divergent thought and view. Once more I protest."

"He accuses us of partiality," cried another, louder still.

"He accuses us of conspiracy," cried a third. "That is how he wants to evade the issue."

The long bearded and shrewd Father Palladius however, had not yet lost his imperturbability. "Well, well," he said stroking his hirsute appendage with a thick-fingered red hand. "How very extraordinary! I am supposed to be accusing my brethren of what they have themselves admitted. Or is it possible that I am not only short-sighted but hard of hearing as well? I seem to remember that in his smart opening address Ambrose, the great Bishop of Milan, called upon us—with the exception of us two, that is—to sacrifice our greatest asset, our Christian forbearance and brotherly love, in defence of the Lord, should the necessity arise."

The holy Bishop, however, remained seated in his saddle, from which it was not easy to dislodge him.

"Let Palladius hold his tongue!" he snapped curtly, but even with these few words his sonorous voice nearly shattered the frightened walls of the sacristy.

Palladius did indeed remain speechless with surprise.

"Let Palladius hold his tongue!" the holy bishop sitting still, repeated. "And if his tongue should refuse to stop, let him grab it into his mouth as hard as he can. Even when burning in the fire of hell, he will still regret that he ever opened it to speak."

"I am listening to you with interest, oh great Bishop of Milan," Palladius said.

"Dear Friends and Brethren," the holy Bishop began, his eyes ranging over the dumbfounded diamonds and rubies, "I entreat your advice. I want to find a way to defend our poor Brother Palladius against his own viciously wagging tongue, which is beyond doubt a hundred times more wicked than his honest, if erring, soul. Or are we to suppose, in spite of all our hopes, and wishes, that his tongue is speaking the truth and betraying what he is harbouring in his inner heart? For, what he has uttered so far, would in itself, suffice, for us to anathematize him and excommunicate him from the Church. No, I cannot and I do not believe his tongue. Beloved forbearing and learned colleagues, I think Christian charity obliges us to give our erring brother a chance to withdraw his rash protest and answer the question we shall put to him one by one."

At his point a great hubbub presumably arose in the cramped sacristy, now blazing in a glorious light as the rays of the sun poured in through the orange-coloured window. "Granted... Granted!" the pious fathers shouted enthusiastically, "let us help and heal the halt and the lame!"

"Listen, Palladius! Ambrose said gently, aiming his long nose at the heretic, "Withdraw the protest!"

"I cannot withdraw it, father," replied the defendant. "Only at the universal and plenary Council convoked by the immortal Ceasar can and will I clear my person and my intentions."

"Very well," said the Bishop of Milan, his distressed gaze once again ranging over the gathering of holy fathers. "As we all know, dear colleagues, the bishopric sees of Palladius and Secundianus belong under ecclesiastical law, among the Western congregations. There is consequently nothing to prevent us, as fully authorized deputies and representatives of these congregations from bringing to account the halt and the lame."

"I therefore rule," cried the burly methodical Bishop of Aquileia, shaking an angelical sound from his chairman's bell, "I rule that the Council, unexpectedly transforming itself into a fully authorized Council of the Western dioceses, intends to interrogate Bishop Palladius and, subsequently, Bishop Secundianus. I hereby declare the procedural debate closed. Contributions are now invited on the merits of the case."

"Honoured Fathers," said Eusebius of Bologna, who, though Ambrose's most loyal friend and adherent, began his politic address, not in a sitting posture, but on the contrary, rising from his armchair. "We have listened abashed to the authentic letter, read to us a little while ago, which Aurius, the impudent heretic, wrote, to Alexander of Alexandria, and in which, impertinently placing himself in opposition to the doctrine of the Holy Trinity, he goes so far as to claim and propagate that

the Father is the one and only eternal,

the Father is the one and only without beginning and end,

the Father is the one and only immortal,

the Father is the one and only wise, good and mighty,

the Father is the one and only judge over all,"

thereby denying the divine origin, being and might of the Son and of the Holy Spirit, that is, the blissful unity of the Holy Trinity. And now, "Eusebius of Bologna continued," we ask you Father Palladius, to tell us what your attitude is towards the foul heretical letter that has been read to us. Or let us, Father, with Christian forbearance..."

"And eager curiosity!" exclaimed Ambrose from his seat.

"...with Christian forbearance ask Father Palladius," Eusebius of Bologna continued, "to refute the false doctrines that have been quoted..."

"He will do nothing of the sort," Ambrose shouted from his seat.

"...to refute the diabolical lies just mentioned," Eusebius of Bologna continued, "or defend them by citing convincing passages from the Scriptures or from the Church Fathers."

"Where should he take them from?" cried Ambrose. "Fabricate them? Such passages do not and cannot exist."

"I ask you Father Palladius," said the presiding Bishop of Aquileia, "would you for the sake of order and greater lucidity, to refute or defend one by one the articles just quoted. First. Does he agree or does he deny that the Father is the one and only eternal?

"He is not fool enough to show his true colours!" shouted Ambrose from his seat.

The fathers looked at one another in amazement, then at the holy Bishop. Never before had they seen him take the field in such martial armour and with a youthful fervour that belied his age against detractors and eroders of the Church, who with carious teeth and stinging tongues were demolishing from within its sacred unity, important above all. However, as the countenance of that little servant of the Lord radiated devoutness so unearthly that in its light even his inornate, harsh speech became transformed, the fathers suddenly rallied behind him to a man and, giving vent to the vulgar, malicious glee and wolf-pack savagery that are latent in every human being, began to jeer and shout, and the towering, solitary Father Palladius was immersed in their laughter and bespattered with their saliva. "He is not such a fool as to show his true colours!" they repeated over and over again, their teeth gleaming, the walls reverberating with their shouts. For this reason the impartial chairman soon rang his bell, and its angelic ringing produced temporary silence, in the confined sacristy.

"As Palladius has refused to return an answer on the first point," said the presiding Bishop of Aquileia, "I shall now ask him the second question. Does he agree or does he deny that the Father is the one and only without beginning and end?"

"His tongue has lost its glibness now!" Ambrose shouted from his seat. "Yet he has not swallowed his beard yet, I see."

"Nor shall I do so, O, Saintly Bishop of Milan," Palladius replied with perfect equanimity.

"As Palladius has refused to return an answer concerning the second point as well," the chairman said, "for the sake of brevity I shall now question him on the third, fourth, and fifth points together. "What is your attitude, Palladius, to the heretic Arius' infamous claim that the Father is the one and only immortal, wise, good and mighty, and the one and only judge over all things?" "We are just wasting our time with him!" Ambrose shouted from his seat. "His attitude is entirely negative!" Once again the assembled fathers burst into a loud jeering, and it was some time before Palladius, after repeatedly opening his mouth in vain, was once more able to make himself heard. "I am sorry," he said in his hollow, diminutive voice, "but I must repeat that I do not recognize this assembly as authorized to interrogate me. But even if I did so recognize it, how could I possibly answer any questions amidst these frothing waves of hatred that reaching to my lips, even to my nose, drive the words back into my throat? I also object to Bishop Sabinus as writer of the minutes, for I have serious doubts concerning his impartiality."

"On mature consideration," the chairman said, "the objection is refused. The recorders have been elected by unanimous vote, the complainants having abstained. Am I to understand Father Palladius as saying that he has seen reason and is now willing to answer the questions put to him?"

At this juncture, Ambrose, Bishop of Milan, rose from his seat for a brief moment.

"Let us make it easier for the halt and the lame to find their way," he said in his sweetest voice. "Let us consider Palladius as not having heard the questions that were just put to him, and let us ask him new questions."

"Well, then," said Eusebius, the holy Bishop of Bologna, "I now ask you, Palladius: Do you recognize that Our Lord Jesus Christ is one in substance with the Father? Or more precisely, that the Father's Son is himself wholly and entirely God?"

"Since I do recognize that He is wholly and entirely the Father's Son," Palladius said, "what need is there for any supplement?"

"According to Arius' doctrines," said Eusebius of Bologna, patron of the virgins," God created the Son out of nothing and only adopted Him and His Son afterwards. By contrast, according to the creed of the Church and to the faith we all hold, Christ too is wholly and entirely God. Do you recognize that, Palladius? Yes, or no?"

"I do recognize," Palladius answered, "that Christ is wholly and entirely the Father's Son."

"We are all of us adopted sons of God," Eusebius said. "What I ask Palladius to tell us is this: Do you admit that Christ is, in essence and owing to His divine conception, wholly and entirely God Himself?"

"I do recognize that He is wholly and entirely the only-begotten Son of God," Palladius replied.

"This is getting us nowhere," Ambrose, the holy Bishop, now cried, apparently at the end—or almost the end—of his Christian forbearance. "Ask him if he thinks our regarding and worshipping Christ as God is at variance with the Scriptures."

Palladius remained silent for a while, and during this time his strapping figure began to shrink, albeit to a small extent, yet perceptible to the naked eye. "I believe in Christ's power and might that is of God," he said at last, casting a look of hatred at Ambrose from the corner of his eye. The holy Bishop now saw that, the heretic in his evident obstinacy could not be forced to show his colours and hence he decided on a clever and commendable flank attack.

"Beloved brethren," he said in his ingratiating, soft voice, "as Palladius, no doubt because his feelings have been hurt, and probably in his vanity, refuses to admit and declare that the Father and the Son—leaving the Holy Spirit aside for the moment—are completely equal in power and might, let us ask him to pour out his heart to us, and we shall listen to him with brotherly love and pray for his salvation."

"What should he pour out of it?" one of the fathers, presumably, asked. "The filth of heresy?"

"Exactly," the holy Bishop presumably said. "The filth of heresy. So he may cleanse himself and rise to higher things. Let him openly confess that he has allowed himself to be dazzled and misled by Arius' doctrines, which, though utterly false, are not without a measure of philosophical beauty and charm. We shall listen to him without anger and indignation and lead him back into the sweet fold of the Church, where no harm shall befall him."

"No harm befall him?" one of the fathers presumably asked. "Shall no harm befall the heretic who has infiltrated into our ranks under disguise, in order to instigate discord and cause disruption?"

"No harm shall befall him," Ambrose repeated. "Provided he contritely admits that, his eyes and mind having been dazzled by the spurious brilliance of a philosophical beauty and virtuosity of sorts, he became a follower of Arius."

"That is not true," Palladius said. "I cannot possibly confess to that, as I am neither a follower nor an adherent of Arius."

"Come now!" Ambrose said.

"I cannot possibly be an adherent of his, for I do not even know him," Palladius said.

Once again the small sacristy became filled with an ominous buzz and murmur almost too thick in substance to be pierced even by the uneasy breathing of Ambrose the holy Bishop. "What do you mean, you don't know him, Father?" he cried, clutching at his blonde—or rather reddish—beard.

"I do not know him," Palladius repeated in his hollow voice. "I have never read a line of his."

"He's never read a line of his!" several fathers, presumably, echoed, shocked, sneering, possibly astonished. "His not having read a line of his is a lie. Maybe he cannot read at all?"

In the sacristy, which the sun now risen to its zenith had warmed up exceedingly, the holy bishops and deans began to perspire with excitement, and the cheeks of the more corpulent among them acquired an apoplectic tint. "Keep cool! Beloved brethren!" Ambrose cried. "We have no reason for doubting our uneducated colleague's word. However, if he did not know Arius, the letter recently read here must have shocked him all the more. Let us give him yet another chance, therefore, to refute and repudiate, one by one or in their totality, the first five points of that letter."

As Palladius' hulking figure, leaning against the column, perceptibly continued to shrink and stoop, Ambrose, the holy Bishop, despite his short stature, was gaining ground visibly. "Come now, Palladius," he cried boldly. "Come on, my erring brother! Go ahead with it!"

"What do you want me to go ahead with?" Palladius shouted back. "I have told you, that I do not recognize you as my judges. The universal and plenary Council called by the immortal Gratianus. . ."

"Be quiet!" Ambrose shouted. "So you refuse the hand I hold out to you?"

"What right have you," Palladius shouted back in his small sized voice, "what right have you, O, saintly bishop, to call me to account? Are you my prosecutor and judge in one? Who ever heard of a man planting the same tiny bottom on both seats at the same time?"

"Be quiet, Palladius!" Ambrose yelled, now giving full rein to his powerful, sonorous voice, and his narrow, gothic head began to shake with wrath. "You are rushing to your destruction!"

"I shall accept none but the universal and plenary Council to judge me!" Palladius shouted back. "How many times do I have to tell you that? Where are the delegates from Spain? Where are those from Britain? Where is Bishop Damasus of Rome, His Holiness the Pope? or the Antipope Ursinus? What sort of guilefully packed Council is this, from which the mightiest pillars and mainstays of the Church are absent?"

"I call you to order, Palladius!" the impartial chairman cried, bringing into full play both his angelic bell and his lungs. "I must energetically repudiate your diabolical insinuations."

"Even Arius' impieties deserve more respect than the opportunist wriggling of this reptile," a perspiring apoplectic father shouted, beside himself.

At this point the powerfully built but by now somewhat bowed Palladius pushed himself away from the column he had been leaning against and made for the exit with long strides and fluttering beard. "Aha" cried Ambrose, he's giving up the fight! Taking to his heels! This action makes his heresy as clear as noonday. What more are we waiting for?"

Before reaching the door Palladius, however suddenly turned and rushed back to his place, his beard a flutter. "Yes indeed,—the Father is greater" he cried again leaning his back against the column, his head raised high. "I request you to consult the holy bishops of the East!"

"Which of them? Ambrose asked derisively. "Father Paulinus, the Bishop of Antioch, maybe? I daresay he would make short work of you."

"Paulinus is *not* the bishop of Antioch!" Palladius shouted. "The saintly Meletius is the only rightful occupant of the episcopal seat of Antioch, elected by the people and consecrated by the bench of bishops. It is his opinion you must ask!"

"In earlier years Meletius was himself an Arian," one of the fathers presumably retorted. "He abjured his heretical views but a short time before being elected—not without reason, forsooth."

"Ask for the opinion of Gregory of Nazianzus, the great Bishop of Byzantium!" Palladius shouted, banging his fist upon the friendly column which had so loyally supported him till then.

"Gregory of Nazianzus," another father, presumably, said, "belonged to the most noisomely heretical Photinian sect until, he saw reason and changed his views so that he might be elected Bishop of Alexandria and then, of Byzantium."

"And would you be good enough to tell us why those fathers have not come to this Council?" a third father presumably asked. "Letters of invitation, worded in cordial and courteous terms, have been sent to their addresses inviting them to honour us with their physical presence and their wisdom."

"Enough of this!" shouted Ambrose in a threateningly thundering voice, through which, if you looked close, you could detect the yellow trumpets of irate angels peeping. "Let us ask Palladius one more question—the last," the holy bishop continued, "if dispiritedly and without hope, yet to reassure our Christian conscience. I ask him to tell us this: Before He was born, was Christ Man or God?"

"I accuse Ambrose, Bishop of Milan, of impiety, blasphemy and ribald sacrilege," Palladius shouted, stretching himself upwards for the last time. "I decline to answer him."

These words were followed by a startled silence, and in his amazement the stout and somewhat slow Bishop of Aquileia put the chairman's bell, which he had been clutching for some time back on the table. "Just what impiety, blasphemy and sacrilege do you accuse our brother and colleague Ambrose of?" he uttered slowly and methodically, his eyebrows raised. "Enumerate those charges one by one and point by point!"

"Only before the universal and plenary Council," Palladius repeated for the hundredth time.

"Brethren" said Eusebius, patron of the virgins," let us stop harassing and plaguing Palladius! How could he be frank with us after having been found guilty of two heresies, condemned as a bishop of the foul-mouthed Photinians ten years ago, and now revealed in the full daylight of his Arian deviation."

"Prove it!" Palladius shouted, his voice increasingly hollow.

"It's up to you to prove me blasphemous and sacrilegious!" Ambrose shouted, his voice more manly and ringing then ever. "But first disavow Arius so we may speak to you at all."

"Anyone lacking the courage to publicly condemn and disavow Arius," the impartial chairman declared, "resembles him and may rightly be called a heretic."

But before the final, fatal and irrevocable, word was spoken, the powerfully built Palladius made a last and futile attempt to secure the salvation of his soul. And realizing that the attempt was futile since the holy wolves of the Lord—carefully hand-picked and with well-timed hunger had apparently met here for the purpose of tearing him limb from limb, his eyes grew dim, his perky beard dropped dejectedly, and his tongue, like the ancient sage's began to falter and stutter, as if a large pebble had been placed under it.

"Fathers," he said "let us stop to-to-tormenting each other if we can help it. Our over-exc-s-s-cited temper have burst into flames, and we have been flinging thoughtless sparks into one another's faces and beards. Let us give ourselves time to cool down and become calm. The rock of the Church will not have been shaken if I and my comrade-in-arms, Secundianus, are left to rot in our supposed heresy for a while, or if those present—or at least a majority of them, are for the time being left under a delusion as to our true intentions. I would therefore, with due modesty and Christian humility, suggest that the learned luminaries here assembled temporarily extinguish their brilliant lights and only let them forth again after a few weeks' repose—on, say, the first Sunday of June, when summer too will have ripened its glow and its fruits, and when people, with contented hearts, will be gathering in the crops from the fields."

No sooner had the heretic's last stammered word been spoken then Ambrose, the great Bishop of Milan, requested leave to speak.

"Beloved Brethren" he said, still seated, "Palladius is obviously seeking to bolster up his lost cause by temporizing. Perhaps he cherishes the hope that by the first Sunday of June several helping hands of dubious cleanness may be stretched out from distant Byzantium, or that he may be able to bring some of them here in a hurry; or he may be hoping for such a change in the present internal and external political situation, that the Lord, owing to pre-occupation elsewhere, will forget about his insignificant person and individual case. Well, let us see how we stand."

At this words, the holy bishop's narrow, gothic face once again began to radiate such devoutness that the Council fathers watched him in amazement and an extraordinary silence descended upon the small sacristy.

"What is a good prince like?" the holy bishop asked, turning to the second question at issue no doubt in order to elucidate the first. "When the avenging angel descended on Israel, King David stood before him and said, "Behold, I the shepherd of the flock, have sinned, I have done wrong; but the flock,—wherein has it sinned? Turn you your hand, pray, against me!" That's how this good prince acted. And whenever insults where heaped upon him, he would not reply to them, but would pray; when his authority was challenged, he was benevolent, kindly and meek in spirit; he was valiant in battle and gentle in ruling his country. Intrigues he would pass over in silence and, as though unaware of them, never recall them by a single word.

"Beloved brethren," the holy bishop went on, "that is the kind of prince, the Lord in this grace has offered us—the immortal Emperor Gratianus in the West and in the East the immortal Emperor Theodosius, both of whom ardently profess the true doctrines of our Church. Every intrigue wherever it may come from, they pass over in silence, and though aware of it, never recall it by a single word. In the West the august Caesar, despite the intrigues hatched in very exalted positions, has lately restored and delivered into our hands Portina's Church along with St. Myrocle's tomb which the accursed Arian heretics had forcibly occupied and stolen from us. In the East no sooner had the great Theodosius begun his pious reign in Byzantium than he drove the heretics from all our churches and forbade them to expose their madness in public. Behold, such are the princes we have."

At this point the fathers, had they not been inhibited by decorum, would no doubt have clapped their jubilant hands in rhythmical applause; but the great Bishop of Milan, ever averse to praise and flattery, hurriedly continued.

"What indeed can the mad heretical dogs expect of such pious princes!" he exclaimed in his golden-chorded, melodious voice. "In the existing internal and external situation what change of advantage to them can they hope for? Are we not acting as we should, when to right and left we clutch these august imperial hands so they may lead and be led as is meet, thus wisely harmonizing the Lord's will and plans with imperial needs? It is for the prince to defend the Church against its mortal enemies; paganism and heresy; for no Christian ruler can be impartial or even indifferent, in matters of faith. True, here the prince's duties end; for he must not persecute anyone, in his person and liberties, in his body and views, for holding a different faith, or force him contrary to his beliefs to attend a divine service that is distasteful to him. Worship of the Lord cannot be regulated through secular legislation."

This time the pious fathers, even if their sense of propriety, had permitted it, would not have clapped their hands, stunned as they were by the amazing inopportuneness of the last sentences pronounced by Ambrose. They knew, however, that Ambrose's thoughts were wont to flash back and forth between the two extremes of his pious spirit like bolts of lightning. They knew that his mouth had two voices that were wont to argue with each other; his intentions two hands, where the right sometimes did not know what the left was doing, but that, when all was said and done, his great soul and graceful little body alike were serving the inscrutable plans of the Lord.

Regaining their composure in this knowledge they continued to listen to his great closing address with eager attention.

"Furthermore," the holy Bishop went on, "princes have no right to interfere in the concerns of the Church with profane hand. Although it is their governmental duty to convene universal and plenary Councils, they must not influence resolutions adopted at these Councils, either by whispered insinuation or by vociferation, and are obliged to give their assent to Council decisions and to implement them without demur. The affairs of God are not subject to imperial jurisdiction. The palace belongs to the emperor; the church, to the bishop. The Church acts within its own holy authority in engaging or dismissing its servants, it alone takes decisions on matters of faith and on its pious policy, down to the minutest detail. The Arians are thus doubly accursed, and in this they are even worse than the Jews—for being ready to play the rights of the Church into the profane hands of the prince."

Although the tensely listening pious fathers were in complete agreement with this, they still refrained from expressing their approval by clapping not least because their minds, far less distinguished than the holy bishops, had not the slightest idea of what the great Bishop of Milan was driving at.

"The church is the property of God, and not of the Caesars," Ambrose cried, his countenance radiant with devotion, his eye raised to the ceiling of the sacristy. "God has given the Church to the bishops on commission and they cannot surrender it to the heretics even at the prince's order. The sacred devotional objects and vessels are similarly the exclusive property of God, and no immortal Caesar may lay hands on them anymore than on the person of the Lord's anointed bishops, who, in matters of morals and faith, are not subject to secular law—although, alas, they too groan under the load of taxation and to this day have vainly sought exemption from this burden."

"Alas—alas—in vain!" numerous fathers presumably murmured.

"Such then, is a good prince," the holy bishop continued. "Thanks be to the Lord, our august Caesars—the immortal Gratianius on the right and the immortal Theodosius on the left (or the other way round)—both of them being devout and true Catholics, know and honour the Lord's pertinent dispensation, and for this reason we may clasp their hands with complete confidence. What, then, can Palladius expect of them? Or does he reckon, perhaps that these distinguished princes, overwhelmed by their wordly concerns, will forget about his insignificant person and his individual case? A case we intend to elevate to the level of universal validity and expand into a precedent by placing it on their imperial desk, in order that the Council's sentence be duly and properly upheld and implemented."

"What, then is the actual state of affairs?" the holy bishop continued, returning with a nimble twist of his mind to the starting point of his excellent if tortuous, statement. "What are the serious external or internal troubles, that might deflect our Caesar's attention from this individual case? Whether you look to the West or to the East, you can see the turbulent surface of the empire becoming smooth and hear the peaceful cooing of doves from the gardens of the faithful. Both here and there the blood-sucking barbarians are being tamed. In the West, the august Gratianus has curbed the ever unruly and ferocious Germanic tribes, the flaxen-haired Alans, the Alemanni, the Saxons, and the Franks, while in the East, the great Theodosius, wisely turning to good account the desperate straits of the Visigoths driven from Transylvania, has concluded a peace with them and invited to Byzantium and feted there Athanaric, their old king (who died of the strains of the celebration.) And I have just recieved news of the death, by act of God, of Fritigern the Goth, Conqueror of Adrianopolis, and ruthless executioner of the pro-Arian august Emperor Valens. Little by little, the provinces that were laid waste are reviving. Roads are being re-paired, fields cultivated, and houses and farms built on the ruins, while the increasingly pacified barbarians are grateful to the wise and benevolent Caesar for having forgiven their misdeeds and accepted them as his allies. The Empire is now recovering from a prolonged spell of military ills. What, then, is Palladius pinning his hopes on?"

Disappointment await those impatient fathers who had been hoping that the holy bishop, after ranging over the vast regions of past and present, would with wordly tact, or for lack of breath, neglect the malleable summits and precipices of the future. "Beware, O Caesar!" Ambrose cried in his incredibly sweet voice, "Beware, O vice-regents, governors and commanders, who, as you tread the now smooth surface of the world, are apt to forget the inferno rumbling beneath your feet! Beware, for in this mundane exist-ence nothing is everlasting: neither peace, nor war, neither wounds nor their healing, neither the crest of the wave nor its trough. Least of all the peace of the human soul, which is but a breathing space between two cock's crows. Beware, my good friend and disciple, Gratianius, who fail to arm yourself properly against the treacherous attacks Roman paganism is prepar-ing to launch, and condone Arian intrigues in your own home and at your court: Beware, for bloodstained shadows are threatening your youthful life! While indulging in your games, on the race track, on the spring-board or in the ring, or while hunting on horseback, with bow and arrow, bears or lions brought at great cost from Africa, remember that more insidious beasts of prey are baring their teeth at you from within the human soul!

Beware, O sagacious Theodosius, lest you go astray in the labyrinth of your fits of anger! I see immense red clouds gathering over your head, which from time to time cast a shadow on your great mind and darken your justice-dispensing imperial hand. Beware, for justice is but the imperfect beginning of charity, which serves God! Beware, lest, in discharging your imperial duties, you should ever come into conflict with the Lord's intentions and plans!"

With this last exclamation, the holy bishop concluded his closing address: and he would no doubt have exhaustedly dropped back into his chair, had he not remained seated throughout his speech. And the tensely listening fathers would now no doubt have jumped to their feet, had they not been standing anyway, for during the last passage they had excitedly risen from their seats, wondering what on earth could have prompted Milan's great yet small servant to such a dreadful and impertinent digression, to such an apparently tactless warning and prophecy. The presiding Bishop of Aquileia, however, true to his methodical, slow way of thinking, reached for his angelic-sounding bell, lifted it and shook it.

"I herewith ask you, Palladius," he said, bending his hulking body forward, "will you after having heard these words, withdraw your apparently thoughtless motion to have the Council adjourned?"

"Dejectedly, though, and without any hope, I once again ask you, beloved brethren," said the shrinking heretic, "to adjourn the meeting until our mutual excitement has cooled down. Then reopening it in due time, let each of the two parties bring along a trustworthy person, that is, a notary public, who will act as impartial judge, and a short-handwriter, who will closely and accurately record the ensuing debate."

On hearing these words, the assembly was so intensely shocked that the fathers stood nailed to the ground, their tongues utterly paralysed, and there fell a silence so deadly that one could hear the thin echo of the chairman's recently rung bell bump against the ceiling as it roamed among the columns of the sacristy.

"Trustworthy persons!" repeated Ambrose, the holy bishop, who even in a sitting posture now appeared taller than the wretched heretic and so actually jumped to his feet and took a few steps forward. "It is not for the world to judge the servants of the Lord," he cried.

"It is for us to pass judgment on the world!"

Having spoken these words, the holy bishop loomed still larger and took another step forward.

"Although we have found Palladius guilty of heresy on several counts," he said with incredible solemnity, "our cheeks would blush if one who declares and believes himself to be a consecrated bishop were to be sentenced by secular personages. For this reason, and seeing that he himself wishes to give our dispute publicity by submitting it to secular personages and bowing his head under their judgment, I here condemn Palladius with all the wrath and contempt at my disposal. And having considered what he has confessed to in the course of his examination today, and what he has kept to himself, what he has condemned and what he has failed to condemn, I declare him to be unworthy of the holy office of bishop and urge the honoured Council to depose him from his office, unfrock him, and excommunicate him from the pious flock of the Church. Anathema!"

"Anathema!" the twenty-nine bishops howled enthusiastically and with the ferocity of a pack of wolves, though it is possible that some did so with flushed cheeks and some with a heavy heart and tearful eyes. "Anathema upon Palladius!" the shout went up, with a force that made the walls of the sacristy tremble in alarm. "Anathema upon the heretic! Anathema upon the traitor who would entrust the judgment of the Lord to the hands of secular personalities! Anathema upon the disrupter of unity! Anathema upon the enemy of Christ and the Holy Spirit, upon the denier of the Holy Trinity!"

And as even the angelic sound of the chairman's bell failed to silence the wolf-pack's clamour, the order-loving Bishop of Aquileia raised his large body, and leaned over his chairman's desk.

"Quiet!" he cried. "Gratianus, the immortal Caesar, having entrusted the sacred Council with considering trying and finally judging the case of the complainants, Bishops Palladius and Secundianus, I now put the case to the vote by roll call. As chairman I open the voting. Anathema upon Palladius, heretic, disrupter of the unity of the Church, denier of the Trinity!"

The great Bishop of Milan—his cheeks pale and his eyes filled with tears— voted next. The third to vote was Anemius of Sirmium, the fourth Eusebius of Bologna, patron and guardian of the virgins, and they were duly followed by all the other brilliant diamonds and rubies, although the minutes record the names of only twenty-five voters. And although it was by now late afternoon and the waning sun was watching the devout assembly with its single bloodshot eye through the western windows of the sacristy, the good fathers also tried the case of the taciturn Secundianus. And as the latter never answered a single question or warning or censure addressed to him, he too was unfrocked and anathematized. Also excommunicated in the same breath was a presbyter from Pettau or Ptuj, a man named Attalus, who had arrived that afternoon and who was a secret agent and spy for that good-looking, hip-swinging, barbarian-necklace-and-bracelet-sporting, venom-filled creature, Julian Valens, whom Ambrose, the holy bishop, had recently driven from the old basilica of Milan.

As other likely candidates were not on hand, no one else was excommunicated; for, under ecclesiastical law, not even the most wretched of heretics
could be condemned without being given a chance to defend himself.

At further meetings of the sacred Council, which took up each day and
hour of the lovely fruit-ripening month of June, the fathers considered the
clandestine machinations of the wicked Antipope Ursinus, discussed the
affairs of the Eastern Church, and finally drafted a written report to the
three joint emperors, the immortal Gratianus, the immortal Theodosius and
the immortal, ten-year-old Valentianus II, on the agenda and resolutions of
the Council—notably the excommunication of the heretics—and begged the
august Caesars to have the goodlooking Arian spy, Julian Valens, who was
subverting the people and stirring up strife, expelled from Milan and to
prevent, by the use of force, the Photinians of Sirmium (the present-day
Mitrovica) from holding clandestine meetings which, for all their being
clandestine, increasingly shocked the good Christian citizens of the town.

Returning to his quarters from a meeting of the Council one night,
Ambrose beheld the towering, long-bearded figure of Palladius standing at
the corner of a deserted street in Aquileia, at the base of a high watch-tower:
the heretic was standing alone in the moonlight, underneath sheets and
shirts that had been hung out to dry; his head was bowed down and one
enormous fist was pressed against his heart, and he was crying loudly; but
in the pious light of the full moon, his inherent heretical wickedness cast
a long shadow upon the wall of the house across the street. On reaching
his quarters, the holy bishop went down on his knees before the crucifix in
his room and passed the short moonlit night in wakefulness.

"What are you doing to me, my Lord and Creator?" he cried, or rather
whispered towards the sky so as not to wake up the bishops and deans who
were sleeping in the adjoining guest-rooms. "Is *this* my mission here below—
to add to the already sufficiently intolerable sufferings on earth of those
poor lambkins? To inflict fresh wounds, while guiding them to You, in
the hope of a healing—alas, how far away? A hope which, however well-
founded, sometimes, I own, flickers out even in me of a night... No!
It isn't true! I trust in You, O Lord, for ever and ever! But where shall I
find the strength to conquer my inclinations, curb my arrogant intellect and
walk upon earth as an avenging angel? Lo! I have been Your servant and
bishop these ten years, and during this short time have on the whole, extermi-
nated heresy in northern Italy, Pannonia, Illyricum... Give me power!...
But to what end?... Do summon me away, O Lord! For I have lost every
wish to go on living. O, summon into Your presence, this poor lambkin,
now all confused and in danger of losing its way!"

REALISM AND THE CRISIS
OF REASON

by

GEORGES CHARAIRE

P hilosophy and literature, when not confounded, as among pre-Socrates scholars or with Lucretius, have permanent connections in all epochs and in all civilizations; quite apart from the general atmosphere created by great religions like Christianity, is there any need to recall all the links that can be established between philosophy and literature—for example, as regards the courtly literature of the Middle Ages? Shall we evoke the Platonism of a Du Bellay in a poem such as "L'Idée"?

> "*Là, ô mon âme, au plus haut ciel guidée*
> *Tu y pourras reconnaître l'idée*
> *De la beauté qu'en ce monde j'adore.*"

Should we discuss the Pyrrhonism of Montaigne or the Jansenism of Racine? Or the general influence of Cartesianism in the 17th century? Need we recall the 18th century in France, this century of brilliance when men of letters became travelling salesmen for English empiricism? Should we speak about the *Aufklärung?*

Do not certain literary schools declare themselves as being founded explicitly on philosophical doctrines, such as naturalism, which claims kinship with the experimental method of the end of the last century? (Here I am obviously taking the word "philosophical" in its broadest sense.) Recently, on the occasion of a ten-day symposium at Cerisy, I had a discussion on the *nouveau roman* with Robbe-Grillet and Claude Ollier, in the course of which the latter claimed that phenomenology was the basis of the New Novel.

Writers keep transposing philosophical conceptions into literature while often in fact distorting them.

As to contemporary literature we should speak about the influence of

Nietzsche or Freud, or about that of Marx (perhaps from the political rather than philosophical aspect), and lastly of existentialism. But here we come to our main argument and I shall return to contemporary philosophies later on.

More particularly, whenever the problem of tradition and modernity has arisen, a philosophical climate has been one of the determining factors; this climate was itself determined of course (here a Marxist explanation—among others—is not to be excluded).

Let us take an outstanding example: the dispute between the Ancients and the Moderns in France at the end of the 17th century. The dominant philosophical feature of this dispute was Cartesianism, with its rejection of authority. Following in the footsteps of Francis Bacon, who said that Antiquity is the youth of the world and properly speaking it is our time that is antiquity, the world having grown older, Descartes said: "It is we who should be called the ancients, for the world is older now than before, and we have a greater experience of things." This was taken up by Pascal, who wrote: "It is in ourselves that one can revere that antiquity which we revere in others."

The question of tradition and modernity was thus clearly raised. If I choose this example of the dispute between the Ancients and the Moderns at the end of 'the 17th century, it is not only because it is one of the most famous, but beecanse it was started in the name of reason.

But if today the moderns are joining in battle against tradition, it has all the appearance of being a battle against reason. This is *the crisis of reason*. So we shall try to trace the main lines of philosophical thought which can determine the problem of tradition and modernity in 1965, and single out the dominant feature that inspires "the moderns."

At first sight we can see nothing but great confusion; nevertheless, we shall limit ourselves to a study of the Western philosophy, which is still occupied with the questions raised by the Greek *logos*. (I am quoting Heidegger from memory.)

Alongside the persistence of a great Marxist current and, like it, having Hegel as their source, we observe the appearance of existentialist trends, philosophies of the absurd that have had the effect of causing turmoil in the Marxist current, in what survives from Freudism and in the degenerate currents of the great philosophies. A new trend, however, enters the scene with Teilhard de Chardin.

These upheavals, this very confusion, call forth the crisis of reason heralded by "the rising tide of the irrationalism of philosophies in vogue today," against which Husserl thought he was pitting the heroism of reason.

It must be said that rationalism in the years between 1852 and 1870, particularly in France, was dangerously compromised: the wine had acquired the flavour of the flasks. Moreover, it was less a question of the positivism of Auguste Comte than of the reign of a positivist spirit waning into a pretentious and cramped scientism, into down-to-earth common sense, into bourgeois utilitarianism, associated with a search for material satisfaction and a lack of artistic and poetic understanding. "Get rich" became a moral rule. This baneful positivist spirit in France appears to have shaped the general atmosphere of this period to a greater degree even than Anglo-Saxon utilitarianism or pragmatism.

It is then that we witness the great Dionysiac revolt of the end of the last century of which Nietzsche is the chief embodiment. This was also when Bergsonism flourished (I am ignoring now the purely literary movements).

And, above all, there is one man who in his time, the first half of the 19th century, had passed almost unnoticed—Kierkegaard. He and his anxiety were destined to take on considerable importance. (Today I was moved by curiosity to look up a 1925 Larousse dictionary, only to find that Kierkegaard's name was not mentioned.) This man's anxiety corresponds tragically to that of men of a world in the throes of great upheavals, where all religious, moral and social values are shaken, where traditional philosophies appear routed, a world where technological revolutions are soon to question the very structure of society.

Yet it was perhaps reason itself that was to deliver the most powerful blows against rationalism. Classical determinism was challenged. Science itself at the beginning of the 20th century was again being questioned. The observer distorted observation; electron and photon became an inseparable couple; light could be at once undulatory and granular; the world continuous and discontinuous. While the quantum theory and Einstein's relativism were about to give a prodigious boost to science, to the glory of rationalism, the philosophers took hold of the new facts and concluded that "there was no longer any objective certainty."

The men of science themselves—among them De Broglie—revised their positions, and unitary theories of the Universe again gave determinism a place of honour. But the "seat" of modern philosophy had been fixed. It failed apparently to re-establish contact with science, or even to seek to perfect itself from it, considering the two as belonging to separate spheres.

So there were no longer any objective certainties. From there to existentialism, to the philosophies of the absurd, was only a step.

Despite all these hasty schematizations, we can find a rational explanation for the atmosphere of our anti-rationalist era, which seems to have over-looked an appalling by-product—nazism. But let us consider anti-rationalism in its peaceful aspects. Here we can distinguish a number of anti-rationalist attitudes which stem from a confusion of the rational and the reasonable. René Allain said recently: "The universe is not rational, and if one must communicate with it, we should accept its infinite madness."

This is the confusion which beset Camus. Confusion is, indeed, the climate in which an exacerbated subjectivity has its origin, an isolated humanism and anxiety—despair. This does not, for example, prevent Sartre, in outright contradiction with the initial theses of his philosophy, from believing in commitment. From this confusion a second-degree confusion if born, the philosophy of confusion, and often—as with Sartre, whom I shall take again as an example—an unintentional philosophy of confusion.

Leaving out a number of factors that have influenced our era, such as the discovery of Negro art, I have tried to explain, in broad outline, the crisis of reason.

In the purely literary field this results in disintegration: the destruction of all the rules, of linear time, of language.

But for literature this strikes me as being far less serious, because litera-ture can produce a harvest even with heresies.

Before proceeding to what will be the subject of the second part of my article, I shall endeavour to foretell what may emerge, or what, in my opinion, it would be desirable to have emerge, from our troubled era: it is quite possible that looked at from a historical perspective this era will be considered as one of the great moments of the Renaissance that began in Europe in the 16th century, a broadening of that Renaissance. The Renais-sance is, at all times, not only a return to the past, but a dynamic step toward the future. That of the 16th century, while rediscovering Greco-Latin civilization, also paved the way towards modern discoveries; the planet was explored, the printing machine invented. In our times, all civilizations, including the so-called primitive ones, are being studied, and the cosmos is being explored. As to inventions, if man is wise enough to use them for peaceful purposes, they will lead to his liberation—an age-old dream. "Slav-ery will cease the day the shuttles work by themselves," said Aristotle, and Gyula Illyés took up this idea in his poem "On the Subject of Shuttles." "It will be the machines engendered by themselves, and not a new race of slaves, that will do our hard labour."

We have reached the Dionysiac moment of this Renaissance, and perhaps only such a moment can shake the torpor of traditions.

What in philosophy is called dogmatism becomes academism, a crystallized classicism, in literature; and I quote here what Lukács wrote in "The Present Significance of Critical Realism": "Revisionism..., cannot be effectively fought unless we first submit dogmatism to an all-round theoretical and practical criticism."

This raises the entire problem of order and disorder. Paul Valéry wrote that "the two great evils of mankind are order and disorder, disorder and order." And Marcel Arland said: "Generations are swaying between the two dangers of order and anarchy. There is no other order for thought than that which existed in the past. Anarchy is a rejection of this order, but to the extent that it contains something fruitful and does not content itself with being a game or a suicide, it represents the search for a new order."

In the programme of the Budapest Pen Club conference in October 1964, the following question was raised with regard to poetry: Does the general tendency lead towards a new order or towards chaos? This brings to my mind this thought of Anaxagoras: "Chaos reigned, then reason came, putting everything in order." It is still reason which can put things back in order, but only reason in the Hegelian sense—a reason ever fighting against itself and capable, for example, of accepting the fact that universal order can be in contradiction with any particular social order.

For this, we have to accept all the inquiries and all the contradictions. Literature is one of the most important sources of inquiry. Even that which is pathological should not be rejected if it helps to enlighten us about man. Goethe called romanticism a sick man in opposing it to classicism. Nevertheless, romanticism thoroughly shook the 19th century.

Provided we do not fall into the current error of "what is, must be" or into fatalism, our era can be rich in lessons. It will be up to the philosophers to extract a broad rationalist philosophy from this chaos.

If the word rationalism has been given a narrow interpretation both among its advocates and its detractors, the word realism, often associated with adjectives, has also acquired very singular meanings.

There is a need to give back to these words all their richness by taking them in the widest philosophical sense in harmony with Hegel's idea: "All that is real is rational, all that is rational is real."

In the light of this definition, we can claim that even the behaviour of fools is real and can be apprehended, in the double sense of the word, by rationalism. So much the better if the literature of our time opens the window on regions that until now have remained unexplored.

To take my examples from the theatre, let me call to mind Ionesco's *oeuvre*. The philosophy inspiring an author—consciously or unconsciously— is of little concern to us. Ionesco has created extremely original works which renew the theatre by raising the problem of communication. And this is an eternal problem.

I recall Beckett's answer when he was asked to explain the meaning of one of his plays: "I don't know," he replied, "I am not an intellectual."

One could say that a valid work, however inspired by a philosophy, can withstand the test of time only if it is not immured in this philosophy. The gods who inspired Maya sculpture are no more; but the work lives on if it is really a work of art, that is, if it expresses Man in his reason or madness.

Besides, certain works have at certain times been the bearers of philosophical messages that, nowadays, are self-evident. If these works are still alive, it is because they contained, in addition and above all, the human qualities of *chefs-d'oeuvre* of lasting value. This is why one can find a common denominator for all the masterpieces of every epoch.

A work of art has a life of its own. The *Tartuffe* staged last season at the Théâtre de France by Planchon is significant in this regard. Breaking with the tradition of an old, obese, dirty and repugnant Tartuffe, he showed us a young, seducing and charming one. Planchon has perhaps thus discovered *the* Tartuffe of the stage, played by Du Croisy, who generally acted the role of a young leading man and was less than thirty years old.

It is the weakness and the strength of literature that it often creates ambigous works. As an example, I refer to Anouilh's *Antigone*. At the time of the liberation, he was attacked for his play by colleagues of his entrusted with the investigation of collaborationist activities, but I learned that at that time his work had been performed in London as an example of the resistance of French intellectuals. The difficulties were smoothed out, and rightly so.

Literary works often have a richer content than the author intended to give them. Take Paul Claudel's *Hostage*. The fervent Catholicism which inspires it could become a forgotten religion, yet, in its admirable form, this play would remain no less of a sublime tragedy on behalf of a great idea.

Art does not grow old; this is its superiority over all philosophies. This perpetually renewed youth, it owes, like that of the earth, to an identification with the real. It enables us to discover the real. The most poetic attempts of art are the boldest approaches to the real.

When I was in Hungary, I was the guest of Miklós Borsos, and before dinner we went to see his studio at the back of his garden. In the flickering candlelight, finished or still incomplete statues evoked man's tragedy. In this retreat of creation the abstract forms attested to the quest for the essential tendencies of reality.

7

From all that I have said, one can see how I interpret realism. Did not Brecht himself have this conception of realism in his theory of "distanciation?"

In conclusion, let me repeat that there are no precepts for art: the theoreticians always arrive after the battle. This was the case with Boileau who wrote his "*Art Poétique*" when nearly all the masterpieces of classicism had arrived at such a magnificent literary florescence.

Although it can create an atmosphere which inspires artists and writers, philosophy, nevertheless, follows other paths. Yet it is the task of the philosopher to seek to respond to the great anxiety of *Waiting for Godot*.

The most rationalist philosophy must draw from the arts as from science everything that reveals man and the universe, in order to approach the Real to the highest possible degree, to give us that modern outlook we look for. Then only can the trends imbued with anxiety give way to great currents of the hope and the joy of poetic reason.

MIKLÓS BORSOS: ORPHEUS

MIKLÓS BORSOS: FISH

MIKLÓS BORSOS: WAITING FOR GODOT
OVERLEAF: SYBILLA PANNONICA

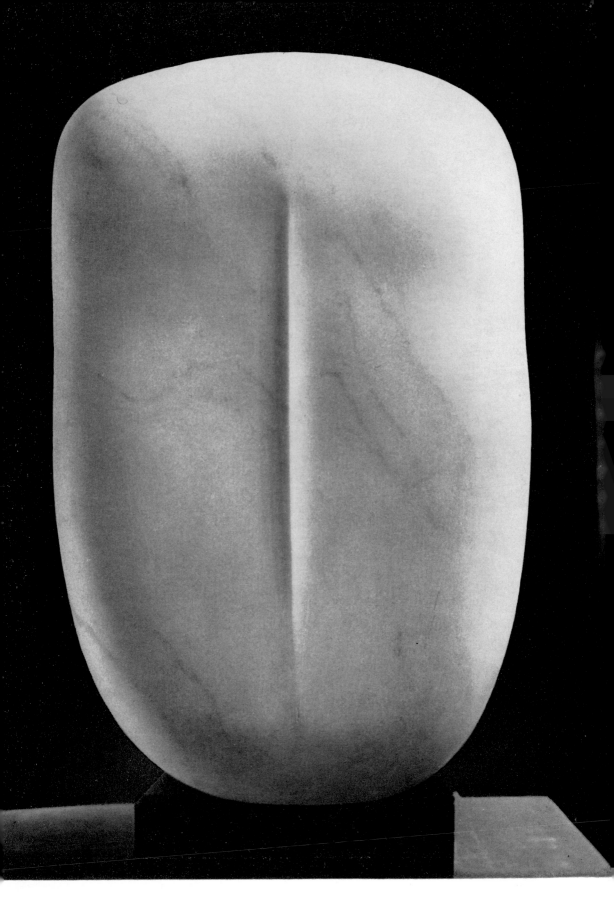

REALITY AND MYTH

The New Sculpture of Miklós Borsos

by

GÉZA PERNECZKY

The most recent sculptures of Miklós Borsos have been on show in the former monastery of Tihany Abbey, one of the most characteristic landmarks of Lake Balaton. The lake landscape, the baroque building and his statues squatting like gigantic pebbles formed a harmonious whole—illustrating one of the artist's principal qualities—that of concentrating his art on reproducing the forms offered by nature. Even after creatively transforming them, his stones can be returned to their original environment without disturbing its unity. The plastic art of Borsos is thus reminiscent of those Grecian and Roman sculptors who do not conjure up the presence of heroic semi-gods but rather make us feel that a human being has passed by and put everything in its rightful place. For all that, Borsos is a contemporary, not an imitator of bygone days; in Hungarian sculpture he has, indeed, perhaps been most successful in utilizing and adapting avant-guarde achievements. On the other hand, the economical orderliness, serenity and harmony radiating from his works do not recall the fundamental position of the avant-garde school—revolt. Borsos's pantheistic gentleness and serenely dignified avant-gardism are his very own.

István Genthon in one of his essays (in *Vol. IV, No. 10,* of The New Hungarian Quarterly) traced this feature of Borsos's art to Mediterranean culture. He was the first to use the term "Pannonian" art, which is now currently used in Hungary to qualify the Latin atmosphere of the works of artists living along the shores of Lake Balaton—a sort of Hungarian Riviera. The rich biographical material and analysis of milieu to be found in his essay can perhaps be usefully complemented by an examination of Borsos's new sculptures as a particular synthesis of European trends and domestic traditions.

It may be affirmed that it was the somewhat sequestered and timidly evolving taste of Hungarian society that prevented the more extreme trends

7*

of avant-gardism from producing any works of high quality. Hungarian art reacted sensitively to the achievements of modern plastic art, but in every instance immediately sought for an antidote, a more harmonious tone. That is why for fifty years the spirit of Maillol dominated sculpture. The former students of Archipenko—among them Bény Ferenczy—paradoxically produced their most mature and profound works in a neo-classical style. Borsos is perhaps the first artist not only to adopt architectonic austerity in his forms, but also the method of the free tracing of forms, and yet to succeed in making a name for himself. His style elastically stretched from the detailed portrayal of face and body to works reminiscent of the conceptual plastic freedom of Brancusi or Arp, while retaining throughout his link with organic forms.

In fact Borsos, in the course of his career, was influenced not only by the human form, but also by the "structure" of stone, and thus, while coming close to non-figurative sculpture, there was always a fundamental difference between his creative method and that based on a purely intellectual approach. Borsos attributed almost the same importance to stones extracted from the depth of mines or the beds of rivers or lakes as to forms created by man. He wished to give these creations of nature the same prerogative acquired long ago by human and animal forms as inspiring Muses. Therefore he was primarily concerned with giving wider expression to nature and not with changing systems of thought or making them more abstract.

This explains why nature as he sees it is not portrayed by itself, but always together with the traditional, as a background for the figures. This is not always to his advantage, but it gives his works a style of their own. Two extreme examples—a portrait and a composition with a non-figurative effect prove this. The red marble portrait of Lajos Kassák, the Hungarian veteran avant-garde poet and painter, is one of Borsos's latest works. In spite of the rigorous structure of the expressive face, the veined fissure and unevenly nodular texture of the red marble suggests almost a second portrait, a second reality. The ascetically simple composition thereby conveys an atmospheric richness and beautiful craftsmanship that lend the bust spontaneity and suggestiveness, though somewhat alien to the personality portrayed. As the opposite extreme to the Kassák portrait I would choose the *Sibyl Pannonica;* the undulating eggshaped form is dominated by a single line suggesting the axis of the face, and this sensitive gesture gives the woman, the whole face and expression of the Sibyl increasingly determined and concrete form.

Borsos holds that polished or granular surfaces are themselves equal in importance to a gesture or a profile. He boldly mixes the two, considering them related, time-honoured brothers. The dimly surmised metamorphosis, always interwoven with play, finally gives rise to a representation of nature peculiar to Borsos, in which he succeeds in eliminating the ambiguous and sometimes eclectic figural and mineral realities and replaces them by a third reality. At the Tihany exhibition the green marble series entitled *Sirens* represents this synthesis: woman's heads with streaming manes and faceless faces—carved around open hollows and convexities—embodiments of water in motion and rippling stone. In Borsos's oeuvre, consisting almost exclusively of motionless stone, standing in petrified dignity, these small, lythe creatures are almost unique. But they were heralded by the coloured drawings in which the stones, the light-swept sky and the rippling mirror of Lake Balaton appear as the components of a single cosmos. In these graphics the elements play the main role, and among them water is the embodiment of motion. In his statues Borsos has concentrated on the immobile world of stone, but in the smaller compositions of the Sirens he has striven to achieve a paraphrase of water in motion and the result is unexpectedly rich. Even in his static compositions Borsos apparently could not forget the haunting influence of rippling surfaces, and here, in the figures of the Sirens, he has revived not only this memory, but portrayed the cosmic picture of nature as a whole, composed of elements in motion.

Undoubtedly this type of nature representation, this galaxy of elements and partly stationary, partly mobile beings made of mineral and water, tends to inspire a mystical interpretation. Borsos's aim, however, is not dramatic; it is not related to Moore's surging primitive forms, but rather to the smooth craftmanship and enigmatic essence of Brancusi's The Egg. His myth too excludes the motive of action, even in the case of his lithe statues, which seem to drift like flowing water.

The Sirens are not dramatic heroines, but a mood, the hallucinative embodiment of one of the elements. His other sculptures also have to be approached emotionally, among them, the Kassák portrait already mentioned, the Sibyl Pannonica, the related women's heads—including the Young Fury —and the robust composition entitled The Fish. The last comes closest to form per se being realized at the moment of mental discovery—the creation of a clearly outlined and abstract work, as in the case of Brancusi. But here again it is more organic nature that prevails: The Fish is not "form" but "basalt," and this difference can be truly felt only if one passes one's hand over a Brancusi statue and over Borsos's pulsating basalt fish. The myths here become impersonal and undramatic, while at the same time retaining their mineral and biological intimacy through the prevailing mood. Even in his most compact statues Borsos creates an illusion, and in his most mathematical ones he has inherited some of the hallucinative technique of impressionism.

For this reason, his myths are "quasi-myths"—impressions that hint at myths through the mood they awake. They have no story, they imply no sacrifice, initiation or cult; they are the quixotic mirages of sun-flooded nature, glowing visions, recalling impressionist paintings. Borsos of course is far removed from impressionist sculpture, such as was practiced by Rodin and his school. He respects the essential elements of sculpture as does every artist, once he has discovered the laws of the twentieth-century plastic and thereby come to understand the essence of new norms of sculpture. But as a social being Borsos has inherited the attitude of the impressionists, scanning as he does the shore with squinting eyes and giving shape in his imagination, to the forms of nature. It is in this attitude that his relative estrangement from avant-gardisme is rooted. Even today he has not given up beauty and the mediatory role of atmosphere; in spite of his robustness as a sculptor, he is a lyrical, dreaming craftsman delving into the golden age of myth.

If Prometheus was the general ideal of avant-gardism or Sisyphus, in the stubborn speculative character given him by Camus, then those poets— and with them Borsos—who chisel their impressions into form are more attracted to the figure of Orpheus. Undeniably all of Borsos's sculptures, whether sensitively rounded or pictorially rugged in structure, have a musical effect. And his Sirens, in which he gives free run to this hidden musical beat, are reminiscent of Debussy. Borsos's Orpheus is almost a self-portrait, symbol of the craftsman mining after forms in the depths of the material. The deep shadowy furrows signifying the eye sockets make it one of the most beautiful sculptures at his exhibition. Two other compositions—the great sanguinary martyrdom, with the dismembered head of St. John and entitled Waiting for Godot—are of comparable value. These two statues seemingly contradict the artist's Orphean attitude, though actually they too are condensed timeless states reduced to their essence: a plate from which an enormous head emerges like a Tower of Babel, and the petrified illusion of hopeless hope. Neither inspires to action, both teach to see and perceive.

Undoubtedly there is in the Orpheus personification a kinship to or a nostalgia for the well-intentioned cunning, recurring in Greek legend, a Ulyssean wiliness and curiosity.

The deepest roots of Borsos's art are the forces determining Hungarian sculpture. He, too is torn in two directions: one is the more conservative tendency, which in a country with an agrarian past is more closely linked to the traditional framework of human existence, and as a result, cannot tear itself away from nature and from its figurative personification—the myth. The other is the influence of Western Europe and with it the attraction of a more sterile mode of production as well as more abstract methods of expression. In Borsos's art these forces reveal themselves the impressionist origin of the "quasi-myths" preserved under the veil of moods, and in the similarity one senses in his works to the mathematical exactitude of Brancusi's sculptures. Tenderness and discipline, lyricism and construction, reality and myth—these are the antagonistic trends that face one another.

But in the case of Borsos both poles can always be discerned; he has denied neither, but condensed both into an individual style of his own.

FROM OUR NEXT NUMBERS

(Continued from p. 57)

LORÁND EÖTVÖS, PHYSICIST AND THINKER
Iván Abonyi

THE LAW IN PRACTICE
György Gellért

COLD DAYS
(part of a novel)
Tibor Cseres

THE DEBATE ON ALIENATION
József Körösi

FIRST NIGHTS OF THE NEW SEASON
Iván Sándor

CHATTING UNDER THE CANVAS
Zoltán Halász

FREUD REVALUED
Mihály Sükösd

(Continued on p. 178)

ON THE SCULPTURE
OF HENRY MOORE

by

IMRE TAKÁCS

1

Bodies, folds, movements,
time stands still,
again the fables have spoken,
the heroes have awakened,
the men and women of the age
are moving into bronze and stone and wood
from gillyflower-scented cemeteries,
from common graves, from urns,
from the cages of an artificial world;
they seat themselves in eternal light,
in eternal night,
they hear a thousand years of din and silence,
and transience with its adornments
they lament and pity and refuse.

2

In their faces the horror they have known:
earth poisoned by human savages.

In their faces creative, tender affection,
abiding struggle for the future.

In their writhing tortured anguish,
millennia stretched on the cross.

In their writhing the good of man,
released and leaping from tree to tree.

In their broken features the balance
of reason's triumphs, reason's defeats.

In their broken features their voyages,
their wanderings from star to star.

3

King of bronze,
from the madness of nuclear fission, protect us!
from the poison of the armaments industry, protect us!

With your black-socket eyes look homeward from history,
with all your body see whither human ivy creeps today!

For man has by now outgrown himself,
and yet in his blood he houses an idol
who sneers at the brightening rays of creation.

King of bronze,
our anguish has stricken us dumb: Do the acrobats in the sky
know the press of thoughts in your time-worn head?

4

This stone sees farther
than any official visionary,
this stone sees farther.

The stone will still have a face after the atom bomb,
even though buried in ashes and soot;
the stone will still have its fragments after the burst,
and they will stretch forth into space.

Here stone is not stone,
no mumbo-jumbo of bearded, long-haired jowls.
Here stone is the pearl of our soul,
hope's newborn babe;
piercing our flesh and our mucous membrane,
this stone is offspring of ours.

Emerging from rust-eaten scraps of iron,
it has congealed in the light.

5

The dry wood's bone-bright surface
gives off a breath of spices.

The fragrant resin's capillary network
is the combed hair of women.

The rippling flow of growth rings
matches the passing breezes.

The vivid shadows of the gnarls
become the thoughts of lovers.

And the pose, the lines, the equipoise
are sensitive omniscience.

6

Steel wires whisper:
there were countries,
there were factories,
and there were
human hands...

Do you still sense your Madonna's body-warmth?

If you sicken at blood from the neck of the headless bull,
are you still able to scream?
To be true to yourself!
To be true to time!

7

A man inhabits the garden.
Statue and flowers are linked
by wonder, by compassion.
Nightly the light of the stars
gropes its way along the handiwork.
And high above on heaven's lathe,
like hill, like sea, like hummock:
into a universe I grow.

Translated by
RUTH SUTTER

BARTÓK'S MIRACULOUS MANDARIN

by

BENCE SZABOLCSI

I

From October, 1918, to May, 1919, Béla Bartók worked in Budapest, chiefly in the suburb Rákoskeresztúr, on the music of his pantomime, The Miraculous Mandarin. The libretto had been written by Menyhért Lengyel during the First World War and published in the 1917 volume of *Nyugat* ("West").* As regards the form of the work, in the later arrangement for four hands as well as in the score it was called a pantomime in one act. Bartók himself said of it: "My pantomime, The Miraculous Mandarin—who knows when it can be performed?" in a letter written in the summer of 1919; at the same time his wife wrote: "The new pantomime is finished, Béla is now doing the orchestration."**

Recent research has revealed that Bartók finished the orchestration of the work only five years later, in the autumn of 1924 (which may provide an explanation for the strikingly novel orchestral tone of the Mandarin, novel even as compared to his style of 1919). Moreover, in 1931 he composed a new *finale* for the pantomime; this version is to be found in the manuscript score of the Budapest Opera House and closely resembles the conclusion in the new edition of the arrangement for four hands.

As indicated by Bartók's remark quoted above, it was predictable that the work would not be performed for a long time. The experimental and

---

* See The New Hungarian Quarterly, Vol. IV, No. 11, containing the text of the libretto.

** Béla Bartók, *Levelek, fényképek, kéziratok, kották* (Letters, photographs, manuscripts, music). Collected and arranged by János Demény, 1948, Budapest, pp. 82 and 90. Menyhért Lengyel's story is said to have been originally intended for the Diaghilev Ballet and was inspired by that ensemble. Bartók came to know Menyhért Lengyel's work only in 1918, through István Thomán. (Information supplied by Béla Bartók, Jun.) Concerning manuscript variants, see the study of O. A. Nirschy (Studia Musicologica, Budapest, 1962.) and J. Vinton: *The Miraculous Mandarin* (The Musical Quarterly, New York, 1964.)

often eccentric avant-guarde spirit of the "Weimar period" might have aroused livelier interest in it on western stages, but the difficulties presented by the music and the choreography constituted a grave obstacle even where "moral concern" was not decisive.

In 1923 a fragment of two pages from the arrangement for four hands appeared in the issue of *Nyugat* published for the anniversary of Ernő Osváth. Two years later the complete arrangement for four hands appeared (as op. 19) in the Vienna Universal Edition; again two years later what is called the *Suite* containing the first part of the composition *(Musik aus der gleichnamigen Pantomime)* was published by the same house. (The two-page fragment in *Nyugat* was headed "Copyright 1923 by Universal Edition.") In the four-hand arrangement for piano the work was broadcast over the Budapest Radio in the spring of 1926 by the composer and György Kósa. The first stage performance—in a strongly expressionistic style—took place in November 1926, at Cologne. To the best of our knowledge Bartók was among those present. The première, conducted by Jenő Szenkár, ended in a scandal and a demonstration, followed by protests from the Church and the authorities, while the conductor nearly lost his post.*

The *Suite*, when given its first performance before a Budapest audience in 1928, was conducted by Ernő Dohnányi. At the same time the Budapest Opera House also began to show interest in the composition. Later, in 1931, and still later, in 1941, preparations were made for its staging, but as described in the memoirs of Gyula Harangozó.** "...the pantomime was banned in both cases immediately before the première." In fact the first performance did not take place here until after Bartók's death in December 1945, when the pantomime was presented in an "adequately purged" form with an arbitrarily changed background scene. Finally it was staged in its authentic and complete form first at the National Theatre of Szeged (in 1949), and then at the Budapest Opera House (in 1956).

There are no records to the effect that the composer actually saw his work performed anywhere besides Cologne; however, the Frankfurt revival in 1954 was claimed to have been staged in the spirit of his one-time

---

* Letters, I, 115. Musikblätter—des Anbruch 1926, No. 10, p. 445.—Prokofiev's pantomime, "The Love of Three Oranges," presented not long before at Köln, had a similar fate.—On the first night in Prague (1927) see the communication of János Demény in *Zenetudományi Tanulmányok* (Musicological Studies), Budapest 1962, October, pp. 201–205.

** *Táncművészet* (Ballet Art), Budapest, 1955, February, p. 53.—As far as I know, at the sight of a rehearsal at the Opera House where the Mandarin was to be "tamed" by a change of scene, Bartók himself prohibited the performance of his work in Budapest. Concerning the vicissitudes of the Budapest first night, see János Demény *(Zenetudományi Tanulmányok,* 1959, Vol. III, pp. 413–416, and 1962, Vol. X, pp. 394–396), furthermore György Kroó, *Bartók színpadi művei* ("Bartók's Works for the Stage"), Budapest, 1962, pp. 187–196.

personal instructions, based on his experiences at Cologne. In Bartók's life-time The Miraculous Mandarin was thus regarded as a failure, though, as set forth in the memoirs of Harangozó, "...The Mandarin must have been one of his favourite works, for talking about it could dispel even his sad thoughts" (just before his emigration, in the autumn of 1940, five years before his death).

What was it that made this work so inaccessible, and what is it that still stirs up debate about it?

It is not difficult to answer these questions. The Miraculous Mandarin marked a turning-point in Bartók's development indicating the composer's entrance upon a novel, steep path. Moreover, this new start coincided with a significant crisis in the musical life of Europe, at a time when the fever curve of music was at its peak in every part of the world. Bartók's third and last work for the stage signified the most dazzling encounter with this crisis and, at the same time, a show-down with and a turning away from it.

The story of the pantomime, which was mentioned with such abhorrence by musical moralists both in Hungary and other countries, is as follows: In a metropolis, somewhere in the Old or in the New World, in a gangsters' den, three bandits bully a girl into beckoning to passers-by from their attic window and enticing them to come up. A shabby old gallant and then a shy, awkward youngster seize their chance and climb up the stairs to the attic; but having no money, both are thrown out mercilessly. The third is a strange and formidable guest, a Chinese mandarin on a visit to the metropolis, with whom the frightened girl hardly knows how to deal. Her seductive dance gradually arouses the awe-inspiring visitor's passion and he begins to pursue the girl with ever increasing ferocity. The gangsters attack and rob him and then kill him three times, first by suffocating, later by stabbing and finally by hanging him, but to no avail. The victim cannot die until he has received from the girl the kiss he so deeply desires.

What did this libretto convey to Bartók, and how did it come to attract his attention? Why did he say of it in spring 1919 in a press interview* that it was... "wonderfully beautiful"? What chord did this ancient motive of oriental tales, the Undying Lover—alter ego of the Undying Hero—strike in his soul?

In his other two works for the stage, presented at the Budapest Opera House in 1917 and 1918 respectively, long before The Miraculous Mandarin, in the Wooden Prince and Bluebeard's Castle, the problem of love was approached from different angles. Bluebeard's Castle, of earlier origin

---

* Bartók Béla válogatott írásai ("Selected Writings of Béla Bartók"). Collected and arranged for the press by András Szőllősy. Budapest, 1956. p. 339.

but presented later, emphasized the hopelessness of a truly close relationship between man and woman; in The Wooden Prince, subsequently composed but performed ahead of Bluebeard's Castle, the symbolical trials of the lovers and the final happiness of their finding each other took place in the optimistic atmosphere of a folk tale. In the Wooden Prince the lovers—the prince and the princess—triumphantly overcome the hostile forces of the surrounding world which stood in the way of their happiness.

In The Miraculous Mandarin this picture became more sombre than in either of the others. Here love is killed by the hostile environment, itself becomes sullied from the very first; here we are faced with the meeting of a prostitute and an exotic spectre, not of the innocent lovers of a folk tale. But who is responsible for this sullied love and for its inevitably horrible end? There can be no doubt about the answer: the predatory world that has condemned men and women to such love, exploits and distorts their whole being and finally flings them into the pit. In The Miraculous Mandarin the environment and the colouring of the outer world turned to darkness, and human passion changed into almost pathological torment. Whereas in the Wooden Prince the obstacles to human happiness were transient, fabulous trials and afflictions that were soon relieved, the milieu of The Miraculous Mandarin was transformed into an inhuman, murderous world, into an enemy that destroyed every form of life.

Bartók hated this enemy; his hatred was incandescent, elementary, and more frantic at this stage than ever before or after.

To conceive such a hatred he had to encounter the object of his hatred; he had to live through a turning point of history that revealed to him the infernal and destructive inhuman forces of life in all their depth.

2

The discontent of the intelligentsia of Europe developed slowly, even after the outbreak of the First World War, but from 1916 onwards it became increasingly aggressive. At the beginning of the war there were those on both sides who cherished the illusion that the war was fought for a "true cause." The socialist and the radical bourgeois was the first to reject this illusion; yet even these strata were long at a loss as to the instruments, the ways and means for starting a struggle against the war. In the letters of Zsigmond Móricz and Béla Bartók it was chiefly from 1916 that the voice of protest against the war became noticeable, and those of our contemporaries who lived through the First World War may still remember that at the same time anti-war propaganda grew steadily stronger in the literature, press and theatres of Hungary.

Musical life reflected the same change, with the difference that under the rather backward Hungarian conditions these characteristic movements, which in the West ever more openly expressed the increasing anger and despondency of the intelligentsia, were less conspicuous in Hungary. Anger and despondency—the two were not reflected in equal measure, but almost everywhere both were to be found and their proportion lent a positive or negative emphasis to these movements. Here we have in mind those trends that branched off from futurism into expressionism and dadaism, which assumed an important role in the western cities, at least in the domains of literature and art, and other disruptive tendencies that with growing insistence called for the annihilation of traditional art forms and, directly or indirectly, of the social system that maintained them.

On the whole these artistic, literary, and musical movements had common slogans and certainly employed similar instruments. They agreed that the immediate past was to be abandoned and replaced by something radically new; they branded the world of bourgeois morality as false and obsolete; they also agreed on using a whole series of novel, hitherto unknown or formerly somewhat ignored artistic means for giving vent to their hatred and protest. Some of them aggressively accentuated distortion and ugliness, in order to reveal and expose the hideousness and wickedness of the existing order; others emphasized the decomposition of forms with a view to proclaiming anarchy as the only way out; a third group elaborated new, speculative systems to stress the necessity of evolving a new way of thinking, a new world order. In all cases, preoccupation with machines and masses was intended to draw attention to the novel experiences of proletarian life and of the big cities.

All these instruments appeared together, often overlapping and inter-penetrating; all were fed by moral, aesthetic, social and political aspirations, and all of them entered into European musical life.

The year 1918 was an important milestone in the history of European music. It was in this year that the greatest French composer of the era, Claude Debussy, died in Paris while the Germans were shelling the town. In the same year the Group of the Six was founded in Paris for the purpose of introducing a new and harsher, "everyday" note into music. That very year witnessed the first scandals and demonstrations provoked by dadaist and expressionist movements in France, Germany and Austria. In the autumn of 1918 The Soldier's Tale was given its first performance on a small Swiss stage, marking the entry of Stravinsky into the musical life of post-war Western Europe. It was in 1918 that the debates around Schönberg became more and more acrimonious in Germany and the vogue of American jazz appeared in the West.

October 1918 was the time of the bourgeois revolution in Hungary, while the proletarian dictatorship was proclaimed in the spring of 1919. In Hungarian literature 1918 saw the appearance of Zsigmond Móricz's novel "Torch" *(Fáklya)* and the last volume of poetry published by Endre Ady, "At the Head of the Dead" *(Halottak élén)*. Both books contained powerful visions of death and rebirth. Móricz was the first to pass judgment on a foundering world, and Ady dealt with the fate of the nation in a kind of *danse macabre*.

It was in October 1918 that Béla Bartók began to compose his *danse macabre* music to The Miraculous Mandarin. By the time he finished it in spring 1919, the Hungarian revolutionary government was engaged in a defensive war for its very existence against the onslaught of superior numbers from every side. All around there was war and revolution, confusion and disaster, visions of threatening death and extermination. There were also visions of a past that could not be continued in the old way—of good and evil, locked in mortal combat, of violence and will to survive, of humanity and inhumanity, of West and East, of chaotic metropolises and rebellious peasants, of civilization and primitive forces.

It was in this period, at the height of this clash of forces, that the Hungarian composer created the music of The Miraculous Mandarin.

3

Until the end of the First World War the music of Bartók and Kodály was rarely played in the West and remained practically unknown to wider circles. Beginning with 1910 some of their pieces for piano or chamber music were occasionally played in French, Swiss and American towns, but they could not become more generally known and new works could not be taken out of the country on account of the war. In 1918 Bartók found a publisher for his works in Vienna (the Universal Edition), and from that time on his compositions reached the West more easily, more quickly and in larger numbers. On his earlier concert tours, from 1904 on, Bartók had been to English, French, German and Spanish towns; but at the time he was known as a pianist and hardly, or not at all, as a composer. Now, he entered European musical life as a composer "published in Vienna" and again as a piano performer from 1919–1920 on. As a composer he was introduced into it by the year of the revolution, as a pianist he was exiled into it by the counterrevolution.

The world that faced Bartók here was absolutely alien to him, confused and in many respects repellent. He did not retreat from it, but observed it with distrust and even anger. He was shocked by the turmoil, the noise and the elbowing in the western capitals, and revolted by the savage ruthlessness with which the weak were swept aside and trampled down in the world of apparently free competition. He was angered by the advertising drive, by the "all-for-sale" market.

It was not long before Bartók turned away from this world and recalled the touching memories of his old tours through the villages, the dreamed-of virginal purity and human depth of peasant life in Eastern Europe. A contributory factor was post-war confusion: the anarchy of social life undergoing reorganization in the large cities, where the morass of war profiteering had suddenly increased to an incredible degree and implicated immense areas; the breathless rush that dominated not only the bourgeois life of these societies but their entire spiritual life as well; the good or evil slogans of the "new art" taking shape in various centres, under various slogans, and proclaiming alternately cubism, atonality, mechanical music, choral speaking or the chaotic language of dadaism as the leading principle.

Bartók was simultaneously attracted and repelled by these movements. Attracted, because he could pick out from them what aroused his instinctive curiosity, what was likely to enrich his own developing language and means of expression, and perhaps still more because with every one of his nerves he sensed this labyrinth, this confused undulation, this all-embracing crisis. He was already a universal artist, sensitive to the manifestations of every nerve of the universe and to its entire nervous system. He may have failed to notice what had happened during the war to that old, ideal world which he carried in his memory; for the (apparent) harmony of the lovely Hungarian, Rumanian, Slovak, and Ukranian villages had been broken as a result of the terrible storm of the war. It was the crisis and the confusion itself that first clamoured for expression in him; but from the very beginning there was also a desire for elucidation, for weighing, for reckoning, accompanied by immeasurable indignation over the corrupt hooliganism of the cities, capable of any infamy.

Bartók's encounter with the metropolis and his conflict with the new forms of life came about in the period after The Miraculous Mandarin; but a premonition was induced by the war, and it was The Miraculous Mandarin which made it evident that within him the "reckoning" had already begun. A man for whom Nature was the principal criterion and the ethics of Nature the highest moral standard may at all events have wondered what would happen if real jungle law were introduced one day in this monstrous human jungle.

More than half a century earlier a great Hungarian poet was seized with a kindred passion, a similar wish for a reckoning, and was roused to similar anger by the inexorable drive of the capitalist metropolis. In Madách's "Tragedy of Man" *(Az ember tragédiája)* the London fair makes Adam exclaim:

> What competition, if one, sword in hand,
> Confront another rival weaponless?
> What independence, if a hundred starve,
> If they will not submit to one man's yoke?

The significant question receives an equally significant reply:

> Deemest thou there is never harmony,
> No system in the workshop of this life?
> Gaze, then, a while with spiritual eyes,
> And mark the work they bring to plenitude.

At the same moment the whole London fair is transformed into a single scene of *danse macabre* where everyone utters his last word, setting forth the single meaning of his life before jumping into the common grave.

In truth, those who posed the question with such moral stress and such sharpness had ever since the Middle Ages been attracted to the *danse macabre*. "Let me go to my death!" were the words the writers of medieval chronicles put into the mouths of their heroes, because it was in the light of death that they could show most clearly the true meaning and lesson of life. Not in vain did the *danses macabres* of Orcagna and Holbein inspire so many writers and artists. When the composers of the nineteenth century, Berlioz, Liszt, Verdi and Mussorgsky, apparently returned to Orcagna and Holbein in their own compositions on death, they were in fact creating the great *danse macabre* of their own age, calling for analysis, decision and judgment.

Béla Bartók's own vision of the *danse macabre* followed in their steps. He passed judgment on his age in an appalling pantomime, the libretto of which could have been no more than a hair-raising, sensual Grand Guignol for anybody else; he recognized in it an appropriate framework for his own merciless sentence. That is why and how he undertook to compose music to Menyhért Lengyel's pantomime at a time when almost every critical issue of his age had become intolerably acute in his eyes.

4

The forces and impulses of the period come on the stage in all their starkness and bareness, simplified in terms of allegory as in a mediaeval morality play. Oppressed and Venal Love (the girl) appears as the forced ally of Murderous Villainy, and the Elemental Impulse of Vitality (the mandarin) steps in; the episodic figures of the conflict are Helpless Youth and Helpless Old Age (the youth and the old gallant). These "simple" allegories acquire an extraordinary emotional and moral impact as, charged with dynamic power, they combine or clash. Characteristically, the figures are in steady dramatic motion and shift their positions in such a way that Bartók's attitude towards them clearly emerges.

The musical atmosphere of the opening is metropolitan, only later is it revealed to be that of the murderers, of Villainy; as such it gives unity to the composition as one of its fundamental themes. The other most significant basic theme—as will be seen—is that of the mandarin; it is remarkable that the third theme, that of the girl, standing between the two, gradually approaches the second, to which it actually corresponds (minor thirds or augmented seconds) and with which it finally joins forces against the first, thus unfolding with it and in it the girl's own denied and sullied affections. However, this attachment gains strength only in the shadow of death.

As pointed out before, the love that unfolds in this pantomime—in a situation and form that is "beyond morality and society"—is branded as distorted, suffocated, crippled, abnormal love. This applies to the young visitor's helplessness and shy desires no less than to the girl's sensuous flirtation and the mandarin's sudden blaze of passion. Love and death —fatal love and fatal death—are, nevertheless, the essence of this work. It is the inhuman world in which the action takes place that has made a mockery of love and death, has maimed and poisoned it.

Love and death: here neither is timely, neither can exercise its power naturally, elementally, but inevitably errs into by-paths; both only serve to cast a still deeper shadow on a sombre and deprived life. Yet, breaking through all this debasement, rising above "the flowers of evil" and thrusting them aside, true love and true death emerge as the decisive laws of life. The victory of this elemental, positive law is, however, due to Bartók's music and not to the libretto.

The musical concept of the work counterposes crass extremes: the civilized confusion of a European metropolis and the "primitiveness" of Asia; corrupt calculation and elemental desire; violence and emotion; life and death. In creating these tremendous tensions, these decisive antinomies, the composer declares his own attitude. Had Bartók written this work in his youth, under the influence of Wagner's Tristan, he would most likely have emphasized that infinite longing can be appeased only by death. In this case death would have been a veritable relief and an escape to a happier world. But here the situation is very different. Even in death the mandarin's desire is a protest, and in satisfying it he triumphs over his murderers, for he has overcome and survived murder itself and been allotted a tragic death of a superior order signifying victory, the supreme victory of life.

In the end it is not the mandarin who is conquered but his murderers. Thus there is no trace of Tristan ecstasy, no escape, no nirvana: desire defies and annihilates murder, derides it and bursts forth in death as triumphant vitality. There is something of this in Tristan too, despite Wagner; at all events this deed of Wagner's, this self-refuting idea, was further developed by Bartók in The Miraculous Mandarin.

It is as if this fundamental idea was expressed by the relentlessly strict symmetry of the work as follows.

INTRODUCTION: METROPOLIS, THE GANGSTERS' DEN

I Thrice-repeated gestures
    of seduction
(Two episodes, two
minor characters)
	IV Thrice-repeated
	    murder

III Mandarin's dance	

II Mandarin's appearance
    Amorous play
	V The Girl's kiss.
	    Death

Thus it is the Mandarin's dance, this fierce burst of passion, this "allegro barbaro" more awe-inspiring than any other of Bartók's compositions, which is in the centre of the work. What precedes it is the presentation of the hostile world; what follows it is the struggle of vital force and of passion against this world, its tragic end—a deathless death that brings victory and exaltation. Before the Mandarin's dance the might of a hostile world is represented by thrice-repeated gestures of seduction, after the dance by a thrice-repeated murder—this is the ordeal the envoy of a remote world has to face. If he can assert himself he will triumph and receive the kiss without which he cannot die and after which he may die. In accordance with the rules of classical tragedy the moment of his downfall fills him with a strength exceeding that of his adversaries. With his entrance greatness appears in this base world and passes from it with his death.

The musical structure emphasizes the same idea. Here the three gangsters are a single amorphous group represented by rhythm and motion rather than tune; the rhythm, as pointed out before, is that of the metropolis. A large city, violence, crime and murder all have the same meaning for Bartók at this turning-point in his life. (His hatred and indignation were to find similar expression much later in his Concerto.)

(N. B. This was the motive of the hero's despair in the Wooden Prince.)

The musical world of the girl is far more human and at the same time more sensuous, though more erratic and indeterminate. These tunes follow the pattern of the princess' movements in the Wooden Prince, but instead of being playful and childish, they are of serpentine intricacy, suffocated and suffocating; they emerge from obscurity and return into obscurity. The domain of instincts here is not serene, but tormenting and tormented and shackled by grim memories.

(Note the triple step accompanying the mandarin's figure.)

The libretto surrounds the figure of the mandarin with a mysterious atmosphere. While for Bartók too it is mysterious, it is, nevertheless as physical as an elemental phenomenon of nature, as the whole of the human world, if we take into account its great motive forces, great conflicts and great destinies. Its impulses are recognized impulses, but, having become overcharged and uncontrollable, they break the bounds of civilization and step into a sphere that this civilization finds mystical and superhuman. The "folk music" that flashes and re-echoes in the composition is represented by the Mandarin's music with its Asian flavour, its "untuned pentatony" whose exotic yet steely brilliance and stubborn progression announces the irresistible will and passion of the hero.

(Rhythmically and partly also melodically these "Chinese" tunes appear to be echoes of well known Chinese pieces of music.)

"The vital force of Asia opposed to the corruption of Europe" was the comment on this figure made by appreciative critics, who saw in this the essence of Bartók's message. Those who subscribed to this view profoundly misunderstood the all-embracing humanism of Bartók, who proclaimed the greatness and beauty of human advance, the heroism and loftiness of the fight against dark and blind fate in every manifestation of naive purity and of popular strength, in the sparkle and thunder of every "allegro barbaro." The object of his enthusiasm was not barbarity, but man maintaining harmony with the great forces of nature in an epoch of distortion, unnaturalness and inhumanity. Béla Bartók, a professed pantheist as early as 1907, a dozen years later dared to stage primeval nature itself as a protest, in Asian disguise, against the free-for-all Europe of 1919 which brought dishonour to the continent.

Only heroes with intense passions can suffer as immeasurably and death-defiantly as does the heroic figure of the mandarin. The theme of his agony and unquenchable desire, reminiscent of a sigh and a moan, already hinted at when he enters the stage, is heard throughout the second part of the pantomime, becoming a chorus of wordless wailing behind the scenes in the most horrible moments; it then declines with the life of the mandarin and flickers out in the orchestra after a last burst of resistance.

(The sobbing of the violas, then violas and violins rising above the chorus tune represents the first trace of the stifled chromatic dirge that was to come into its own twenty years later in the second movement of the Divertimento.)

In general, an outstanding role is assigned in the music of the pantomime to tunes or fragments of tunes that remind one of sighs, cries and gestures. The appearance of such gesticulating, sometimes feverishly projecting and loose melodic lines that virtually beat the air, may be followed in Bartók's music since the Second String Quartet, especially since 1915/17, i.e., approximately from the time when melody based on fourths began to play an important part in his musical language. This kind of theme predominated till about 1923, up to the elaboration of the Dance Suite, and then waned. The music of The Miraculous Mandarin stands in the centre of this creative period, as the most powerful summary of the composer's achievements in this period, i.e., the years around 1920. Only two earlier works approach it in importance—The Wooden Prince and the Second String Quartet.

Here a few words have to be said about some other peculiarities of the Mandarin's music. For a fairly long time the work was held to be atonal. This attitude seemed to be justified by the circumstance that it is not easy to define the central key of the composition and that the tonal functions are in most places blurred by a structure resting on chords by fourths. However, Bartók's later words: "...at one time I approached a kind of twelve-tone music, but even my compositions of that period are unmistakably constructed on a firm tonal basis," apply also to The Miraculous Mandarin.* As a matter of fact it contains scenes with a clearly recognizable tonal centre, and the whole pantomime is built up around such loosened centres, from the first seduction, through the great central dance, to the scene of death. (Thus the three seductions are in A, C and E, respectively, the great scene of the mandarin's persecution is in A, while the murders are in C sharp and B, and the end is in F.)

* *Bartók Béla válogatott zenei írásai* ("Béla Bartók's Selected Writings on Music"), Budapest, 1948, p. 17.

As has been mentioned before, the use of fourths played an outstanding part in loosening these centres. Chords by fourths appeared also in the last compositions of Liszt, while Skriabin evolved a whole system based on fourths. However, at this time, it was not their example that encouraged Bartók to apply chords by fourths. Later Bartók declared that . . . "the accumulation of peculiar fourth steps in their old tunes provided the initiative to build chords by fourths."* In this connection one may also think of the influence exerted by Schönberg's compositions.

Apart from these chords by fourths there are many more novel features in the music of The Miraculous Mandarin. Mention has already been made of the "untuned pentatony" which in the scenes of the Mandarin furnished a basis for the most singular combinations; to this we may add the Arabic or Javanese scale which had enriched some movements of Bartók's works from the Suite for Piano (op. 14), to reappear not only nearly twenty years later in the Mikrokosmos (On Bali Island) but also in the first movement of his posthumous Concerto for Viola. Equally striking is Bartók's dramatic chromaticism, which easily leads to the growth of a tissue woven of second and seventh dissonances; his dramatic rhythm, which instinctively avails itself of asymmetrical "Bulgarian rhythms"; his treatment of the orchestra, which in this work completely abandons the school of Strauss and shows a link, if any, with Stravinsky alone; the staggering and disquieting effect of the wordlessly wailing chorus, which had to be dropped from the Suite, the orchestral adoptation of the work. It may be stated in general that in the first period of his activity up to 1920, and even much later, right up to the Cantata Profana, Bartók did not compose any symphonic work that equalled The Miraculous Mandarin in power, courage and dramatic truth.

5

The years that followed The Miraculous Mandarin brought a change in the problems that aroused Bartók's concern. The issues of love, instinct, desire and fate receded, to give place to much sharper contrasts, like man and nature, and the duality of civilization and freedom. The free man, the figure of Homo Naturalis, who engrossed Bartók's fancy in this period, sometimes simply bore the name of Peasant, another time he appeared as a mandarin or a mythical stag, hinting at the atmosphere of the Hungarian Great Plains or Rumanian forests or Chinese mountains. Meantime, not only did the principal figure assume another shape, but behind it also

* ibid. p. 23.

the mountains, the forest, the lowland farms in the background, indeed Bartók's whole natural and human world.

At the time of The Miraculous Mandarin Bartók entered the lists as a warrior in the chaotic struggle designed to rescue the human dignity of European art: the defence of humanity against violence, barbarity and inhumanity. Eleven years later, under a menacingly overcast horizon, when Bartók again raised the disquieting question of "saving humanity," his reply did not issue from such close-at-hand wrestling, but from a more removed height, and therefore more triumphantly. The great work we have in mind is the Cantata Profana and was composed in 1930, at a time when Bartók had set himself the clearly defined target of helping to create "a brotherhood of the peoples." The letter in which he described his creed was addressed to a Rumanian acquaintance. His friendly relations with Rumanians and his passionate inquiry into Rumanian folk music ten years later caused official Hungary to bring against him the ridiculous accusation of high treason. The virtually unprecedented renewal of his musical language at this time was promoted by the abundant treasures of Rumanian folk poetry. The words of the Cantata Profana, also derived from Rumanian folk poetry, were intended to be the opening item of a series of major cantatas linking several nations.

Of the planned series only one was completed, the "profane cantata" on the mythical stags, protesting more convincingly than any explanatory words could have done and sounding a warning alarm against the approaching horrors. Bartók saw only one way to avert the underground, insidious movements setting peoples and nations against one another: away from the lowly cottages, back to nature, reject all the old lies! He who has returned to nature, who stands on the mountain top and again holds up his head freely may again become master of his fate and keep clear of base contagion. That is how the mythical stags of the Cantata Profana stop on the summit of an imaginary mountain, the mountain of freedom, calling on humanity longing for liberty to follow them.

The battle to be fought was fought by Bartók from this mountain top alone, from a great altitude and distance. His anger did not burn so fiercely or so closely as in The Miraculous Mandarin. In the Cantata a surprisingly big role was assigned to narration, to depicting the situation, to epic elements, to reminiscences. In his review of the première of the Cantata Profana in Hungary, Aladár Tóth wrote on November 9, 1936 "...Here the composer relates... how he was transferred in his dreams to a vast, fabulous, legendary, trackless forest, where he found a new life without any limitation or compromise. He describes... the demoniac relief he felt when, his heart filled with youthful, bold and boundless love of freedom, he broke through the virgin wilderness"; "... he tells about the revolt of the young against their fathers"; he, "...the most daring of the warring young generation, describes the terrible pain caused by breaking away for ever from the happiness and comfort of home life that he who leaves and those who remain behind experience with equal vehemence. Having vowed to live for freedom, he will drink no more from a glass, but only from a pure spring..."

This passionate declaration, though following logically from Bartók's former development, was nevertheless an entirely new feature. Equally new was his rejection of all compromise, of any "parleying"—even of the direct contact involved in fighting, wrestling and meeting the enemy. With a single prohibitive gesture he swept aside for his heroes and for his own liberated self all possibility of coming to terms with the old world that was clamouring for his return home. This is not a contest between generations, but between slavery and freedom, between those born to be slaves and modern man born to be free. Bartók's disillusionment, his breaking away from the "world of cottages" was so consistent and incisive that his austerity, his boundless adoration of nature tend to make him appear almost inhuman. Discerning contemporaries, however, recognized that it was not man as such whom Bartók hated, but the coward who has degraded himself to servility and denies the great truths of life.

"This titanic music is the Song of Wolves in an age of servility," wrote Aladár Tóth. "At the same time it is an excruciatingly painful message that grips us to the depths of our souls by its warm humanity; it is the message of a poet whose eagle soul has broken out of our everyday life into eternal freedom—into solitude... Yet perhaps it is really he who speaks the truth of our time and of all times as he boldly and sublimely utters the secret and suppressed truth of our souls. Listen to the rumbling applause of the young thronging the gallery! Who would dare to say that the proclamation of human freedom elicits no response in our century?"

By now we know that Bartók did not stop at committing himself to breaking out of prison (and society), to this detachment, but went still further, another step higher. For, obviously, the next step was that of peopling his pure and superhuman Nature, the primeval wilderness of the Cantata Profana, this crystalline vehicle of freedom, so that it should one day become humane and human. This great step was taken in Bartók's last works, another fifteen years after the Cantata Profana, most likely as a result of the composer's last ordeals. His return into mankind's midst had actually begun long before; the Music for Strings and Percussion (1936), the Divertimento (1939) and the Concerto for Orchestra (1943), with their finales recalling folk festivals, can hardly be imagined otherwise.

This return characteristically coincides in the works themselves with the tormenting visions of the Second World War. Such extreme poles as deepest mourning and loudest rejoicing, despair and certainty, were already present in them; only the last, reconciling unity and the final summary beyond contradiction were still missing. They were realized in Bartók's last masterpieces.

As in the last works of Beethoven, the austerity of the suffering composer was mitigated by love of mankind, sympathy, confidence and humanity at the highest and most glorious level. The humanity of Béla Bartók's art is embodied in the warmth of his last great compositions. The sylvan hymn of the Third Concerto for Piano transformed the grim natural world of the Cantata Profana into the happy summer wood of our childhood. The homecoming wanderer enters eternal silence in a happy reverie, like one who at the end of his struggles lies down peacefully at the threshold of his birthplace.

SURVEYS

LAJOS MARÓTI

TWO CULTURES AND WAYS OF THINKING IN CONTEMPORARY AMERICA

TURNING THE PAGES OF "DAEDALUS"

I have been turning the pages of the first 1965 number of *Daedalus*, quarterly of the American Academy of Arts and Sciences (Harvard University) with twofold interest. It has been a bit like finding a letter in one of those bottles cast into the ocean, enabling me to catch up on the intellectual activity of a distant world. Here in Hungary we get our information about the mind and mood of contemporary America from two sources. The outstanding living (or only recently deceased) representatives of American *belles-lettres* constitute one source; the other is American scientific literature, which our specialists carefully sift and analyze just as specialists the world over sift and analyze the publications of their colleagues abroad. But what practically never reaches us is the happy medium between these two extremes, the American *essay*, which would give us a direct and first-hand insight into the specific qualities of intellectual life. Accordingly, the first thing I looked for in *Daedalus* was that missing clue to the *ways of thinking* in contemporary America.

The other half of my twofold interest was more personal. Entitled "Science and Culture" and edited by Gerald Holton, this volume contains fourteen essays on the interrelations between the various sciences and culture, and raises a question on which there had been heated discussion in Hungary a couple of years ago—that of the "two cultures." As the perpetrator of the essay which

started off that debate, I regret that this issue of *Daedalus* could not have come in time to provide us with additional ammunition. Yet there are lessons to be learned from it even now. Although the controversy has died down in Hungary, it is still interesting to observe how substantially the same subject is handled in a part of the globe which is separated from us by thousands of miles, half a continent, and a whole ocean.

I

On the basis of a single volume it may appear a rather rash and ill-founded undertaking to try to outline a "way of thinking," even for home use. But in certain respects there are noticeable differences of method in our thinking, and comparisons intrude themselves so insistently here that I cannot resist the temptation.

The most obvious point of departure in approaching the problem is a definition of the term "culture." Some of the contributors to *Daedalus*, just like some of our Hungarian authors, introduce their remarks with an analysis of the concept of culture. And the differences begin right here. Among the various approaches we find again and again a term that never figures in our definitions of culture—"behaviour." (Viz., as quoted by the Briton E. R. Leach from the American R. Bain, "Culture is all behavior mediated by symbols.") This focus on "behaviour" is no doubt related to the systems of philosophy which have been so influential in the United States—John Dewey's pragmatism, J. B. Watson's behaviourism; but this is not particularly pertinent for us here. It would be more accurate if we pointed out that this term, as well as those concepts of culture which we are about to discuss here, arises from a mode of thinking centred on action, which we Europeans regard as characteristically American.

It would take us too far afield if we listed here all of our epistemological objections to pragmatism and behaviourism. Let us stick to the concept of culture and to outlining our differences on that. It would appear that to us in Hungary the state of involvement in culture is not directly related to behaviour but to *orientation*, the way one sees things, the quality of one's picture of the world. Culture to us is not primarily a guiding principle, a guide to action but rather a storehouse, a mass of knowledge which—in accordance with the antique meaning of the word—has the capacity to form the basic character of the spirit, and which is valuable for its own sake. This helps to explain why public opinion in Hungary still means "humanistic" culture when it says "culture." The whole point of the passionate polemics of recent years was precisely the recognition that this general impression had long since been outdated by time and practice.

The concept of culture based on "behaviour" signals a deeper difference in thinking, which explains why those who implement it sometimes think, as does "Science and Culture," along quite different lines than we do in questions of detail. Which does not mean, of course, that the vistas thus revealed may not provide us with a curious and thought-provoking spectacle. On the contrary, what probably surprised us the most in this volume of *Daedalus* (and what would perhaps be most provocative, if it were possible to conduct a debate) were the essays whose authors examined the subject of

"science and culture," in its relation to contemporary conditions and social and political movements, from the viewpoint of the action-oriented sociologist, ethnographer, social scientist. (For instance, essays by the Americans Talcott Persons, Don K. Price, Oscar Handlin, and Daniel Bell, and the Briton Edmund R. Leach.)

II

The reviewer is confronted with an embarrassment of riches in the variety of ideas presented in "Science and Culture." To simplify his task, let us confine ourselves here to just one of the themes dealt with—that of the "two cultures." This expression, as I see it, is used in different senses. I would like to concentrate for the moment on that sense which—in accordance with the original intentions—tends to demonstrate that the development of the leading role of the natural sciences today leads us to reckon with a type of person whose culture is based on a specifically scientific kind of thinking, unlike that of his predecessors, whose culture was based on the "humanities."

Several authors in this issue of *Daedalus* oppose this formulation by C. P. Snow and his view of the situation. To quote from the criticism by Harry Levin of *The Two Cultures*, "Beneath its well-meaning truisms there lurks one striking novelty, which has scarcely been tested by all the discussion, the implication that science can stand by itself as a culture. This assumes not only a total separation from the humanities but also an internal unity among the sciences..." "...Furthermore, it is dangerous and divisive to interject the number two, as Sir Charles Snow duly warned us when he did so. It would be better to acknowledge the coexistence of further subcultures, one large heterogeneous culture, democratically split up into numerous professional lobbies."

There is undoubtedly substance in these critical remarks. To begin with, it is certainly a mistake to represent scientific and humanistic culture as irreconcilable opposites. Culture is an organism; a closer investigation shows that no matter what sector of our culture we contemplate, it is deeply connected with the other sectors, without which the development of the entire culture is unthinkable. It is interesting, for instance, to trace the question in the system of lyric poetry, where we discover how productively the scientific view of the world influences development of the poet's *expression*. (It goes without saying, of course, that we are thinking of the very best lyric poetry, which is in essence a system of complicated two-way associations, excluding thematic elements. Obviously if an attempt were made to transpose Kepler's laws into verse, let us say, the result would not be lyrical poetry.) And vice versa, science in our time is simply unthinkable without the continuous assimilation, strictly speaking, of humanistic culture. According to Einstein, physical theories have to meet the following requirements: "The second point of view is not concerned with the relation to the material of observation but with the premises of the theory itself, with what may briefly but vaguely be characterized as the naturalness or logical simplicity of the premises... This point of view, an exact formulation of which meets with great difficulties, has played an important role in the selection and evaluation of theories since time immemorial. The second point of view may briefly be characterized as concerning itself with the inner perfection of the theory..." If we look closer we will see that this is by no means a *sui generis* viewpoint of physics. It comes nearer to an aesthetic one. Its roots are not in the natural phenomena we examine but in our thinking, more exactly in the Greek thinking which ours is based on. And yet without this axiom of selection, our contemporary science would in all probability simply never have developed... Another example: Balmer discovered the series named after him—whose importance in the development of modern

physics need not be emphasized—not by applying pure physics to his analysis, but by persistently tracing and working out an analogy connected with musical sounds, based on his belief in the primitive harmony of the world... Again: "It is plain to see in the works of Max Planck that his thinking was influenced and fertilized by humanistic culture," said Werner Heisenberg in pointing out the contribution of antique Greek philosophy to modern nuclear science... Thus scientific and humanistic culture, it appears, cannot be split asunder with the radicalism of the accustomed formulations of our time.

On the other hand, even if we accept—as we finally must—the fact that scientific and humanistic culture respectively continue to present two differing pictures of the world, is it correct to speak of "two" cultures? In my essay, for instance, the one that started off the debate, I indicated three main diverging cultural trends: humanistic, scientific, and technical. But if we are to be consistent, and if, above all, we are adequately to define culture, we must state that each activity induces a different type of "culture" in the individual engaged in it, and that in the last analysis there are as many types of culture as there are intellectual occupations and not merely two. (For lack of a better expression, I did not speak of "two cultures" in the first place, but of the fission of culture.)

It is evident that Snow's conception and terminology are open to serious criticism. But this criticism does not dispose of the symptoms he put his finger on and exposed. For we might as well confess that if we place side by side the mechanisms that activate the thinking of the humanist, the scientist and the technician—let us say the engineer with a university education—and compare them, it becomes obvious at once that we have here three different ways of "thinking," three ways which are broadly identical with the thinking of other representatives of their respective categories. And if we recall the original meaning of "culture" (*cultura animi*

= formation of the soul), no doubt remains that the natural sciences and technology must be considered the specific constituents of the shaping and creation of culture. We could, of course, re-define culture in such a way that the natural sciences "fit" or "do not fit" the definition, thus making the definition itself a primary factor in causing the split. But none of this alters the fact that the unprecedented development of science in our time has created an imbalance somewhere and a feeling that something is wrong*.

This is how we summarized the state of affairs a few years ago at the end of the first major phase of the controversy in Hungary: We know that the word "culture" has at least two meanings. It can mean the sum of certain values; or it can mean the condition of the "soul" brought about through the possession of those values (new faculties, aptitudes, and above all enriched by a unified viewpoint of the world). In our days, the word "culture" in both its meanings undergoes a curious change. Parallel with the necessary specialization of modern life, a cancerous inward growth starts developing in the various spheres of intellectual values which make up culture, to such a point that if viewed from outside—and worse still from inside—it is no longer possible to see the connecting links between the spheres. This process also affects the individual's outlook and state-of-being-cultured, because, if for no other reason than the limitations on his time and energy, he bogs down in the details of his own specialty and thereby loses the most important positive benefit "culture" had offered him up to date—the certainty of general orientation. This must result in a general malaise.

It is reassuring and worthy of note that the factors I have mentioned (but also the

* To quote René Dubos: "The two cultures may be an illusion, but in practice science is still regarded in our communities as a kind of foreign god, powerful and useful, yes, but so mysterious that it is feared rather than known and loved."

ones I neglected here, such as the role of specialization, the significance of technology and its effect on this process, etc.) appear almost without exception in the thinking of the *Daedalus* essayists too, sometimes in formulations very close to those published in Hungary. Let us take a single example by way of illustration. "Only complete acceptance of the world which is developing can make our lives genuinely acceptable. Such acceptance involves two tasks: to advance in every field to the furthest frontiers of knowledge possible today; and to combine and communicate all such knowledge so that we gain the sense of structure, the power to see our world as an interconnected whole," wrote George Kepes; compare this with our summing up above. In any case, it is an interesting fact—which shows that perhaps malaise is really the problem at issue—that of all the authors in Daedalus it was precisely an artist, whose primary task is self-expression, who formulated these ideas with the greatest plasticity.

III

It was not our generation, however, that discovered the existence of the "two cultures." The representative bourgeois thinkers of Europe's intelligentsia prepared the way for our present sensitive reaction to the symptom of "fission"—nor was this symptom without precedent in the development of human culture. This is perhaps the only factor which, I am sorry to say, is not mentioned in the "Science and Culture" volume of *Daedalus*.

It is obvious that recognition of the divisibility of the values created by the human spirit (and of the ability to classify them in order of merit) necessarily coincided with the beginnings of the ideation process of culture, the systematization and identification of knowledge that marked the birth of science. By dividing "*cultura animi*" from "*cultura agri*" and opposing them to one another, consciously differentiating between cultivation of the "soul" and material culture, we set up a barrier between them and imply a priority of the one over the other, generating acceptance of the existence of "two cultures"—however we may define them. That this division already existed in the consciousness of ancient man (even though he did not postulate such theoretical differentiations or organize debates about the "two cultures") is indicated by his attitude towards the two types of human creative activity, one of which he selected as being worthy of "free" man, while he condescendingly relegated the other to the competence of slaves. The precise content of this discrimination between "culture" in its narrower sense and "civilization" in the sense we use today, has of course changed again and again in the course of time, but I have the feeling that in its essence it could be detected in any period of European culture, for instance in the educational system of various eras, from the "*septem artes liberales*" of the Middle Ages right down to the bourgeois school system of recent times. The first concealed but very real separation of "*cultura animi*" from "*cultura agri*" is latent in bourgeois thinking and becomes manifest and quite acute in our century (also showing we have to dig deeper to get at the roots of the idea of culture). In one phase of this process the thinkers on science such as Dilthey, Windelband and Rickert made a strict distinction between *Geisteswissenschaften* and the natural sciences, which had first emerged at the beginning of the seventeen hundreds, and grown in importance in the course of the next two centuries.

The confrontation of culture and civilization became so self-evident in the thinking of some representatives of bourgeois philosophy in the twenties of this century that it became a programme. Oswald Spengler divorced culture from civilization and opposed them to one another not only theoretically and as a system but temporally as well, and considered civilization a phase of degenera-

tion, "the inevitable doom of culture." The halved category—like the two halves of the Marquis in the novel of Italo Calvino—began a double life and developed into the two basic categories of a theory which employed a method of analogies in attempting to give a complete explanation of history —but this is of no immediate concern to us at the moment. It should be mentioned, however, that what Spengler "...meant by civilization (was) above all technology." (Ortega.)

We would be digressing too far if we expatiated on the weaknesses of the historical scheme Spengler built on this rigid, metaphysical contrast between civilization and culture in order to evolve a theory that would explain as agony symptoms of "Western culture" the crisis phenomena he observed already before World War I, and to which he opposed—to make his formula quite unambiguous—the Germanic sense of vocation, thus leaping headfirst into the shallow waters of the brownshirt ideology. Considering the glittering and imaginative rather than well-founded structure of Spengler's theory, with all its contradictions, anyone can imagine how easily historians pulled it to pieces. History could be forced into the Procrustean bed of this system only by the mightiest efforts, and then only after lopping off inconvenient chunks of it here and there. As to the rigid metaphysical confrontation of culture and technology, and the idea that technology was "burnt-out culture", the bourgeois viewpoint on culture could not accept this either. "According to Spengler, technique is what remains after interest in the fundamentals of culture has already dwindled to nothing. I cannot share this belief. Technique is itself science in its essence..." (Ortega.)

But whether or not these ideas are defensible, Spengler did not simply get them out of his own head or out of the air. Distorted as they may have been, they obviously and necessarily reflected real social problems, actual contradictions, which prompted reac-

9

tions from other bourgeois thinkers as well. From our point of view, Ortega y Gasset is the most interesting of them.

"Barbarism of the specialists": I first came across this expression in "The Revolt of the Masses." According to Ortega, the specialist barbarian is the most typical representative of "mass man." Mass man, who "revolts," penetrates every sphere of life and settles down there, is characterized, according to Ortega, by the complacency of intellectual sloth, which regards the culture and civilization of the twentieth century as being natural as air. It never occurs to him that without his active help, this civilization—if he does not continue building it up—will soon collapse over his head.

The arbitrary category of mass man and the naive construction built on the revolt of this type of man are obviously outdated; but one is bound to agree with Ortega's remark that "the specialist with his one-sided education," the "specialist barbarian," is a somehow inferior type of human being. "...In the old days people were simply classified as learned or ignorant, as more or less learned or more or less ignorant. But the specialist does not fit into either of these categories. He is not learned, because he knows nothing outside of his specialty; but he is not ignorant either, because he is "a scientist," and he knows his little nook and corner very well... In specializing him, civilization sealed him hermetically in his own smugness; but this smugness and delusion of strength makes the specialist think he can call the tune outside his special branch of science as well. Which causes this man, who is supposedly the ultimate in skill—a specialist—i.e., the exact opposite of mass man, to conduct himself in almost every sphere of life without skill and like a mass man."

Leaving aside for the moment the question of why Ortega regarded the one-sided scholar as an unhealthy phenomenon, it should be pointed out that he actively tried to prevent the spread of this one-sidedness. Like László Németh in Hungary, a writer

and thinker of rare universality whom Ortega undoubtedly influenced in many ways, he did this, partly by example through the many-sidedness of his own spirit.

Although this by no means exhausts the subject, we have probably succeeded in indicating through the few examples given that the problem of "two cultures" had its antecedents in the bourgeois thinking of the recent past, both in Hungary and abroad.

*

There is actually a difference, not only one of object or of method, but one of values, too, between *"cultura animi"* and *"cultura agri,"* values that contribute to our spiritual self-improvement and values connected with our physical existence; between "the humanities" and "the natural sciences," between culture and civilization. The predominance of the latter is a symptom of danger. Spengler pushed to extremes a contradiction which even without the prodding of the Great Pessimist we were able to absorb from the subject matter and the spirit of the history lessons given in our humanistic grammar schools. We received this contradiction ready-made... The man whose prototype is the one-sided specialist barbarian "becomes ipso facto primitive...," Ortega warned. It would appear that when we regard the fragmentation of culture and the acquisition of nothing more than an ingredient of culture, our misgivings have also come to us ready-made...

Our own statement of the problem, even if we cannot agree with the original motivation of either Spengler's or Ortega's quoted assertions, appears to be extraordinarily parallel; the correspondence of the formulations and terminology is almost exasperating at times. I might mention in passing that László Németh used the expression "two cultures" as early as the thirties, but his use of the term referred to a different contradiction from the one that appears, as in Snow's formulation, two decades later. It contrasted the natural "primitive" folk culture with artificial, "officially produced" culture. The question arises whether our polemics have added anything to this long-standing formulation of the question.

After the controversy in Hungary on the "two cultures" I tried to make a sort of summing-up. Although it will not be possible here to analyse it all, I would like to conclude with just a few words on it.

The answer to the question is contained in the delimitation of the differences. How do we arrive from fundamentally different starting points at the same symptoms and, through them, wind up, perhaps, with fundamentally different conclusions?

If we look closely, we will see that the precursors of the culture problem arrived at these questions as the by-product of a thought-process. For Spengler the duality of culture and civilization was on the one hand a fact and on the other hand an historical phenomenon, and, as such, basic and immutable. To Ortega and László Németh, it appeared similarly basic, and while it might perhaps be just possible to find a solution in their own practice (or in the select circle of those who understand), *in general* this was not to be thought of.

In the contemporary debates the point of departure *was the function of culture itself.* (Occasionally there was even the danger that this would turn into the function of an "ideal" culture which existed independent of space and time.) *We expected culture to be complete and to give something complete* in the name of "man," —man complete and liberated from any one-sidedness that had been foisted on him. And this we wanted *en masse.* With the help of certain data I tried to give a sketch of the cultural relationships of a restricted little stratum of the intelligentsia. How did Hungarian public opinion react to this debate? After the second article, there was a heated clash of views as to what should be done to guarantee, in future, the sanity of the culture of the *masses.*

What follows from this? In contradistinction to Ortega and to the youthful László Németh, we believe, even without fully understanding or elaborating what has to be done, that the problem of one-sided culture is only a *symptom,* and that it is curable, not easily or immediately, perhaps, but historically. It can also be concluded from this that our view of cultural fission and our approach to the symptoms behind it differ radically from those of the philosophers of culture whom we mentioned above, including the László Németh of the thirties. This despite the fact that we refer to identical, or at least analogous, symptoms, and that our formulations do not even differ very much.

Cultural fission is a symptom of crisis. This is our reaction to it. There is no need to prove this assertion because practically everyone agrees with it. (Not only we but Spengler and Ortega also consider it a symptom of crisis.) The question is only what crisis it is the symptom of.

And here is the second and decisive difference in the statement of the problem today and the statement of it by the bourgeois thinkers nearest to our time. In the eyes of Spengler—to whom cultural life itself is history and its conversion into civilization the actual doom of the *Kulturkreis*—the coming of the technical age, its declaration of independence, is not a warning but the fact of the crisis itself. From Ortega's viewpoint, in the system of elite-mass coordinates making their appearance in history, the one-track and fragmented culture of the mass man who is merely civilized means the likelihood of crisis.

We, who consider culture a superstructure, regard cultural fission—the crisis of culture—as a signal only, a projection on a spiritual plane of the crisis of society. In contrast to the earlier controversy, the discussion on cultural fission has been characterized in Hungary recently by an assumption that the problem reflects a social contradiction.

9*

The question is how to define that social contradiction, which is the background and the root of the problem. My feeling is that the separation and counterposition of culture and civilization today (which in its sharpest form treats the humanities as an exclusively cultural factor and civilization as a symptom of final dissolution) is the last stage of a process. I suspect that the starting phase of this process was the formation of the concept of "culture" which we inherited from the very beginnings of culture in Europe, when the classical arts, to the exclusion of all other activities, were grouped under the protection of the "nine muses." Such a concept of culture could obviously only be born in a society where one group "destined for culture" and independent of physical labour could regard disdainfully all activities which adapted nature to human needs—activities which were directly productive. This separation and counterposition of "the culture of the soul" and "the culture of the material," and the profound subordination of the latter to the former, essentially reflects the structure of class society; and while its direct cause was the historically necessary division of labour, its basis is ultimately the contradiction between intellectual and physical labour.

And all this can be turned about. To make a programme of resolving the problem of cultural fission, one must see a realistic possibility of resolving the contradiction between physical and spiritual labour, between the systems of values corresponding to these, between "civilization" and "culture."

And here again we find an interesting concurrence of views: I came across this very idea, which I had formulated as the most essential conclusion of our debates in Hungary a few years ago, where I expected it least—in an essay in *Daedalus*. Herbert Marcus writes: "The integration of cultural values into the established society *cancels the alienation of culture from civilization*" (author's italics) "thereby flattening out the tension between the 'ought' and the 'is' (which is a real historical tension), between the potential future and present, freedom and necessity."

I need only add that one necessary condition for this is the liquidation of class divisions in society.

PERCY M. YOUNG

MEETING POINT

Among the insidious maxims that come up out of a distant past—in which in a puritanical environment every occasion prompted a moral precept—the most irritating is that which says that travel broadens the mind. In fact when one is travelling, unless in chosen and congenial company, and in a long-distance railway train, the mind shrivels almost to non-existence. Especially is this true of the mind that is packaged by an airline and then carried off into the unknown. They told me that I was to go to Nigeria. Disbelief in suspense, I was (according to the hand-out) taken there at 600 miles an hour and at a flying altitude of 10,000 metres. After ten hours and a continent and a half I found myself in Lagos. A tropical night of half-sleep, and a morning jaunt in a small aircraft. We touched down at Ibadan and Benin, and at lunch-time made Enugu, the capital of Eastern Nigeria. From there a car took me to the University of Nigeria, at Nsukka.

About this bargain-basement Odyssey

there was quite enough to remember to have satisfied my old moral preceptors that some mind-broadening—in their sense—had taken place. I had been in a VC 10, had visited Lagos, briefly seen two other cities with exotic names, and for good measure had crossed the Niger. But after that I was for three weeks to live in Nigeria. What was more I was to work there. That is the point at which one starts to live again. For working with means thinking with, after which one is not the person that one was before. What broadens the mind is what happens after the travelling has ended.

When one takes one's first walk in an unfamiliar land one is liable to see the problems of the world laid out for inspection. This is especially true on the African continent. Most of all is it true for an Englishman visiting a country which was once governed by the British and which is still in membership with the Commonwealth. One has one's national past to live with—and in some respects down—and a newer conception of relationship to live up to. The exercise is made somewhat easier by experience and by a philosophy of unity in humane affairs. In the world in which I normally live the political credo of an artist is often suspect; yet without one the artist is in the long run impotent.

An artist, of whatever sort, must believe in one world. The aim of the artist is to help to create at least a general belief in the credibility of one world. In this case he posits some kind of absoluteness in respect of equality, and at once one must recognize an equality as between national traditions. This is not, and never has been, easy to accept. Even vocabulary militates against out best-founded intentions; for the word "under-developed" has a number of unhelpful connotations. What, we incline to think when duped with self-esteem, can we do for "them"? It is, perhaps, more generous in some particulars to see what "they" can, or will be able to do for "us."

A musician is concerned with music; but he is also concerned with the people who make music and as to why and how they make it. It is at this juncture that this peripatetic English musician turns himself towards the Hungarian self that—as a result of immersion in Hungarian affairs in general and the music of Hungary in particular—evinces itself from time to time. In Hungary, one recalls, music throughout the centuries has been a positive factor in national development. More than that, a highly distinctive national music has not only preserved its integrity but has irradiated the whole of musical culture. Hungary has put two composers of world stature, not to mention a large number of executant musicians, on the international scene. Thus we (who are not Hungarian) appreciate that certain of the processes that made this come about constitute, at least a set of guiding principles, at most an inspiration.

After two days in Nigeria, therefore, I was considering my immediate task—to examine and to advise on musical education within the University—in the light of my Hungarian experience. Noting through the press the recent establishment of a Hungarian Diplomatic Mission in Lagos I envisaged the exciting possibilities latent in a general sharing-out of cultural experience in the not too distant future.

We may now particularise, shaping the problems and the prospects. Nigeria potentially is a very rich country. Exploitation of natural resources can in a reasonably short time lead to an enviable prosperity. This process involves modernisation, but this in turn brings problems of some gravity. On any main road it is possible to see on the one side the world of a thousand years ago, and on the other familiar symbols of contemporaneity. Reverence for the latter can be overdone, and not only in Africa: the quest for prestige breeds dangers, chief among which is a disrespect for cultural truth. One feels that some of the values of "the West" are both over-valued and mis-understood. In the ambit of music and of musical education what is second—even third-best in the European musical tradition is accepted as efficacious. The musical historian looks back with alarm to the damage once wrought on native skills in Europe by a bourgeois regard for often indifferent alien reputations.

Here again I return to Hungary, where the start of a new era of musical authority came when nourishment was taken from the grass-roots. Unlike Britain (where the Industrial Revolution took effect earlier) Hungarian folk-art was still vigorously alive when at the beginning of the century Kodály and Bartók with creative perspectivity led it into a new milieu, thus ensuring that the village would in one sphere at least conquer the town. The folk-art of Nigeria (what is said in this context also applies to other African countries) is indescribably rich and vigorous. Nor is it one art but a collocation of independent, if inter-related, arts formulated in separate tribal groups and cultivated by groups within these groups. There is the art of the Hausa people of the north; of the Ibo people of the east; of the Yorubas of the west; and of the countless smaller tribes. The arts, in which ancient Sudanese and Egyptian influences linger, are even now socially effective and symbolically meaningful. Music, poetry, and drama of traditional order still maintain their place in the village and fulfil their integrating and therapeutic function. "To every Ibo," says Dr. W. Echezona, "life has a melodic and rhythmic orientation," and in his essay on *Ibo Music* (*Nigeria Magazine* March, 1965) he gives many examples to fortify his statement.

Since the languages of Nigeria are tonal and the precise relation between the pitch of one syllable and another is of great significance it is clear that where words end and melody begins is difficult to determine. It is also clear that to set African words to melody as conceived in a European sense raises a particular problem. This very problem, indeed, tends to strengthen a barrier created by a limited nationalism which will presently be referred to; that which threatens to place antagonism between the two main traditions of art and culture. In the Hausa country, where Emirs maintain courts, there are yet court musicians who contribute to the *mystique* of monarchy. Throughout the country the folk dance easily grows into the art-form once familiar in Europe as the *morisco* or the *masquerade.**

The visitor sees these manifestations of traditional art and is readily lost in a romantic haze. I was jerked back to reality by the lady who observed that folk-music in this country was beautiful, and then went on to add that it "must be preserved." What she meant was that those who live in the bush according to ancient precept should continue to do so—in order to "preserve" folk-art. To preserve it that is as a curious relic for visitors. Here in a nut-shell is the narrow view. The broader view—as of the Government of the country—is that health and education services must be expanded, and communications improved, so that the general quality of living may be improved. Somewhere of course, the folk-arts fit into this broader view, but not sterilised by preservative agents.

Let it be said that in so far as there is a great wealth of folk-music still practised in Nigeria, there is work for many scholars for many years. The scientific methods perfected in this department of musicology in Hungary could be invaluable. But there is a more important consideration than this. Mr. A. V. King, for some years on the staff of the University of Ibadan, who has done invaluable research in the field of Hausa music, speaks in a recent paper** of the necessity for "...the ability of the tradi-

---

* *Nigeria Magazine*, published by the Government of Nigeria in Lagos, and *A Journal of Yoruba Edo and Related Studies*, published by the Ministry of Education, Ibadan, are particularly to be recommended for their generous exposition of all aspects of folk-art.

** *Music Tradition in a Changing Society*, Nsukka, 1965.

tional music of a particular society to adapt itself to extremes of social change and yet retain its continuity."

Up to a point the literary tradition of Nigeria (necessarily exposed to the world through the medium of English) has found out how to adapt its traditions, and a developing school of novelists promises to bring much-needed freshness of outlook and expression to the contemporary English—American scene. As a composer one becomes sensitive to what is politely called "atmosphere," which can be translated into more practical terms. Ibo instrumental music, by pipes, by crwth-like stringed instruments, by a miscellany of zithers, harps and cylophones, and drums (including "speaking-drums") and other percussion, leaves impressions that should at least show that the "advanced" techniques of the "Western" tradition of orchestration can still learn as much as Debussy thought they should when he was captivated by the colours of Javanese *gamelan* music in Paris in 1889. There are rhythmic patterns, improvisations in ensemble, and melodic contours, to enrich the imagination. Within the masquerade is material for ballet (and Nigerians move poetically by nature). Of the short stories that I read at least half-a-dozen would make splendid opera libretti. But just as *Háry János* could only be composed by a Hungarian, so the new, developed, music of Nigeria must be composed by Nigerians.

It is sometimes said that some nations are by nature more musical than others. Basically I disbelieve this, but would accept that social conditions may either make it appear so or give opportunity to certain innate musical skills to show themselves. We are back with folk-music. Nigerian students aiming at a higher musical education were brought to me for examination. What they *knew* about music was slender. What they could *do* was enviable. Their sense of pitch and of rhythm

is impeccable. Their emotional contact with music is close. Their imagination is boundless. They sing and they dance without inhibition. There is every reason to suppose that in the next generation or so Nigeria may provide the world with a great composer. But only if musical education is devised to suit the background and the present needs of the nation.

At the moment one sees on the one hand folk-music somewhat uneasily dropped as a "national" duty into the educational system, on the other the allurements of the "rules" of western academic music. Development within the educational system (as in other faculties) depends greatly on the exchange of ideas; more on this than on methods as such.

In a moving and informative autobiographical book* a young Nigerian writer wisely observes: "One cannot, for any reason, completely abandon one's culture to make room for another. There must be a spirit of give-and-take in cultural matters. Peoples and nations, like individuals, pride themselves on their peculiar characteristics.

"It is, of course, very necessary for us to know what other people do, but how can we make the best use of the experience of others if we do not sufficiently understand ourselves?

"What then do we understand by a Nigerian culture? Is it the culture of our cosmopolitan township? No! Then communities are unrepresentative. Where then do we find our culture? We find it in our villages—there is the reservoir of our cultural heritage."

Something very like that we have read before—from Budapest. Thus—with a Spenserian enthusiasm for the imagery of rivers—I came home looking for a confluence of Niger, Thames, and Danube.

* Dilim Okafor—Omali, *A Nigerian Villager in two Worlds*. Faber and Faber, 1965.

ANDRÁS KLINGER

REASONS FOR DIVORCE

The results of a number of statistical surveys dealing with divorces (marriages which have either been dissolved or declared null) may provide a certain amount of information on the divorce rate in the light of personal information about the divorced individuals, but they fail to reveal the real reasons for divorce, and particularly to explain the unreasonably high rate of divorce in Hungary.

The 1953 Matrimonial Act abandoned the previously enforceable rule that substantive grounds for divorce must exist: the Court was bound to grant a decree of divorce on a number of statutory grounds. Under the new Act the Court may only dissolve marriage if the resumption of conjugal relations is considered past hope on account of the profound and irrevocable nature of the breach. A general definition of this character makes it incumbent on the Court to state reasons for the judgement, and also to take into account the circumstances making for divorce.

The judicial practice established by the new Matrimonial Act has enabled a more accurate and exhaustive study of reasons for divorce to be made. The demographical department of the Central Statistical Office, the Demographic Research Committee, following preliminary investigations, recently completed a comprehensive study of the causes of divorce covering the years 1957 and 1962. The detailed results of this research for the year 1962 have been published (1965) by the Demographic Research Committee (together with the principal data of the year 1957)*. We are proposing to discuss in this article the findings of the Committee on grounds for divorce.

* "Reasons for Divorce."—Statistical Survey of the Demographic Research Committee of the Central Statistical Office. Vol. 5. 1965.

This detailed investigation of the causes of divorce covers a sample of 10% of all marriages dissolved in Hungary in 1962. The sample was taken from the statistical cards drawn up for each marriage dissolved during the year.

In order to increase the accuracy of estimates based on these cards, the material was arranged partly geographically by county, partly by separating the men into five-year age-groups to obviate unbalanced differences between those under and those over fifty.

The material was thus broken down into 160 groups and the sampling within the groups was carried out on an individual basis. As a result of this procedure 1,741 divorces out of 17,410 marriages dissolved in 1962 were examined. There were four reasons given for the divorce in 718 cases, three in 624, two in 322, and one in 77. The average number of grounds for divorce was consequently 3.1.

Taking the 1962 picture as a whole, in relation to the total number of cases, only one-tenth of the grounds for divorce were already in existence before marriage, and nine-tenths appeared in the course of married life. The highest percentage was taken by adultery (31%), while cruelty, leisure spent away from home, drunkenness and incompatibility were represented by 11%, 9%, 8% respectively. These figures—compared with those of 1957—show a certain decrease in reasons in existence at the time of marriage, but the percentage for estrangement and drunkenness has increased considerably.

Principal Reasons

In terms of the first and principal grounds for divorce, grounds already existing before marriage take a considerably higher place (20% of the total). Adultery (18%),

Total and principal grounds for divorce (%)

Grounds for divorce	Total		Principal	
	1957	1962	1957	1962
1. Total	100	100	100	100
2. Grounds already in existence at the time of marriage	10.8	9.3	21.3	19.6
3. Grounds arising in the course of marriage ..	89.2	90.7	78.7	80.4
4. Breakdown of grounds arising in the course of marriage				
a) Estrangement	11.5	14.1	13.2	15.1
b) Drunkenness	5.7	8.4	11.1	16.9
c) Cruelty	9.4	11.4	4.8	5.1
d) Adultery	34.8	31.3	19.5	18.1

drunkenness (17%), estrangement due to incompatibility (8%), leisure spent away from home (7%), cruelty and the forced sharing of accommodation with parents (5%) follow in that order. Three to four per cent of the marriages were dissolved on ground of estrangement due to jealousy, lack of mutual understanding over sexual problems, or the education of the children.

Subsidiary Reasons

There were two or more grounds for divorce given in 96% of the total divorce cases in 1962. If we analyse the principal reasons in conjunction with other secondary reasons we discover that the grounds for divorce are frequently more than one. Drunkenness and cruelty are the most frequent reasons given, and generally appear together. Where drunkenness was given as the principal reason, in 60% of the cases cruelty was secondary, and drunkenness was a secondary ground in 14% of the cases where cruelty was given as the principal reason. Drunkenness and cruelty were the principal or secondary grounds for divorces in 35% of all divorce cases.

Adultery is also very frequently found as a subsidiary reason where the principal reason given is lack of mutual understanding over

sexual problems (35%) and it is—of course— particularly common where either the husband or the wife spend too much time away from home (39%).

Reasons According to Sex and Age Group of Parties

In 69% of the total number of divorces granted the husband was responsible for the breach (this figure was slightly lower in 1957). This also means—at least according to the statistical data—that in two-thirds of the cases under review husbands had been held responsible for the divorce. If you take secondary reasons into consideration, the position of husbands is slightly better (65%).

The reasons for the divorce of husbands and wives differ considerably. More husbands are divorced for drunkenness and cruelty and more wives on grounds of estrangement and extra-marital love.

The principal grounds of divorce initiated by wives are mainly estrangement due to jealousy and the sharing of accommodation with parents (three times as high), chronic illness and lack of mutual understanding over sexual problems (twice as high).

It is noticeable that the principal grounds adduced for divorce vary according to the ages of the parties. Grounds already in existence at the time of marriage account for almost half of the divorces among younger people and gradually decrease with age. A striking fact is that such a reason is nonetheless frequently invoked by older people; 14% of husbands aged sixty or over asked for the dissolution of their marriages because they had been based on financial arrangements. Younger people (21% of the husbands under 25 and 25% of the wives under 20) obtained divorces on the plea that they married irresponsibly. Eight per cent of the men under 30 obtained divorces because they had married before or during their military service and their marriages had deteriorated owing to their long absence from home. Young people frequently cited as grounds for divorce the fact that they had entered marriage merely to legalise premarital relations; 6% of the wives under 20 and 5% of the husbands under 25 gave it as the principal reason. Compared with the data for the year 1957 grounds for divorce already in existence at the time of marriage decreased considerably amongst people under 30. A decrease of 7% among husbands and 14% among wives indicates that more consideration was being given to the decision to marry.

The rate of divorce in which estrangement appears as one of the reasons appearing after marriage gradually increases with age. Particularly significant is the increase of estrangement due to incompatibility, e.g., less than 4% of husbands under 25, but almost 17% of husbands over 60 obtained divorces for this reason. (As a reason for divorce adduced by wives it has increased from 3% to 14%). The divorce rate on grounds of jealousy is highest in the 50–59 age group as regards men, and the 40–49 age group as regards women (6% and 7% respectively). The rate is lower amongst younger people (2–4%) and it is quite rare among couples over sixty.

Adultery is the reason most frequently adduced for divorce by husbands aged 35–49 and by women over 35. Divorces for adultery

in these age groups amount to 21–22%. This reason is less frequently given among younger people, 9% by husbands and 10% by women under 25. The rate of divorce based on adultery committed with a person employed at the same place of work is highest in the 35–39 age group. Divorce for drunkenness is also very frequent among couples aged 35–39 and the percentage of divorces on this ground amounts to 22%. Divorce on grounds of cruelty is highest among husbands aged 25–29 and women aged 20–24 (8% and 7% respectively) and it is also high among husbands aged 50–59 and women aged 40–49.

Among the other reasons for divorce lack of mutual understanding over sexual problems is the most frequent reason given by husbands aged 25–34 and again at 50–59 (4%) and also by women under 20 (6%) and between 20–29 (4%). This reason is scarcely ever given by elderly couples. Leisure time spent away from home is the principal reason for divorce proceedings brought mainly against husbands aged 25–35 (8%). It appears less frequently among the reasons given by middle-aged couples. Sharing accommodation with parents as a reason for divorce is mainly found among younger people (8% of the marriages of couples under 30 have been dissolved for this reason).

Marriage Period, Children

If we analyse the principal grounds for divorce according to the length of marriage we find the same variations as in the study of divorce cases based on the age of divorced couples. Grounds already in existence at the time of marriage in cases of marriages of short duration form a high percentage of the total (more than 50% of the marriages lasting less than one year and 33% lasting from one to three years were dissolved for such reasons) and the figures dropped steadily as the duration of the marriage increased.

The rate of divorce on grounds of estrange-

Principal grounds for divorce classified according to the age of the parties (%)

Classification according to the age of divorced husbands

Principal grounds	Under 25	25–29	30–34	35–39	40–49	50–59	Over 60
1. Total	100	100	100	100	100	100	100
2. Grounds already in existence at the time of marriage	47.2	26.9	18.4	11	10.4	16	25.3
3. Grounds arising in the course of marriage	52.8	73.1	81.6	89	89.6	84	74.7
4. Breakdown of grounds arising in the course of marriage							
a) Estrangement	7	10	14.2	15.1	18.4	21.5	24.1
b) Drunkenness	9.2	15.3	18.7	22.3	19	12.5	12.6
c) Cruelty	3.5	8.3	3.7	4.1	4.7	5.5	3.8
d) Adultery	8.5	13.5	19.2	22.4	22.3	19.5	12.6

Classification according to the age of divorced wives

Principal grounds	Under 20	20–24	25–29	30–34	35–39	40–49	Over 50
1. Total	100	100	100	100	100	100	100
2. Grounds already in existence at the time of marriage	54.3	31.6	19.8	17.5	12.7	13	15.9
3. Grounds arising in the course of marriage	45.7	68.4	80.2	82.5	87.3	87	84.1
4. Breakdown of grounds arising in the course of marriage							
a) Estrangement	5.7	10.4	12.9	13.7	14.2	22.6	21.6
b) Drunkenness	2.9	15.3	16.9	18.7	22.7	16.7	11.2
c) Cruelty	2.8	7.2	4.8	3.8	4.2	5.9	4.7
d) Adultery	8.6	9.8	18.2	19.4	21.6	21.1	22.3

ment gradually increased with the duration of the marriage. In cases of divorce on other grounds we cannot discover any correlation between the duration of marriage and frequency of these reasons as grounds for divorce. The percentage for drunkenness appears to remain steady, with occasional fluctuations, and in cases of marriages of short duration is almost negligible. Cruelty as grounds for divorce fluctuates considerably. It is highest in cases of marriages lasting less than one year, but it is still high where the marriage has lasted from three to fourteen years, while it is relatively low in marriages lasting one or two years or more than fifteen years. Leisure spent away from home is the most frequent reason for divorce in the fifth or sixth year of marriage, and the least frequent in marriages of one or less than one year's duration. Divorce for adultery is highest in long-standing marriages (28% of marriages lasting more than fifteen years have been dissolved on this ground) and it is worth noting that the rate is fairly high in marriages of shorter duration (10%) and lowest in marriages of not more than one year (less than 6%). Lack of mutual understanding over sexual problems mostly appears as grounds for divorce in the fourth or fifth year of marriage (almost 7%) and is the least of the reasons adduced in marriages shorter or longer than that period. A rather high percentage of marriages lasting less than five years broke up because the couple had to share accommodation with parents.

Some deviation is caused in the whole picture by another factor, namely, the number of earlier divorces either party to the marriage had had before the present one. Adultery as grounds for divorce is less frequently involved among people who have already been divorced before, and estrangement rather more.

In one-fifth of the divorces under review premarital intercourse took place between the parties; and in half of these (i.e., one tenth of the total number of divorces) a child resulted. In these cases the grounds for divorce already existing at the time of marriage are frequently invoked, and adultery occurs more often than among parties where no premarital intercourse took place.

The divorce rate, both on grounds which were already in existence at the time of marriage and for estrangement, is highest in marriages without children and decreases proportionally with the number of children. The trend in divorces on grounds of drunkenness, however, runs in the contrary direction: the number of divorces increases with the number of children. A third of the marriages with four or more children were dissolved for this reason, while divorces of childless couples for drunkenness were only 12%. The divorce rate for cruelty is almost identical, with the exception that where there are three children of the marriage it is very low. Perhaps there is no direct connection be-

tween the increase in the divorce rate for these two reasons and the number of children in the family, but it might be due to the fact that the couples divorced on these grounds as a general rule belong to the social groups where larger families are to be found.

The divorce rate for adultery is highest in marriages with two children (more than 25%) and still high in families with three or more children. It is relatively low in childless marriages. The figures for leisure spent away from home as grounds for divorce are different. They are relatively high in marriages with one to three children and lower in childless marriages or where there are four or more children.

The age of children also affects the whole picture. In families with young children estrangement is rarely found as a reason for divorce while drunkenness, cruelty and adultery are frequently adduced. It is interesting that leisure spent away from home as grounds for divorce is frequently invoked in families where the children are less than 7 years old. Where there is no child or more than two, these grounds are less frequently invoked.

Social Status and Educational Level

The social status of the husband also plays its part in the grounds for divorce. Divorce is relatively rare among agricultural labourers. Here most of the reasons for a divorce are based on grounds already in existence at the time of marriage. This does not apply to the professional classes, where estrangement plays a larger role than among manual workers. The difference is particularly noticeable in cases of estrangement for reasons of incompatibility, which make up 10 per cent of the divorces of the professional classes while it is only 6–7 per cent among workers.

Significant differences are apparent among the other grounds for divorce: drunkenness accounts for 18–19 per cent of the divorces among manual workers and only 12% among the professional classes. Adultery is relatively rarer amongs peasants (15%) while in the other two groups it is 18%. The frequency of divorce for drunkenness and leisure spent away from home shows similar trends. Sharing accommodation with parents plays a higher role in peasant divorces (6%), accounting for 4–5% in the other two groups.

The fact that as a general rule the wife works as well not only increases the number of divorces, but it also alters the picture as a whole. These differences, however, are not very significant, save that estrangement causes more divorces among the dependent than among wives in employment. It is also

Principal grounds for divorce classified according to social status (%)

Principal grounds	The social status of husbands		
	agricultural worker	non-agricultural worker	professional classes
1. Total	100	100	100
2. Grounds already in existence at the time of marriage	26.1	20.2	15.3
3. Grounds arising in the course of marriage	73.9	79.8	84.7
4. Breakdown of grounds arising in the course of marriage			
a) Estrangement	13.3	14.6	16.9
b) Drunkenness	18.4	18.7	12.3
c) Cruelty	4.1	5.3	5
d) Adultery	15.1	18.4	18.8

Principal grounds for divorce classified according to employment or dependency of the wife (%)

Principal grounds	employed wife	dependent wife	employment category of wage-earning wife		
			agricultural worker	non-agricultural manual worker	professional worker
1. Total	100	100	100	100	100
2. Grounds already in existence at the time of marriage	19.8	18.9	29.2	20.7	15.1
3. Grounds arising in the course of marriage	80.2	81.1	70.8	69.3	84.9
4. Breakdown of grounds arising in the course of marriage					
a) Estrangement	14.7	16.9	9.7	14.2	17.2
b) Drunkenness	17	16.6	16	19.5	12.7
c) Cruelty	5.1	4.6	5.5	5.2	4.9
d) Adultery	18.2	17.5	15.3	18.8	18

of interest that divorce for adultery is not significantly different when invoked against wage-earning wives or dependent wives, and adultery with fellow workers causes less than 4 per cent of the divorces under study.

Differences in the social status of the couple are reflected in the grounds for divorce in cases where the man belongs to the professional classes and the wife is a manual worker. Adultery for instance, accounts for only 19% of divorces where both parties belong to the professional classes, but it rises to 27% where the husband belongs to the professional classes and the wife is a manual worker, though only to 17% where the position is reversed.

To sum up, similarity or difference in the social status of the couple does not greatly affect the grounds for divorce. Where it is apparent at all, it is usually the case that the husband belongs to the professional classes and the wife to another social group.

A study of the grounds for divorce of persons in the same social group, according to the age of the parties, reveals the same variations as above.

The percentage of divorces on grounds already in existence at the time of marriage in the case of agricultural and non-agricultural manual workers under 30 is 35%, while only 24% amongst members of the professional classes. The figures for estrangement as grounds for divorce give a different picture: as regards men, the percentage is 30% for professional workers over 50, and 23% for non-agricultural workers of the same age, while it is only 11% for agricultural workers. It is also interesting to note that the contrary is true for women: the rate is 30% among agricultural workers over 50 and only 16% among professional workers.

The educational level of each of the parties appears to have the same effect as their social status. Grounds for divorce already in existence at the time of marriage decrease proportionally with the rise in educational levels, and at the same time estrangement

as grounds for divorce increases. Drunkenness is mainly invoked among couples with the minimum educational level, i.e., primary schooling. The divorce rate for cruelty is still more revealing in the effect of educational levels; it is high among persons who have received no education, and in the case of men having completed only the first five classes of primary school, it is highest.

Divorces on grounds of adultery are unconnected with the educational level of the couple. The divorce rate on these grounds is the highest of all, both among those with high as among those with low levels of education.

Differences in the educational levels of the parties greatly affect the grounds of divorce. Where the educational level of the husband is higher than that of the wife the divorce rate is highest on grounds of estrangement, adultery and leisure spent away from home. Where, however, the wife has the higher educational level, the main grounds for divorce are estrangement and cruelty.

Housing Conditions

The divorce rate is greatly affected by housing conditions. Divorces are particularly numerous where accommodation is shared with others: only half the divorces were among couples living alone, although three quarters of the families involved in divorce according to the census data of 1962 had their own separate accommodation. The divorce rate, therefore, of people sharing accommodation was double the rate of families living alone.

The divorce rate among couples sharing accommodation with parents was particularly high (20%) but the divorce rate for couples living in furnished rooms was also double the average.

Among the principal grounds for divorce already existing at the time of marriage, living in subleased rooms was mentioned in half of the divorces.

Principal grounds for divorce classified according to the educational level of the parties (%)

Principal grounds	No educa-tion	Primary school years completed				Secondary school years completed		Univer-sity educa-tion
		1–3	4–5	6–7	8	1–3	4	
A. Husbands								
1. Total	100	100	100	100	100	100	100	100
2. Grounds already in existence at the time of marriage	25	20.4	16.2	21	20.3	20	16.8	18
3. Grounds arising in the course of marriage	75	79.6	83.8	79	79.7	80	83.2	82
4. Breakdown of grounds arising in the course of marriage								
a) Estrangement	10	10.2	17.6	12.6	15.3	15	21.5	16.4
b) Drunkenness	5	24.5	15.7	23.6	16.4	11.6	6.7	3.3
c) Cruelty	5	8.2	6.2	5.1	4.6	5	6	2.5
d) Adultery	40	16.4	16.7	16.3	19.4	26.6	12.8	22.9
B. Wives								
1. Total	100	100	100	100	100	100	100	100
2. Grounds already in existence at the time of marriage	14.3	18.3	20.3	18.8	22.1	20.4	11.5	16.7
3. Grounds arising in the course of marriage	85.7	81.7	79.7	81.2	77.9	79.6	88.5	83.3
4. Breakdown of grounds arising in the course of marriage								
a) Estrangement	14.3	10	13.7	14.1	13.9	24.7	19.7	22.2
b) Drunkenness	14.3	20	17	22.7	16.7	7.5	6.5	—
c) Cruelty	9.5	3.3	2.8	5.6	4.8	6.4	8.2	1.8
d) Adultery	28.6	28.3	20.7	19.1	16.4	14	11.5	24

Adultery

Adultery on the part of either of the couple may directly or indirectly influence the dissolution of marriage.

In 43% of marriages dissolved in 1962 the husband, and in 31% of the cases the wife, committed adultery, while in 14% of the cases both of them were unfaithful.

Only a fraction of adulteries led directly to estrangement. Compared with the total number of divorces this applied to only 20% of the husbands, and 15% of the wives. Only in 2.5% of all cases of adultery leading to estrangement was adultery committed by both partners. Only after marital relations were broken off was adultery committed, in 15% of the cases by the husband, in 13% by the wives, in 4% by both. The marriage in fact was dissolved for other reasons, and the adultery occurred later on.

From one to five years elapsed between the breaking off of marital relations and the final judgement in 40% of the divorces. In more than 20% of divorces co-habitation had ceased for periods ranging from six to ten years, or in 17% of the cases even from eleven to nineteen years. It is also significant that in 6% of the cases marital relations had not existed for over twenty years. Marital relations had been broken off for less than a year in only 17% of the cases.

The period of the breakup of a marriage also considerably influenced the grounds for divorce. Where this period was short, most of the grounds for a divorce were already in existence at the time of marriage, while in cases where matrimonial relations had broken down for a considerable period the most frequent grounds invoked were estrangement and adultery.

Re-marriage

Husband and wife re-married in 27% and 30% respectively of the cases after the dissolution of the marriage. There is no evidence of any intention to re-marry in 48% and 49% of the cases. In 6% the parties made it clear that they intended to marry again. Where both of them intended to re-marry the grounds for divorce already

in existence at the time of marriage were higher, and estrangement was less frequent.

In 9% of divorces the husband and the wife respectively had a child from another person.

*

It can, in sum, be averred that the demographic conditions applying to the parties, i.e., their ages and the duration of their marriage, considerably influence the reasons adduced for divorce, as does their social and educational background.

The high divorce rate in Hungary can probably be explained by the fact that young people have tended to marry without due consideration. (It is pleasing to note that this trend is gradually decreasing.) Analysis of the grounds for divorce also points to a high consumption of alcohol and consequent cruelty as an important cause of marital breakup; 20% of divorces in 1962 were caused by these two factors. It is also regrettable to note that the divorce rate on these grounds has lately been increasing. To some extent the changing nature of society is responsible for divorces on such grounds as estrangement, sometimes due to ideological differences between the parties, changes in social status and disparity of cultural outlook.

LÁSZLÓ MÁRKUS

DÁNIEL KÁSZONYI

Life of a Nineteenth-Century Hungarian Revolutionary

To cope with the organizational inroads of the counter-revolution in 1848, the Hungarian Government proceeded to raise an independent army. This army was based on Hungarian forces serving in the Hapsburg imperial army and was garrisoned beyond the frontiers of the country. Dániel Kászonyi undertook to persuade the *Nádor* Hussars to return to Hungary. It was a dangerous mission to be sure, for if caught he would have been sentenced to death. Although the return of the Hussars has become one of the legendary episodes of the war of independence, the person of Kászonyi, the "instigator," for a long time remained shrouded in mystery. We publish herewith some new facts about an interesting figure in the Hungarian War of Independence, who later became the pioneer of the Hungarian labour movement.

Dániel Kászonyi was born in Vienna on the 2nd of October, 1813. His father, a landed aristocrat of the Borsod district, was an official at the Hungarian Royal chancellery. Dániel was three years old when his father resigned from his post and moved to Kassa. This was the town that formed his personality up to the age of seventeen; his friendship with Marcell Dessewffy, who was older than himself, particularly influenced his intellectual development. He went farther than his contemporaries and became, through the guidance of his friend, a devotee of the French enlightenment, of Voltaire, Rousseau and Diderot. His interest in literature, philosophy and art led him to acquire a well-rounded education, but in the last analysis it was Diderot's rationalism that determined the basic trend of his *Weltanschauung*. He revolted against all kinds of authority, but at the same time he had an unshakable belief in humanist morality and the power of education to shape character. He was a fanatical truth-seeker.

For a year he was a cadet with the Radetzky Hussars. He was fired with enthusiasm for the Polish revolution and with a number of companions tried to run away to the aid of the Poles. Then he quit the army and enrolled in the Academy of Law. In 1832 he came as a law assistant to the Parliament in Pozsony, where he became involved in political struggles. The speeches of statesmen who advocated reforms aroused a deep response in the young men of the Parliament; they stirred up political currents and became a considerable power in forming public opinion. This youth movement began with torchlight processions and demonstrations at the theatres, but later it took on organizational forms. Dániel Kászonyi was one of the initiators and founders. Metternich's secret police very early got wind of the developments in the organization which purported to be an educational and reading circle, and an informer was smuggled into the "Young Hungary" movement. The membership fluctuated in numbers and was heterogeneous in character. Immature ideas, zeal, personal ambition, and various shades of rebellion, reformism, and willingness to compromise could all be found side by side in this organization, which described itself as a Conversational Society. Nevertheless, within a year and a half, the movement spread to the law students, and unwittingly paved the way to the creation of Lajos Kossuth's party. In April, 1836 the Lovassy brothers, members of the left wing of the movement, were arrested. Kászonyi, too, was tried by the Royal Court of Appeals. He and several of his companions were told that they would never again qualify for a position in the royal administration. He was only twenty-three and already his career was wrecked. But his confidence was by no means shaken. He lived first in Vienna, later in Budapest. It was then that he first tried his hand at journalism, which in the course of a life full of vicissitudes eventually became his profession.

On hearing the tidings of the Vienna revolution of February, 1848 Kászonyi did not hesitate to enter the lists. He hastened to Pozsony and offered his service to Kossuth. His romantic inclinations, his proficiency in languages, his resourcefulness and trustworthiness, his courage and his cultivation predestined him for confidential missions. But his outspokenness, his pride and his radicalism prevented his coming to the fore. On the 1st of March he conveyed Kossuth's speeches to Vienna, and in accordance with his instructions got in touch with university students and the democratic intelligentsia. Soon he also became acquainted with that section of the working class which supported the struggle of the bourgeois opposition. These workers made a very deep impression on him. Together with the "Aulists" he visited the workers' districts because, as he related in his memoirs, "I knew it was there that I would find the most susceptible hearts. Nor was I disappointed, for these rough working people everywhere constitute the marrow of the revolution. With their common sense they immediately recognize who their friends are, just as they recognize a just cause." While these lines betray a certain naiveté, they testify to their author's democratic leanings, and record the fact that even then he was already interested in the working class; the social content of his radicalism was far more advanced than that of the radical Hungarian nobility of 1848.

He stayed in the imperial capital from spring to October, a period when the people of Vienna erected barricades more than once. He took part in the armed uprising of May 15th and as an active witness of that time wrote: "How often the argument against everyre volution is reiterated—that freedom degenerates into anarchy! This is intended to discourage support of democratic systems. Those who believe it should have been Vienna at that time to see how utterly false their argumentation is. What they choose to call the rabble is the most revolutionary and yet the most honest section of the people."

The October events in Vienna—the uprising of soldiers and workers in defence of the Hungarian revolution—had a decisive influence ai d lent strong support to the left wing. Kászonyi was a participant in the October events. He was an intermediary between the university students and the Hungarian chargé d'affaires. He was present when the sentence passed by the people on the Minister of War, Latour, was carried out; severil times he acted as a courier between Vaenna and Kossuth, he delivered arms to the "Aulists," organized the uprising in the Pozsony district, was an intelligence agent for the Army of the Upper Danube, a liaison officer between General Görgey and Kossuth during the Northern Campaign, a Government Commissioner of the City of Eger, and then confidential courier for Kossuth and Csányi. In the summer of 1849 he fled from Világos to Komárom, and after the castle was surrendered went into exile with the other defenders who had been granted honourable withdrawal.

The defeat of the 1848 revolutions established the sway of reactionary forces all over Europe. Bitter years in exile awaited Kászonyi. Like all other political exiles, the Hungarians had to struggle through crises that were not primarily physical, but moral. Between the backwardness and the theoretical insecurity of the Hungarian exiles; between the political antagonisms and the personal frictions that were inseparable from them; exposed to a motley collection of adventurers, careerists, informers and impostors, Kászonyi became inured to many tempests in those twelve years. During the ups and downs of that period he lived by teaching languages and fencing, giving piano lessons and translating books. Meanwhile he took part in the political campaigns of the exiles. Although a follower of Lajos Kossuth, he was drawn increasingly towards the left.

The London Society of Democrats, led by János Xantus, had already been established in January, 1851. Dániel Kászonyi was in the Presidium of the Society, which was connected with the Chartist leader Julian Herney. Kászonyi was present at the international demonstration held on February 11th, 1851 termed "communistic" in a report by the London agent of the Austrian secret police. Later he became a leader of the New Buda Settlement Committee which rallied the left-wing, revolutionary elements.

Not even at the outset had the Hungarian exiles ever constituted a homogeneous group. In their left-wing tendencies they were most closely related to the revolutionary democrats, as indicated by the fact that the London Society of Democrats joined the Central Democratic Committee. At the same time they continued to support Kossuth, and the name of Dániel Kászonyi is to be found among the signatories of the London Declaration of the February 19th, 1852. During his exile in London his activities were many-sided and complex. He also made contact with German exiles who were professed socialists.

No practical results came of the political activity of the exiles after the 1848–49 struggle for independence was defeated. The primary reason for this is that they did not recognize in which direction the social movement was tending. They failed to base their activity on objective reality. Instead they oriented themselves on their subjective desires. Yet the mere existence of this group of political emigrés was a significant moral factor in the determination of political currents at home. As a left-wing activist in the group of political exiles, Dániel Kászonyi represented a moral and at the same time political force. He remained faithful to the nonconformist ideal, which Lajos Kossuth symbolized for him.

The years he spent in exile in London deeply influenced Kászonyi's ideological development, independent of his political activity. His experience with a well-developed capitalist society and with socialist doctrines opened up new perspectives to him. The majority of the political refugees remained bogged down in their chief and practically only demand—for national independence; but Kászonyi's democratic orientation, derived from the teachings of Diderot, enabled him to break through nationalist limits. He even condemned the policy of the Hungarian Cabinet of 1848 as "utterly false" because of its attitude towards national minorities. On closer acquaintance with the revolutionary democrats, and particularly with the labour movement, he became increasingly convinced that revolutionary movements are strengthened by the common action of different nations. When, as a Hungarian political refugee, he based himself on the cosmopolitanism of Diderot and Voltaire, he was unconsciously committing himself to the path of socialist internationalism, which even in the nineteenth century was being developed to a higher stage.

As a British subject, and under the name of Thomas Miller, he returned to Hungary at the request of Lajos Kossuth. The suicide of László Teleki,* however, made his missions pointless. For a time he earned his living as a tutor, and wrote novels—in German. The compromise with the Hapsburgs in 1867 so bitterly disappointed him that he left the country again. For ten years he lived in Leipzig, where he wrote his autobiography in German. In this book he was sharply critical of Hungarian social conditions although his viewpoint was largely subjective. He made direct contact with the German Social Democrats in Leipzig, and by the time he returned to Hungary in 1877

* See The Favourite, László Teleki's historical tragedy in Gyula Illyés' adaption, in Vol. IV, No. 12, and Vol. V, No. 13 of The New Hungarian Quarterly.

his views were even more revolutionary than before.

At that time the developing Hungarian labour movement was headed by Leó Frankel. * The Independence (Kossuth) Party ignored social problems and proposed nationalism as the only salvation. It was under these circumstances that at the age of 66 Dániel Kászonyi undertook to edit the journal of "those who had no franchise"—the *Krónika*, newspaper of the workers. In doing this he was siding with the persecuted and dispossessed, the *"pétroleurs"* (adherents of the Paris Commune), their party and their ideology. The principles of the *Krónika* had not been clearly established, for at that time the Hungarian labour movement was only just becoming acquainted with the tenets of socialism. Yet Dániel Kászonyi and this movement were already linked with international social democracy. And in his assessment of Hungarian conditions Kászonyi was fighting in the vanguard of progress. The ideals of national independence and of social progress—two objectives that seemed to be mutually exclusive and to take opposite roads—harmoniously complemented one another in Kászonyi's mind. There was no contradiction for him between patriotism and internationalism; he felt that they were intellectually related. Critically examining both his own views and the aims of the Young Hungary movement he stated in his paper that he was looking forward to socialism and that the rebirth of the country would be brought about by the proletariat.

When the Universal Workers' Party was founded he became editor-in-chief of the Party organ, *Népszava*, (a daily paper still existing in Budapest) and a leading member of the Party presidium. He resolutely stood out against former comrades in arms and against the Kossuth Party's press when they accused social democracy of being unpatriotic. "They reproach us," he wrote in the

* On Frankel see p. 150 of Vol. IV, No. 10, of the N.H.Q., in János Jemnitz's Keir Hardie in Hungary. (Ed.)

August 14th, 1881 issue of *Népszava*, "of not loving our motherland. We have stated a thousand times that our country is the earth and that our brothers are mankind, but we also love those who are nearest to us, the children of this land who speak the same language as we do, who understand our thoughts and share our feelings. The love of mankind includes the love of one's country."

Although nearly seventy years old, he was indefatigable in his efforts; as an editor and a journalist he explored the entire range of domestic and foreign politics; he was equally conversant with revolutionary movements in Russia, the activity of the Irish Fenians, and the struggles of the German socialists. He prophesied that if the European Governments unleashed a war it would "be followed by a European socialist uprising." Recalling the March, 1848 revolution he appealed to the young people in his paper: "Prepare for the liberation not only of your own people but of the whole of mankind!" Virtually up to the last moment, he attended party congresses, submitted proposals, and took the chair at workers' rallies, although one of his contemporaries wrote: "He considered himself fortunate when he and his family could eat their fill of stale bread once a day."

He died on the May 11th, 1886. Only a few people accompanied him to his final resting place. There was no official mourning. What he had predicted in the preface to his autobiography came true: "Since I intend to disregard the powers—that-be and bring to light many episodes that have been hushed up, I will make enemies both high and low." This statement is typical not only of the memoirs but of Dániel Kászonyi's whole career, ideological development and character.

*

This brief outline of Kászonyi's activity illustrates one subjective aspect of Hungarian history. This disciple of Voltaire and Diderot, this follower of the rationalists and Encyclopaedists, this radical of the Reform era and of 1848, remained faithful to the ideas of progress to the very end. The question he raised as to whether socialism could strike roots in the soil of nineteenth-century Hungary was answered by his own life. Despite reversals, betrayals and humiliations his own consistency gave him a renewed impetus again and again. His non-conformist attitude inevitably led him to the most significant and progressive camp of the oppressed at that time—to social democracy. In the age-old struggle between cold intellect and warm heart, it was always the latter that emerged victorious at decisive moments. Even though he was disillusioned by the outcome of the French revolution he never abandoned the ideal; as a young man in the Pozsony Parliament he was enraptured by the *"Marseillaise,"* and as editor of *Népszava,* he published the new working-class version of the song.

His career was marked almost exclusively by failures, a reflection of the revolution and of a significant tragic era in Hungarian history. His solitude resulted from the defeat of the revolutionary movement in Hungary, his activity was an organic factor in the struggle for progress in Hungary.

Dániel Kászonyi embodied the finest traditions of Hungarian journalism-revolutionary thinking and intellectual courage. His career points a moral. It reminds one of "The Pilgrim's Progress," where John Bunyan makes his hero, look back from the shores of death over the arduous struggles of his pilgrimage and exclaim: "And yet, I regret nothing!" And with all the pride of a man leaving a fortune, Kászonyi quoted in his will Bunyan's famous words: "I leave my sword to him who follows me on my pilgrimage; my courage and skill to him who can acquire them."

JÁNOS JEMNITZ

MIHÁLY KÁROLYI AND THE ENGLISH LEFT

Correspondence 1921—1939

In an eventful life Mihály Károlyi (1875–1955) the well-known Hungarian statesman and President of the 1918 Hungarian Republic, twice spent periods of several years as a political refugee in Britain. The first was in the interwar period up to and during the Second World War, when he contributed to the British press, lectured extensively and maintained close relations with many leading personalities in English cultural and political life. The general outline and facts of these periods of his life are by now well-known. We believe, however, that the work and thought of Mihály Károlyi have not as yet been properly appraised. It is true that his

memoirs* with much interesting information, were published in London in 1956, and in 1964 a selection from his writings** in two substantial volumes was published in Hungary. For much of what we know about Károlyi's personality and thinking we are indebted to his wife and closest collaborator, Katalin Andrássy, his companion in his political struggles, who gave an account of her husband's life in a number of lectures as well as in a foreword to the Hungarian selection of his works. It was also Mrs. Ká-

* Memoirs of Michael Károlyi, Jonathan Cape, 1956
** *Károlyi Mihály válogatott írásai* — 1920–1946, Budapest, 1964, 512, 679 pp.

rolyi who gave an impetus to further studies by making most of the Károlyi letters available for research.

A striking feature of Károlyi's political attitude was the rapidity and directness with which it emerged. Himself a member of the aristocracy and one of the country's wealthiest landowners, he was already the leader of the radical wing of the Független-ségi Párt (Independence Party), and had fought for the extension of democratic rights, and against the First World War, before it began. The same period saw the formation of his first links with the labour movement. It was this political background which qualified him for the position of President of the Hungarian Republic which emerged from the successful revolution of 1918. After the right-wing assumption of power in 1919, as an exile, he continued in agreement and cooperation with the various revolutionary and socialist movements of the time, of which he considered the communists the most efficient and the nearest to himself.

In the twenty years following 1919 Károlyi devoted all his intellectual and financial resources and practically the whole of his time to the advancement of the workers' movement and the cause of human progress. His primary objective was to be of service to Hungarian people in their struggle for democracy and socialism, but his support was equally unqualified for the anti-fascist battles of the Austrian or Spanish workers, for the Chinese in their revolutionary campaigns, for the Mexicans in their liquidation of the whole reactionary establishment in their country, and for the Soviet people engaged in creating an entirely new social system. Mihály Károlyi was free from all nationalist bigotry; progress for him meant progress on an international level. And keeping in touch as he did with the world on that level, he came into contact with a great variety of representatives of progressive ideas. His own role among the heterogeneous elements of the progressive camp was both interesting and peculiar. He was able to maintain warm and intimate relations with bourgeois democratic politicians as well as with the social-democrats and communists. He paid close attention and gave support both to the communist and a section of the social-democratic movements, but although ne participated in their activities and frequently acted as a mediator between them, he did not spare his criticism. And later consideration has shown that more than once this criticism was justified, as for instance his criticism of the illegalities under the Stalin régime and his opposition to the opportunism of the leaders of the Second International. The analysis of these events, a new appraisal of the history of the workers' movement in that critical epoch is, however, outside the scope of the present introduction.

In the post-1919 period Mihály Károlyi put forward a constructive programme for Europe in general and the Hungarian people in particular, setting as a final objective the goal of socialist transformation. Some of the detailed sections of the proposed transformation, such as the scheme of land reform, he worked out himself. But the greater part of his activities was devoted less to the construction of specific programme than to the day to day struggle he was conducting against the forces of reaction and various fascist factions.

Already before 1914 Károlyi had discovered that the feudal-militarist caste had no scruples in resorting to the most brutal and drastic methods of a safeguarding its own interests and suppressing popular movements. Once again, in 1919, he was faced with the bitter realization that the aristocracy, the great landowners and capitalists, and even a part of the middle classes, were prepared not only to accept the atrocities of this White Terror without protest, but also to conceal them from the world, and even on occasion to approve them—purely in order to assure their economic power.

It was then that Károlyi finally abandoned any illusion that these strongholds of Hungarian reaction would yield by peaceful means, and the recognition of this fact led him to ally himself with the revolutionary political groups. By this step Mihály Károlyi, former President of the Republic, and the magnate who distributed his lands among the peasants, made himself one of the most hated outcasts of Horthy's Hungary. Nor was his heart less open to the fate of the persecuted. With his connections, reputation and moral authority, he set out to mobilize all the progressive elements in Europe and overseas to fight fascism and to save the lives of those condemned by fascist régimes.

The present publication is specifically designed to throw light on these activities; it confines itself exclusively, however, to those cases where Károlyi was urging progressive elements in Britain to take action, and was cooperating with British democratic groups.

The first phase of this cooperation goes back to the early 1920's. Although at the period Károlyi was in closer contact with French circles—he had successfully appealed to the Clarté group as well as to Pierre Renaudel and Jean Longuet to condemn the Hungarian counter-revolution—through the intermediary of the Vienna Socialists he had begun to establish relations with Labour Party circles in London. In this he was helped by Zsigmond Kunfi and more especially Pál Szende, two Hungarian Social Democrats in exile in Vienna, as well as by Sándor Garbai, a veteran Social Democrat living in Paris, and Vilmos Böhm, former Minister of War in Károlyi's 1918 Cabinet and later on the influential leader of the Hungarian Social Democratic emigrés in Vienna, with whom Károlyi maintained friendly relations for more than twenty years. In London Károlyi also undertook the task of political propaganda, drawing the attention of the Labour and Liberal press to articles from the Hungarian Social

Democratic daily *Népszava*, and to the horrors of the White Terror in Hungary. These activities are reflected in his letters to Frederick Kuh and Wickham Steed published below. It was in pursuance of this activity that he approached a number of influential figures from the Labour party for help to save the Hungarian Communists whose lives were threatened by the special courts introduced by the counter-revolutionary régime in Hungary. (The letters of Arthur Ponsonby and Sidney Webb, quoted below, relate to this subject. We might also draw attention to Fenner Brockway's autobiography, as judging by the letter from G. B. Shaw included in this selection it seems justifiable to assume that the approach made to Fenner Brockway to take up the cause of "Fritz Karik"* (was part of a drive initiated by Mihály Károlyi. (Fenner Brockway, Outside the Right, Allen & Unwin, 1963, p. 224)

To round out the picture it must be added that the tone of these letters was, though polite, rather evasive. The same applies to the letter of G. B. Shaw's which Fenner Brockway quotes.

Characteristically, their writers seemed to doubt the effectiveness of their intervention, expressing the fear that their protests might have harmful repercussions. Up to the present no trace has been found of any representations made by them to the Hungarian Government of the day. On the other hand, it is a fact that Károlyi was successful with both the American labour organizations and the French socialists, and that protest telegrams poured in from France, the United States and Germany. Many of these telegrams are preserved in

---

* Frigyes Karikás (1891–1938), Hungarian Communist writer. Took part in the Moscow Revolution of 1917, then in the formation of the Hungarian Communist Party in 1918. In exile after the collapse of the 1919 Hungarian Soviet Republic, at intermittent intervals he was in charge of the organisation of the illegal Hungarian Communist Party.

the archives of the Institute for Party History, Budapest.

Another group of the letters deal with the campaign to denounce German fascism, and were directed towards the staging of an American counter-trial in answer to the Leipzig trial. Mrs. Károlyi took a prominent part in organizing this campaign, and her indefatigable efforts succeeded in winning over a large number of humane and liberally-minded British personalities to the work of extending the drive for support for the anti-fascist campaign. This time, again, the letters reflect only a limited success. It should be pointed out that other letters in addition to the letters quoted here have survived from the period, from John Strachey, for instance, who assured Mrs. Károlyi of his sympathy, and even supplied her with letters to American democrats.

The third group of letters is concerned with the Spanish Civil War. Once again Károlyi and his wife were not only sympathetic to the Spanish Republican cause, but took an active part in the movements of solidarity, made material sacrifices, and lent their support to the campaign organized by the Labour Party. The three letters by Ellen Wilkinson are both proof and illustration of their connections with the campaign.

In conclusion, the fact that in the course of his activities in support of the anti-fascist movements, Károlyi took part in the work of a number of international organizations, where he came into contact with British Labour politicians and other democrats, is not without interest. In the Comité International d'Aide aux Victimes du Fascisme Hitlérien, for instance, he worked in collaboration with Ellen Wilkinson and Lord Morley. The ideals of anti-fascism were closely related to anti-militarism, to a condemnation of aggressive policies of war. As before 1914 and later during the First World War, Károlyi remained throughout the inter-war period an ardent advocate of all pacifist movements,

and exchanged ideas with British anti-militarists, as witnessed by several fragments.

In consequence of these activities Károlyi came to enjoy a high reputation in progressive circles throughout the Anglo-Saxon world, a fact proved, among others, by a host of personal invitations and letters of congratulation. His correspondents included Bertrand Russell, Julian Huxley, R. W. Seton-Watson, Dorothy Thompson—the wife of Sinclair Lewis—and many others. When in 1925 the Horthy régime instituted legal proceedings against Károlyi, Bertrand Russell declared his full solidarity; "Many thanks for sending me the article against the slanders on yourself. I was myself supposed during the war to be a German spy, but alas, the Kaiser never recognised my services!" Victor Gollancz and Julian Huxley expressed their best wishes for the successful staging of an anti-fascist counter-trial in America, and Huxley also provided Károlyi with advice on whom to approach for further assistance. From beyond the Atlantic, Upton Sinclair repeatedly sent his greetings to Károlyi and both Sinclair Lewis and his wife sprang to his defence, when on the diplomatic intervention of the Horthy régime, the US government raised difficulties about his lecture tour in America and practically compelled him to silence. It was at this period that Dorothy Thompson, in a letter dated September 2nd, 1928, wrote to Károlyi, "I wish my husband and myself had been in New York to welcome you on your all too brief visit to the land of the free. It would have been a great pleasure to have seen you again. I am only sorry that Europe still seems to be a more satisfactory meeting ground. If ever this Government—or its successor—lift the idiotic ban against you, I hope you will plan to come and stay with us wherever we may be." Another element in these relationships and the anti-fascist attitude in general, denunciation of the Munich policy, was referred to in a letter from R. W. Seton-Watson of November 29th, 1939 where, in addition to personal greetings, he informed Károlyi in advance of the fact that he intended to wage "a frontal attack on the whole Chamberlain policy" in his forthcoming book.

The clear and unequivocal political position adopted by Károlyi, democratic, anti-fascist and anti-war, won him many friends and laid the foundations for his increasing influence on British public opinion in the years of the Second World War. By successfully building a bridge between the British and Hungarian progressive forces, he was in fact contributing to the creation of the common front which came to unite anti-fascists of the most varied shades of opinion all over the world.

The Daily Herald
                    Vienna, August 5, 1921

My dear Mr. Károlyi,

Mr. Jászi* has been in to visit me this morning, and mentioned that you never received a copy of the Herald, containing a copy of your telegram. I regret exceedingly that I have not saved an early edition of that issue (as you know there are three editions daily); for in the earlier number, your statement appeared *in extenso*. I have, however, succeeded in unearthing this abbreviated clipping.

I have also just written a review of Windischgraetz "Memoirs", just published in London, of which I shall send you a copy next week.

Mr. Jászi also mentioned to me the possibility of you communicating with me by post in future, in case some event of importance arises. I shall, needless to say, always be delighted to hear from you and to do whatever I can to bring your viewpoint before British Labour through the Herald.

During my visit to London last month, I had conversations with a number of leading politicians, both of the Liberal and Labour Parties, and to my consternation found them very inadequately informed about Hungarian affairs. Even men with the insight and integrity of Colonel Wedgwood** are labouring under the delusion that much is to be hoped from the Partei der kleinen Landwirte, which they naively believe to be a thoroughly democratic group. Naturally, I have done my utmost to make clear that this is a thinly camouflaged party of feudal landlords and a mainstay of the Reaction. But it would be highly desirable that some respected Hungarian, whose political reputation is beyond reproach, should go to London and explain the situation as it actually is.***

I trust that you will find time to keep me informed—directly—about significant developments in the Hungarian situation, which come to your attention, and which are not available through ordinary channels.

I shall be glad to have you call on me whenever I can be of service.

With cordial wishes to you, and confidence in the future of a socialist Hungary. I remain

                              Faithfully yours,
                              Frederick Kuh

Special Correspondent,
The Daily Herald.

                                        13.8.23.

Dear Count Károlyi,

In reply to your letter of 11th instant, I should, of course, be glad to see you in so important a matter, although I fear there is

---

* Jászi, Oszkár (1875–1957), sociologist, a leading personality in pre–1914 Hungarian bourgeois-radical movements. Minister for National Minority Affairs in Károlyi's Cabinet, he later went into exile in the United States and became a professor of Oberlin College (Ohio).

** It should be mentioned that despite his many undoubtedly admirable activities, Col. Josiah Wedgwood injured the cause of Hungarian democrats when he signed a declaration in 1921 to the effect that no one in Hungary was being illegally persecuted. Subsequently, however, he consistently took up the cause of the persecuted.

*** We have, unfortunately, no conclusive evidence of whether the interventions requested in fact materialized.

nothing that I could do to help. You will naturally have been seeing other people more likely to be influential in the case.* Unfortunately I am now living in the country, and I have engagements keeping me here for the next week. Moreover, either Lord Ponsonby or Lord Parmoor or Mr. Henderson would probably be more helpful to you. One never knows whether intervention from another country may not do more harm than good. Have you tried the *Manchester Guardian?*

If you think it worth while, my wife and I would be delighted to welcome you for luncheon here at 1 pm. Tuesday or Wednesday next, 16th or 17th August. It is only 47 miles from London, down the Portsmouth Road. Perhaps you could telephone or write.

Yours very truly,
Sidney Webb

19th September, 1925
Dear Count Károlyi,

Thank you for sending me the translation of the Népszava article ** which I have read with much interest. I shall certainly hope to have the pleasure of seeing you when you are next in London.

Pray give my respectful regards to the Countess and believe me,

Very sincerely yours,
Wickham Steed

13. VIII. 32.
Dear Count Károlyi,

I am sorry I am away and I am just going still further afield so I shall not be in London.

* The letter refers to the legal proceedings instituted by the Horthy régime against the leaders of the Communist Party (Imre Sallai, Sándor Fürst, Ferenc Karikás and György Kilián). As the Government had already introduced special courts, Károlyi tried to persuade responsible British politicians to lodge a protest, in order to prevent these summary proceedings.
** The "Népszava" article to which the reference is made cannot be identified.

But as a matter of fact I have already had the case of Karikás fully explained to me and I have talked it over with sympathetic friends. There is only one person who I think could have any influence at all and that is the Prime Minister. Unfortunately I am not in a position to approach him or to be listened to by him even if I did.

I cannot help thinking, however, that if you wrote to him direct he might pay some attention although I know his official mind is always reluctant to interfere with internal concerns of other nations.

I can think of no other method of bringing pressure to bear on the Hungarian authorities from this country.***

Yours very truly,
Ponsonby

June 6th, 1934
Dear Countess Károlyi,

I am extremely sorry that I cannot do what you want. In the first place, the notice is much too short and I have too many things on here in the next few weeks. I hope you will be able to find someone who will satisfy your requirements to take my place. I am not sure, in any case, that I know enough about Americans to be able to treat them in the right way. But at any rate it is impossible for me to go.

I do indeed remember very well the time when we saw you and your husband at our house. What a much worse world it has become than even in those bad days. I do wish that I had known where you were a week or two before, as Lady Trevelyan is now in Germany and is going on to Budapest to attend a conference. It would have been a great thing for her to have seen you and heard something from you of your country. I don't, of course, know what kind of connections you are able to maintain there; she

*** It has proved impossible to ascertain whether any protests reached Budapest on the part of the British Government or the leaders of the Labour Party.

might have passed on a friendly word from you to the friends. I think she gets there next Monday for a week.

Yours sincerely,
Charles Trevelyan

12th June, 1934

My dear Countess Károlyi,

I have written to Raymond Buell of the Foreign Policy Association, and enclose herewith a copy of the letter. You will see that this leaves it for you to communicate with Buell, should you decide to do so, concerning the deputation.

I hope you will be able to get Kingsley Martin to go. Perhaps you may care to let me know before you leave what arrangements you have been able to make. Anyhow, I believe we are to have the pleasure of seeing Count Károlyi here in the course of a few days in connection with the Library of the Burned Books.

It was very pleasant to have the two talks the other day. I am sorry that your engagement with Elisabeth Bergner afterwards prevented our being able to discuss our impressions of the Olympia meeting—which must have been something of a surprise to you about British manners and customs. However, I much hope before very long to have another chance of talk.

Yours sincerely,
G.E.G. Catlin

Dear Monsieur le Comte Károlyi,

Thank you for your letter. I shall very much look forward to seeing you when you arrive in London and having the opportunity of talking matters over. It is a great source of gratification to me that you have been prepared to accept the international treasurership of the Library. Perhaps you could be so good as to send me a note letting me know when I may expect you, and your adress, or in the alternative, telephone so that we may be able to make arrangements as soon as convenient.

It was a great pleasure to see the Countess Károlyi here the other day.

Yours sincerely,
G.E.G. Catlin

News Chronicle   June 19th, 1934

Dear Countess Károlyi,

It was a great pleasure to meet you the other day, and I should much like the opportunity of a further talk with you.

I do not know how long you are going to be in London this time, but if you are free at lunch time any day, I should be very pleased if you would come to lunch with me.

Yours sincerely,
Gerald Barry

June 29th, 1934

Dear Countess Károlyi,

Thank you for your letter. I heard after writing that you had returned to Paris. I hope to have the pleasure of seeing you next time you are in London.

May I offer you my best wishes for you anti-fascist campaign. I am acting on your suggestion and cabling a message to the Committee.

Yours sincerely,
Gerald Barry

8th December, 1938

Dear Madame Károlyi,

I have heard from our relief organisation in Spain that you are willing to go to Spain in connection with our relief work on behalf of the child refugees. It is very good of you to promise to help our relief committee in this way and your report will be most valuable. It is specially necessary to have information as to whether the distribution of relief is working well, and in what way it could be improved. If you consider there are special needs which are not being met I should be grateful if you would get in touch with Dr. Audrey Russell, who is our medical officer there.

Yours sincerely,
Ellen Wilkinson

20th January, 1939

Dear Madame Károlyi,

I was so glad to hear from you, but was sorry to miss you on the phone. At the moment I do not think we have any delegation going to Spain. I will let you know when one is going and will fix you up. As regards the actual committee, would you like to join the Duchess' Committee for Relief for Spain as the political committee is restricted to MPs and a pretty rigid balanced collection of bigwigs. Are you available for meetings yet or would you prefer to wait till after you have been to Spain?

Please forgive my typing this letter, but I am in a terrible rush of work.

Best wishes,
Yours sincerely,
Ellen Wilkinson

8th December, 1938

Dear Madame Károlyi,

I do not think there would be any harm in your going to Spain so long as you went as a member of a Relief Committee. We would gladly include you in any group which we are sending. I have sent you a wire saying that there is a party going on Saturday, leaving Quai D'Orsay at 8.15 on Saturday evening. If you get in touch with Otto he will give you all the necessary details.

I am enclosing a letter which will establish your *bona fide* as a member of a group sent by our Relief organisation.

Yours sincerely,
Ellen

P.S. This sounds formal. If you can manage. If not, another group goes in January.

JÁNOS GYÖRGY SZILÁGYI

JÁNOS HONTI
(1910—1945)

János Honti, one of the foremost Hungarian folklorists, was killed twenty years ago in a forced labour camp, at the age of thirty-four. He obtained his degree at the Budapest University, and then worked at the Hungarian Ethnographical Museum in Budapest. In the period between 1934 and 1939 he spent several years in Paris, on French and Hungarian scholarships. The outbreak of the war brought him back to Hungary, where he remained on the staff of the National Széchényi Library until his untimely death.

One may justly call Honti an infant prodigy—one of those peculiar phenomena appearing less and less frequently in the scientific world of our century. He had not yet finished secondary school when his first paper was published as Volume 81 of the *Folklore Fellows Communications* in Helsinki. The work he carried on so relentlessly throughout the short span of his life resulted in several hundreds of scientific publications. His main interest was directed to research in the epic genres of folk-poetry, more particularly the folk-tale. The first result was the volume referred to above, published during his school years, a synoptic tabulation of tale-types relating to the stock of Hungarian folk-tales published up to then.

Honti acquired a university degree in modern philology, and it was his exceptional talent as a philologist, coupled with an excellent command of languages, that determined the direction of his folkloristic work. His first book was based on his acceptance of the principles established by the Finnish "historico-geographical school." Accordingly, he fitted his classification of the Hungarian material into Antti Aarne's system of tale-types. At that time, the Finnish school was at its height as the authority in the field with research centred on elaborating the methods for ascertaining the original form of a tale, the time and place of its emergence, the path of its migration, and the mode of its variations. Comparative examinations of the largest possible number of variants were made in order to reconstruct the "archetype," the "original" form of a tale. Efforts were also made to determine the probable place of origin of a tale or of a single motive, as inferred from the chart of diffusion of the tale. This method can be regarded as a remarkable achievement of 19th-century rationalism, and the synopsis of tale-types elaborated by that method—together with the amendments subsequently applied to it —proved to be readily applicable in practice. The synopsis was established on the pattern of textual criticism, classical philology's perfectly elaborated method for reconstructing the authentic original text from extant later copies.

Honti's career was still at its initial stage when the crisis of this classical method became obvious. It was at this time that the first serious clash took place between conventional and new principles: in 1929 a Florentine Professor, G. Pasquali, published a comprehensive review of Paul Maas's small manual on the classical methods of textual criticism. Originally three times the size of the manual under review, Pasquali's work finally grew into a big volume, published in 1934. Without belittling the results achieved by classical methods, the author pointed out the often misleading results arrived at in the reconstruction of the "original text," when formal logic and a somewhat mechanistic approach to extant texts were applied. Pasquali emphasized that copies of later origin are not necessarily less authentic than the earlier ones, that certain variants may have their historic significance even if they are of minor critical value, and that descent from a single archetype does not constitute the only possible form of transmission. Hence, the genealogy of a manuscript may in some cases be entirely illusory.

Honti's first important works criticizing the methods of the Finnish school in folktale research sprung from this spirit of revising the traditional methods of textual criticism. In 1931, Honti, still a student, published his German paper "Volksmärchen und Heldensage" as Volume 95 of the *Folklore Fellows Communications*. In this paper he demonstrated, by means of textual analysis, that Aarne's supposition according to which originally each tale-motive belonged to a certain tale-type, is theoretically untenable. This first step was later completed by further investigations, in which Honti naturally took other scholars' achievements into account and which eventually grew into a comprehensive and systematic criticism of the methods of the Finnish school. The essential traits of his concept were disclosed in various papers, written by him in several languages, but as a comprehensive whole his criticism exists, up to this day, in Hungarian only. His main work, *A mese világa* ("The World of the Tale"), appeared in 1937. In it, he always starts out from the extant text-material of the epic tradition and with the aid of his exceedingly keen dialectic method reaches the conclusion that the notion of "tale-type" is a mere abstraction, just as is that of "tale-motive." Neither of them exists in reality. What actually exists, i.e., what one can read or hear, is the prevalent form of a tale: the individual variant. As an example, he cites the tale-type of "The Princess on the Glass Mountain," comparing it with a hitherto neglected Egyptian variant, in order to expose the shortcomings of the methods directed at determining the place and time of origin of the "arche-tale": "A pre-conceived idea may find much data to back it —and a more or less involuntarily neglected trait demonstrates the inadequacy both of method and means used till then."

It would, nevertheless, be unjust to accuse Honti of sterile agnosticism. In spite of his grave theoretical scruples, he insisted that folk-tale explorers must not relinquish the aim of tracing the origin—and perhaps even the original form, if any—of tales. Honti, moreover, never failed to emphasize that Aarne's concept "almost completely met practical requirements." All the same, it was not only the insufficiency of the methods of his day and uncertainty of the results to be attained by them that induced Honti not to focus his investigations on the main problems of the Finnish school, but above all the one-sided approach to these problems. He claimed that the method of comparative tale-research at best reconstructs the skeleton plot of the original tale, but is obliged to ignore both its structure and its formal characteristics. Hence, the comparative method abandons the aim of examining form and content of a tale together. "The analytical method of the Finnish school of folklorists seems to have made them forget that besides a number of motives there is also the tale as a whole."

The tale as a whole—this concept has a double meaning. On the one hand, it denotes the tale as one of the genres of epic tradition, i.e., as a literary form; on the other, it incorporates a certain way of looking at the world, expressed in the particular form of a tale. Perhaps these two aspects of the tale can be considered the main object of Honti's subsequent work. He thus gave an entirely new meaning to the tasks of determining the origin of a tale and of setting up a systematic tabulation of folk-tales. The solution of both these tasks called for the prior solution of the boundary issue. This is where Honti realized his most valuable scientific achievements, this is where he best revealed his extraordinary judgement regarding intellectual and literary forms, together with his philosophical learning, his qualities as a philologist and his vast knowledge of world literature. The basic question he set himself was as to what makes a tale a tale. He wanted to determine the point where tales diverge from the rest of the epic genres, to discover the world picture mankind had been seeking to reproduce and comprehend by creating the tale.

In defining the world concept reflected in the tale, a problem considered by Honti as the ultimate question to be answered by folk-tale research, he was assisted by three important contributions. One was André Jolles's "Einfache Formen," a monograph published in 1930; the second was the new school of research into the history of ancient religion best represented by Walter F. Otto, the eminent Frankfort scholar; the third was Leo Frobenius's teachings regarding the morphology of culture. It was his adherence to Károly Kerényi that brought about Honti's connections with Otto and Frobenius. Ever since his university years, Honti had been a member of a circle composed of classical philologists, egyptologists, ethnologists, archaeologists, philosophers and poets, a circle which, presided over by Kerényi, was diametrically opposed to the narrow-minded, backward thinking then for the most part reigning at Hungarian universities. Ideologically as well as politically, these young scholars resisted the cultural policy of Hungarian officialdom, which helped pave the way for the approaching German occupation of the country.

While maintaining his spirit of criticism, Honti greatly appreciated his indebtedness to the men who, directly or indirectly, had shaped his development. Indeed, he was among the first to recognize certain factual distortions in the work of Frobenius and to reject the irrationalist tendencies of the Frankfort school, leading towards the racial myth of Hitler Nazism. His acute sense of criticism never left him, when faced with new and different theories, nor could elaborate theoretical constructions break his bonds with the material he was primarily concerned with: the actual texts handed down by epic tradition. It was these bonds that assisted Honti in applying his accumulated knowledge to evolving a clear, consistent and independent system of his own.

In determining the world of the tale, he started from the work of Jolles, but what he built up led him much farther. His concept of the tale-world included a characteristic trait: the correction of the real world. In the tale, all boundaries existing in reality are disrupted, the contradictions of reality cease to exist, possibilities are unlimited. All this, however, must not be deemed merely a playful and aimless product of fantasy—on the contrary, tales serve a well-defined and definable aim: to replace the actual order of things by another, imaginary but desired order. The world as reflected in the tale is not what it really is but what it ought to be.

Elements which by this approach may be defined as tale-elements can, however, be found in various literary forms, in most genres of epic tradition. In the course of a comparative study of these forms, Honti produced brilliant analyses, delimiting tale and legend, tale and *saga*, tale and *novella*, tale and myth. His chief concern remained the problem of distinghishing between tale and myth. The question of priority in time of these two had long been discussed and examined by scholars. Honti claimed that while the worlds of tale and myth are different, one does not exclude the other. Myth explains the world and man's place in it, whereas the tale tries to improve both. Hence, it is utterly senseless to bring in the notion of priority. The problem which remains to be solved is, however, the correlation of the stock of epic motives of tale and myth.

Honti's approach to this as to other questions was based on an amazingly vast knowledge of his subject. His new results constituted an organic continuation of his early publications. He held that the motives—the "building-bricks" of the tale—may at the same time act as building-bricks of other epic forms too. Actually, one should never speak of epic motives in the sense of narrative elements whose occurrence is apt to determine the genre of an epic narrative; hence, the essence of a tale is not inherent in the narrative or in parts thereof. "The epic elements which are appropriate for expressing the world of the tale, for building up the

world of the tale, may be found anywhere in the vast domain of epic tradition."

This negative result unavoidably led to the following question: what, if not the epic elements, distinguishes a tale, renders it palpable, recognizable and definable? Honti's answer to this question was rooted in his examination of tale-structure. Thus, he immediately tackled the problems of the history of the tale. According to his view, the individual genres, among them the tale, gradually branched off from the main stream of the oldest form of epic tradition. The tale obtained its characteristic form and function mainly due to its particular structure and structural elements. Honti again and again reverted to the examination of certain tale-elements which "have no significant role in connection with the subject matter of a particular tale, which in themselves are often incomprehensible, and yet cling to their place in the tradition of the tale with amazing persistence." As an example, let us take the so-called "double scenery of the tale"—a feature he treated in a separate paper—meaning that the scenery of the tale itself is not identical with the scenery of the adventures of the hero. It is this second scene, that of the hero's adventures, which constitutes the background of the tale-world, the boundaries of which are usually stressed in the tale with great emphasis. Honti's ultimate conclusion is that the genre of the tale, which in all probability evolved during the Middle Ages until it reached its present form, is characterized precisely by the emergence of tale-elements and of the tale-world within the specific tale-structure.

This constitutes only the first point of the poetics of the tale, to which Honti made a number of further important contributions. In one of his papers he emphasized the significance of the fact that the narrative of the tale always has a biographical character and that the tale takes place in the present. This latter feature is generally stressed by the closing formula of tales, in contrast to the opening formula. Searching for the reasons why the differentiation of epic forms occurred, and analysing the properties of the tale from the point of view of poetics, Honti arrived at the problem of the tale along a new road. His approach permitted him to consider the evolution of the tale on the basis of a much wider historical background than did and could the adherents of the Finnish school. In his last papers, as well as his last reflections never committed to paper, he rounded off a new and momentous project —that of telling the history of the tale from the aspect of its social function, of including in the history of the tale the story-teller as well as the audience, and of considering the tale and its historical changes in its human and social medium.

This latter problem fitted organically into the last phase of Honti's career as a scholar, a phase in which his main endeavours were directed at extending the range of tale-research. These endeavours were in full conformity with his ever-searching, restless and sensitive spirit. Certain limitations inherent in the methods of the "historico-geographical school" and in the conclusions arrived at by Hungarian scholars induced him to study the medieval epic tradition of Northern Europe.

In his last years, Honti devoted considerable time and interest to such studies, which included even textual criticism of Irish and Norse tradition. In addition to tackling problems of genre in epic tradition, this trend of Honti's researches contributed to his new ideas on the relations between folk-tale research and the history of religion. In the meantime, he published a Hungarian folk-tale variant—collected by himself—of the Cyclops-story of the Odyssey, wrote a number of important and valuable contributions about certain tale-motives to *Handwörterbuch des Deutschen Märchens*, and investigated in detail the Egyptian tale of the Predestined Prince, attempting to reconstruct its lost ending. He then turned with increasing interest to the great works of world literature. Following his comparison of Odysseus's figure in Dante and Homer, he wrote an excellent paper on Villon. In another, posthumous paper concerned with tracing a parallel between Orestes and Hamlet, he analysed the difference between medieval and ancient concepts. It is easy to recognize in this analysis the reference to modern times, hidden between the lines: "The sublime purity of Apollo's reign has yielded to that of the human mind, ravaged by fever." These lines are to be found at the end of a paper he finished in the last months of the war, working amidst the horrors of a forced labour camp. Needless to say, this allusion to the present is neither cheap nor anachronistic—it merely voices the convictions of a scholar whose work was never separated from his life and who always bore in mind the ultimate meaning and humanistic aim of scientific work. In another place he says: "Beside his scholarly side, the researcher has to rely on his human side too. As a human being, he is searching for human experience and human truth... His unavoidable weaknesses may sometimes have misled him in the course of collecting and arranging his material. Yet by preserving his human outlook on human things, he may arrive at the truth... what we need is a human point of view in science."

These words, defining Honti's attitude towards life as well as science, epitomize the creed he professed throughout the darkest days of his personal fate. Not even in the depth of his sufferings did he give up his firm conviction that the achievements of the human mind will not have been in vain, even though the near future did not seem hopeful. "When I think of the future," he wrote in his last letter, "I know that humanism and philology will be of paramount importance in it... the tiny candle light entrusted to man's care must be salvaged and carried through the embers of the devastating flames now consuming the world. This small light is man's most valuable possession."

MAGDA RADNÓT

PROBLEMS OF OPHTHALMOLOGICAL RESEARCH

The problems of ophthalmological research can no more be separated from the general development of biology and medicine than any other branch of science. The ophthalmological aspect of modern research in genetics, microbiology and molecular biology are beginning to receive more attention. The progress of biochemistry particularly makes itself felt in ophthalmology, making it possible to examine under more favourable circumstances the metabolism of tissues such as the crystalline lens, the vitreous body and the cornea, which have no veins.

Much of ophthalmological research is basic research. In the past few years special journals have been published in the field of theoretical ophthalmology such as *Experimental Eye Research, Investigative Ophthalmology*, and *Vision*, none of which publishes articles on clinical practice. Special institutes for eye research have recently been established in Europe—in London and in Bonn. They have departments for biochemistry, electron microscopy, histology, etc. These institutes, originally connected with clinics, began training qualified specialists after becoming independent institutions. In the United States there are several laboratories for eye research. The Helmholtz Institute in Moscow has certain similarities with the London Institute, although its various departments are mainly devoted to practical research. The Academy of Sciences in Czechoslovakia has a research department. The Budapest Eye Clinic No. 1 is now developing a similar department, where various groups carry on research in pathological histology, microbiology, electro-physiology, and the use of computor technics and cybernetics in these subjects.

Research in morbid histology has a more serious tradition in Hungary than in most European countries. The first edition of "Ophthalmological Pathology," a Hungarian work published by the Academy Publishing House in 1951, preceded similar works published in the U.S.A., France and England. It ran into five editions. Many papers treating pathological histology appear in American journals. Their emphasis is experimental, as they concentrate mainly on the morbid histology of eyeballs which have been removed.

In Hungary this question is still open. Removal of the eyeball is undertaken much less frequently today than it was ten or twenty years ago. The reason for this is, in part, the improved treatment of lesions. In a number of cases removal of the eyeball is necessitated by delay in the operation. The therapy of growths in the eye is usually removal of the eye along with the tumor. The examination and the assessment of a removed eyeball must, however, be made by an experienced ophthalmologist who has an adequate grasp of pathology. Many more such specialists should be trained. At the moment a great deal of valuable material is being lost both to pathological instruction and to research. In the past year, eyeballs were removed in 206 cases, and of these 66 were studied, but the aim was chiefly to establish or corroborate a diagnosis. Only preliminary steps have been taken in the field of electron microscopical examinations, although these examinations yield results mainly in connection with microbiological examinations. Ophthalmologists also perform research on circulation, particularly in regard to glaucomas or retinopathies of a vascular origin. The diagnostics of glaucoma with the aid of gonioscopy, but mainly with aplanatory tonometry and tonography used for measuring eye pressure, has made considerable headway, although it is still far from solving the pathological origin of glaucoma. We are unable to diagnose glaucoma at an early stage without adequately calibrated tonometres. These must be imported, and we do not yet have enough of them. One to two per cent of the population over 40 years of age have glaucoma, so it is imperative for Hungary to acquire reliable instruments for gauging eye-pressure. Tonography and aplanatory tonometry, which are at the disposal of the ophthalmologists of the major clinics and hospitals, demand a considerable staff of assistants, and this is one reason why they cannot be used at small polyclinics.

Successful research is being done in Hungary on the connection between general circulation and the circulation of the eye. Outstanding results have been attained through the use of mechanical models. Proceeding on the principle of the analogy between the current of fluids and electric current, the first analogic model was constructed at Eye Clinic No. 1. Even fields of research which were inaccessible up to now may yield results with the aid of this model. Research of this character necessitates the cooperation of scientists who have had mathematical training, but also of technical experts familiar with the unsolved problems of medicine and biology. Physicists or technical experts who have not spent years on a given medical problem cannot possibly achieve the needed results, for the assistance they can get from their medical colleagues will not compensate for lack of experience. We are not thinking of the training of some sort of technician-physician, which is unlikely, but of a technician who, after several years of experience, has then spent additional years on biological questions.

Experience has shown that a medical research team may need several such engineers for the solution of the various problems. A natural bent for research is essential in this field, for no results could be attained by urging young engineers into medical research

against their inclinations. And experience has shown that such experts do exist; one must only look for them. These experts are themselves researchers; so in referring to them we are not speaking of mere technical workers who are needed for the solution of problems that necessitate the use of complicated instruments or for the purpose of repairing flaws in the instruments. Even though these are matters of considerable importance in Hungary. Our instruments are imported, and there is no repair service here. Still, if the research institution has an expert with the qualifications just described, then a technician in addition to him should be adequate to solve the purely technical problems.

The daily press has devoted quite a lot of attention to the medical and primarily ophthalmological aspects of laser rays. It is true that research in this field is being carried on all over the world. Nevertheless, at least, in ophthalmology, laser rays are a long way from being used in daily practice. Instruments for this purpose have been made in the United States, but the question of their safety has not yet been clarified. The laser may be used in ophthalmology where foci are brought about in the retina, thus leading to the formation of scar tissue and, through it, to the closing of the tear on the retina. Or the laser may be used for the destruction of some growth, possibly for creating a new pupil where the original pupil is missing as the result of some disease. At present this being effected by means of the photocoagulator. This instrument has been in use for years, and the specialists have compared notes on it. Their initial enthusiasm has subsided to sober criticism. It is true that the "operations" are "bloodless" but the old tried and tested diathermic surgery is just as efficacious in many cases and photocoagulation cannot be undertaken in every case. This surgery can be performed only in cases where the distance between the lesion in the retina and the pigment stratum is from one to two centimetres. Excellent results can doubtless be attained through the heat effect in certain carefully selected cases without any surgery. In Hungary we must try to prepare the way to apply photo-coagulation in as many cases as possible.

The causes of blindness are quite different today from what they were 20 to 30 years ago. Among the infectious diseases, gonorrhoea is rarely a cause of blindness any more. Neither is lues. Trachoma has not yet disappeared in Hungary, but it has been "tamed." Its complete liquidation has been hampered by a new form of disease that has been occurring recently—epidemic conjunctivitis. Formerly, there were sporadic cases of conjunctivitis, but it first occurred on an epidemic scale in 1962–63, and resulted in 20,000 cases in Budapest alone. Its pathogen is adenovirus 8. Kindred viruses may also cause conjunctivitis, often with concomitant pharyngitis. Eye diseases caused by TB are not rare either, but they occur more or less sporadically and unevenly in different regions of the country. However, the malignant cases of the past are no longer found, for we have excellent anti-TB agents at our disposal. Thus infectious disease as a cause of blindness has been relegated to the background, while diseases of the veins and eye lesions caused by old age have become very frequent.

Eye diseases resulting from thrombosis are generally known. A frequent type is thrombosis of the veins in the retina. Construction of the main branch is graver; less serious is thrombosis of a minor branch. Treatment administered in time can ward off grave sequelae. Diabetics attain a higher age today than they did ten or twenty years ago, but cases of lesions of the fundus, which only become noticeable when the diabetes is at least ten years old, now occur very often. Indeed the diabetes remains latent in many cases. An eye specialist often diagnoses diabetes in patients who have had it for 5 to 10 years, who in fact have hyperglycaemia, and know nothing about it. However, eye diseases with quite different

causes often prompt the patient to turn to an ophthalmologist. Nowadays even patients aged 80 or 90 undergo eye operations. Special preparations have to be made for such operations, most of which are for cataract. The results of this surgery are usually very good, despite the age of the patients. In fact, such operations, if properly prepared, are to be highly recommended for the aged, because eye sight is of decisive importance in the relations between the patient and the outside world; the loss of eye sight often leads to accelerated development of gerontological and geriatric symptoms.

Not only laymen but also doctors who completed their medical education a long time ago tend to regard ophthalmology as a branch of medicine only connected with the eyes, and one often hears the opinion that fewer medicaments are needed in ophthalmology than in any other branch of medicine. The supposition is that the medicine for eye-diseases must always be dropped into the eye. The truth is that a grave eye infection is more inaccessible to medicine than any other organ, because of such veinless eye structures as the crystalline lens and the vitreous body. Medicines for an eye infection must be administered internally or through injections, just as in the case of infection of any other organ. Conjunctivitis alone is accessible to local treatment, with the eye-dropper. The problem of resistance to antibiotics also occurs in ophthalmology. This requires preliminary surgery, and it is becoming increasingly difficult to effect a cure.

Ophthalmologists find in too many cases that patients have taken drugs unnecessarily or for an inadmissible period, and this has serious consequences. Formerly penicillin and other antibiotics were used, and are still being used, causing eczemas and resistance. Then when the drug is really needed, it remains ineffective. The same difficulty is encountered with the anti-inflammation hormone of the *suprarenal* gland—cortisone and its derivatives. Many patients carry it about with them in their pockets and take it at will, never suspecting how dangerous it is to make a habit of taking cortisone in this amateurish and undisciplined way. Taking too much cortisone deprives the eye tissues of their normal protective reactions, and can cause lesions and serious inflammations. Taking it over a long period of time can even cause glaucoma and cataract. Taken judiciously, where the case warrants it, the hormones may prevent grave lesions. Medicines taken during pregnancy can also lead to serious lesions in the embryo's eye, the drug thalidomide (contergan) so often mentioned in the press, has caused cataract as well as other abnormalities.

The daily press devotes major attention to immoderate dosage with various medicaments. Day after day the ophthalmologist is consulted by patients who complain that they have eye trouble when doing close work. They blame their spectacles—they often wear glasses with a strength of 3 or 4 D—and take more and more sedatives because of a nervousness due to asthenopia and general lack of stamina. This, of course, leads to still more trouble. Many drugs that influence the nervous system—sedatives and barbiturates—unfavourably affect the capacity of the eye to adapt and concentrate, thus hampering close-range work; the most usual complaint is about reading, because the drugs taken make it harder and harder for the patient to concentrate. The ophthalmological aspects of pharmaceutical research are still unexplored. People think of consulting an eye-specialist only when it becomes necessary to deal with medicaments affecting the eye, not realizing that medicaments taken for other diseases also affect the eye. Suffice it to refer in this context to the well-known atropine effect. Atropine derivatives may, under certain conditions, cause glaucoma.

The foregoing indicates that ophthalmologists are compelled to approach their tasks from many angles. On the one hand, they must attend to problems of basic research; on the other hand, they must find a solution for urgent problems in everyday practice. Various types of ophthalmological research are being carried on at present in Hungarian clinics. However, the future and the requirements of progress urgently demand the establishment of special research institutes. Such institutes are gradually being established, both here and in other countries. The Association for Eye Research, now being formed, is a part of this trend. Its aim is to unite on an international level ophthalmologists, chemists, biologists and other specialists engaged in ophthalmological research.

BOOKS AND AUTHORS

A GENERATION MIRRORED
IN HUNGARIAN LITERATURE

Landmark is the title of an anthology of Hungarian literature published in six different language editions on the occasion of the twentieth anniversary of the liberation of Hungary from German occupation (April 4, 1945)*

The title, however, at once concrete and symbolic, leads to speculation whether this anthology is meant to be a milestone in the national history of Hungary or in the history of her literature.

Without trying to create an artificial antagonism between the two, one cannot but note this ambivalence which can be seen as the background of the editors' labours; or, rather which—let's make no bones about it—made them an uphill task. Miklós Szabolcsi and his co-editor, Zoltán Kenyeres, had to make up their minds whether the work was to be a comprehensive anthology of a national literature, or a literary survey of a certain period. The sub-title of the anthology—*Hungarian Writers on Thirty Years of History*—makes it unmistakably clear that the editors of Landmark opted for the latter alternative: they have tried to give as comprehensive and accurate a panorama as possible of the period immediately preceding, and the twenty-year period following the end of the war; of the process which has created the Hungarian Present. This intention is demonstrated in the chronological organi-

* *Mérföldkő*, Corvina Press, Budapest, 1965. English edition: Landmark, Corvina, 1965.

zation of the volume: it is the chronology of the subject-matter, not the date of birth or literary authority of the author, or the date of composition, which determined the order in which the works are printed in the anthology. This editorial concept may be open to question or criticism, but it cannot be ignored in any appreciation of the book. All the more as this schema of the editors designed around an anniversary must have simplified their work in one direction, while complicating it in another. Helpful because it offers an invisible historical framework, or a line on which you string the literary works of the twenty years under review, thus providing a ready-made schematic skeleton for the anthology. At the same time, however, the dangers inherent in a concept based on a historical panorama must not be underestimated. In the first place one is faced with the almost unavoidable risks of an illustrative arrangement; i.e., that an anthology of the literature of the last twenty years selected on subject-matter is almost certain to be found wanting—and not only as regards the demand for a choice representative of the whole literary spectrum. In the main it is because an editorial policy designed to cover a certain subject from all angles may impose aesthetic compromises, which in turn inevitably lead to an anthology of selections of very varying levels of literary craftsmanship. Authors may be represented not by their best work, but by something select-

ed for the sake of historical completeness—
and perhaps of little consequence in terms
of literature. It is possible that by stressing
one theme or another the editors may find
themselves unable to select material by
purely literary criteria.

The editors of Landmark have been only
partially successful in avoiding this pitfall.
On reading the volume one is struck by the
uneven standards of the writing in it; admirable writing side by side with mediocre and
indifferent performances; in some instances
one is left with the impression that a little
more severity in sifting the rich harvests of
the last twenty years might not have come
amiss. Anyone with a knowledge of Hungarian literature will agree that some of the
pieces selected in this volume do not do
justice to their authors. Jenő Józsi Tersánsz-
ky and László Németh are certainly greater
writers than the selection of their work in
this volume would suggest.

But even though this needed to be said
it must be made clear that the editors have
been alive to the possible implications of
their historico-literary design, and have deliberately made every attempt—often with
success—to avoid these dangers, and to expand their literary chronicle of the last
twenty years into a panoramic view of the
literature of the period as well.

The Past

The volume makes a start with the name
of Attila József. The picture of the Hungary of the 1930's emerging from the lyrics
of this working-class poet is one of unreliev-
ed gloom. In the obscurity of the working-
class districts, "mould traces a map of the
country of want"; the wretched poverty of
the peasant is only exceeded by his utter
helplessness; unemployed workers, hands
in trousers pockets, lounge outside the factory gates. Peasant girls leave their villages and drift up to slave in Budapest tenement houses; the out-at-elbows

teacher in the small village has his meals
provided in rotation as the child of a
different family brings him his lunch
each day of the month. Every line, every
stanza in this early section of the book cries
out in protest, and this categorical opposition transcends all differences of ideology
and age. Agreement on the subject-matter
does not, however, necessarily involve a
monotonous similarity of form. This section
of the book, largely drawing on the works
of the great writers of the time, provides
a far-ranging selection of matter; the first,
a dramatic short story by Zsigmond Móricz,
is followed by a "documentary" along the
lines of cinéma-vérité by Lajos Nagy, and then
by a piece of atmosphere by Andor Endre
Gelléri, a writer who extended the frontiers
of Hungarian realism to embrace the beginnings of surrealism. Those who followed
the controversies and debates of the Hungarian literary scene in the 1950's may be
intrigued to find here a chapter from Tibor
Déry's The Answer, a novel which was bitterly criticized by the literary pundits of the
day. The chapter printed here is a description of a famous event in the history of the
Hungarian working-class movement, the
mass demonstration of Budapest workers on
September 1, 1930, the first blood-drenched
lesson in history to be learned by Bálint
Köpe, the young worker hero of the novel.
With consummate skill, Déry angles this
chapter of his novel around a subsidiary epi-
sode which took place during the demonstration, thus avoiding the dogmatic approach
so easily implicit in the theme, and pinpoint-
ing the essential in the trivial—the sweeping force of communal emotion in the crowd
chasing the canary that had escaped. A searching compassion going straight to the heart
of the matter characterizes György Bálint's
A Man Weeps, the only contribution by
a journalist in the section of the book devoted to prewar years, in which the writer con-
siders the reasons which may have brought
bitter tears to a man, whose appearance suggests a worker.

BOOKS AND AUTHORS

BOOKS AND AUTHORS 167

The first section of the book is also designed to illustrate the resistance to the Nazi reign of terror. A soul-shaking witness to those years of the apocalypse was a poet who fell a victim to Nazism himself. Miklós Radnóti. A poem by János Pilinszky, expressing the anti-Nazi views of the survivors, is unhappily published here—presumably owing to difficulties of translation—in the Hungarian edition of the anthology only. On reading this section of the anthology, a slight misgiving is bound to stir the mind, a doubt whether the overall picture of the anti-Nazi resistance of the Hungarian community that emerges from it is not painted a shade brighter, a size larger, than the reality justified. In one of the stories here—a tale by the young writer András Tabák—among the pieces on the immediate post-war period, the author recalls the past history of a factory under Nazism. In a scene referring back to a moment of past history, two workers charged with sabotage are standing in the factory yard, surrounded by two thousand watching fellow workers. The two are executed in the presence of two thousand silent witnesses, with not a single fist or a single voice raised in their defence. Brief vision of helpless submission to terror appears as a piece of rather isolated reality in the anthology.

Eleven Years

Four thousand days is not a very long time in the life of an individual, let alone a nation... Or so anyone unacquainted with contemporary history might think—if he were not warned by the dates which act as exclamation marks framing the period reviewed in the second part of the book; several historical periods in Hungary, not one, were packed between the two dates of 1945 and 1956. Liberation from Nazism, national reconstruction, land reform, the nationalization of large industrial companies, the introduction of a new

school system—were so many milestones on the path, successive stepping-stones of material, social and cultural progress. This section of the anthology, spanning a period of eleven years, is the part where the literary standards fluctuate most widely. The selection dealing with the period of reconstruction such as the contribution of Lehel Szeberényi—reveal unmistakably the stamp of the oversimplifying dogmatism of the fifties, echo the naive belief that socialism was a continuous triumphal march. However, in the best of the writing published here, we can feel a passionate, compelling quest for truth, including an open analysis of the contradictions of the time.

From all the countless aspects of reality it is not easy to select the essential points to express the truth which give an authentic reflection of the time. In his contribution to this book, a sequel, as it were, to the sociological study he wrote in the 1930's, The People of the Puszta, Gyula Illyés records that great turning-point in the life of the Hungarian peasantry, the land reform of 1945; in this historic reportage he remarks: "Here, too, the great historical moment is quite simple and ordinary. One is reminded of Stendhal's hero, Fabrice del Dongo, who was an eye-witness and took an active part in the most decisive event of his time, the Battle of Waterloo, while being the last man to realize it. Were we, one wonders, aware of being participants of history when actually lived through those moments ourselves?" The characters, the heroes, who crowd the pages of Landmark are, in fact, witnesses—witnesses of history in the making. One cannot use the word hero without making it clear that these heroes have no connection with the "heroes" moulded from the dogmatic aesthetics of Zhdanov, they are not great muscled supermen, not heroes-on-cothurni, they are down-to-earth, man-size human beings. There may be nothing more to their heroism than the action of the musician in István Sötér's short story, A Crossing from

Buda, standing on the Buda bank of the Danube immediately after liberation, when all the bridges were down, who voluntarily surrenders to a young father the boat pass which will enable him to cross the Danube to the other side to see his newborn child. Is this heroism or just a manifestation of human fellow-feeling? By now we have an idea that these two qualities are very closely related. It must be a strange experience— particularly for readers unacquainted with the developments of postwar Hungarian literature—to see in one and the same volume the two extremes in the treatment of character in juxtaposition. On the one hand, there are the deliberately exaggerated portraits of ordinary people magnified into heroes as they go about their workaday business that we find in the work of Lehel Szeberényi or Boris Palotai; on the other, as in the work of the young writer György Moldova, the anti-heroes of ordinary life, under the stress of some extraordinary circumstance, like a flood, finding themselves performing genuine feats of heroism to save human lives. Incidentally, this last piece (Six Lights over the Water) adds a touch of the peculiar flavour of the realist tradition in Hungarian fiction: we have here the bizarre talent of an Angry Young Man of the twentieth century with a leaning towards nineteenth-century romanticism, and a novelist of extreme sensitivity. Another instance of the anti-heroic attitude in the study of character and one which is perhaps more typical of recent trends in Hungarian fiction, is found in the short story by Endre Fejes. Fejes, in his picture of a contemporary family, The Scrapyard, has created in the tragicomic figure of Ignác Vonó, the little man who would like to storm the heights of history, a character, who longs hopelessly to be able to transcend the limitations of his fate and his character, but is quite incapable of doing so, except in boastful words; hopelessly pusillanimous, he curries favour with the losing side in the historical game.

Adequately to register the achievements which have transformed society in the last twenty years is a task worthy any writer. I thought Zoltán Molnár's Inauguration, was a story which brought to life the first day after the nationalization of factories with all the authenticity of an eye-witness. The book would, however, inevitably be guilty of falsifying history if it only included accounts of achievement and success, and excluded all expression of the tragedies which afflicted the nation in the fifties. From the available body of literature on this theme, the editors have selected one of the most moving stories ever written, Tibor Déry's Love—which describes the return to freedom of a man who has served a prison sentence on a trumped-up charge. The drama of the first few minutes of freedom regained, the unspoken poignancy of his reunion with his wife, suggest the presence of forces which the author brings out with the utmost restraint. Often enough he employs only an epithet here or a half-sentence there to suggest the reactions of people facing the questions asked them by history.

Changing World

The latest period—as yet unfinished—dealt with in the book in a separate section, begins with the year 1956, and the subjects and problems are directly connected with the present time. In fact, however, the historical and the literary fail to coincide. Endre Vészi's conventionally dogmatic story, Disciplinary Record, is reminiscent of the writing of the 1950's, and Lajos Galambos's The Tirpaks, an analysis of political leaders who have lost contact with the people, would seem, in its subject at least, rather to belong to the works of the preceding period.

There is one outstanding feature in the selection of the last part of the volume which demands comment. Generally speaking, the editors have not restricted themselves to any one type or *genre* of literature, but have extended the boundaries of fiction to include reportage, the sociolo-

gical study and literary journalism. Towards the end, however, these forms of literature tend to predominate, the better part
of the pieces published here approximating
more closely to documentary than to fiction.
An extract from an essay by László Németh,
a reportage by Sándor Csoóri, Ferenc Erdei's
sociological writing, and the journalism by
György Szabó all concentrate on factual
realism. The quest for concrete truth is
obviously a reaction from the unrealistic
dogmatism of earlier years; it is likewise a
flexing of muscles in preparation for the
greater literary efforts that lie ahead. At
the same time, the dominance of this type
of writing is a reminder that the short story
truly dealing with contemporary problems
has yet to be written, the attempt to paint
a contemporary panorama of genuine literary value has yet to be made. The explanation of their absence lies in the present state
of Hungarian literature.

One single work of fiction has nevertheless been written which merits special attention. Its documentary character—in the form
of a reporter's investigations—is merely the
form; the writing itself bears all the marks
of a work of literature which may well endure. Ferenc Sánta's Twenty Hours* deserves special mention; it should be pointed
out that this extract from Sánta's short novel
can at best give readers only an idea of the
excellence of this modern and authentic
account of the transformation which has
taken place in the Hungarian countryside.

The English-language edition of Landmark is somewhat smaller than that of the
Hungarian original, probably for reasons of
finance. Although one must, by and large,
approve of the cuts, this reviewer greatly
regrets the omission from the third part
of two pieces in particular; Gyula Illyés's
superb poem Moving World, and Gábor
Goda's satirical sketch Protocol. The former

reflects the outward signs of the changed
mentality of the peasant with magnificent
poetic beauty, while the latter would have
filled a lacuna in the volume, which is thus
deprived of the only piece of satirical writing that is found even in the Hungarian
edition. It may be assumed that English-
speaking readers, despite the local references,
would have welcomed this witty caricature
ridiculing the socialist *arriviste*. It is equally
hard to see any reason why, after the elegant-
ly plain cover of the Hungarian edition, the
English version should have had the misfor-
tune of being saddled with such a repulsively
garish dust-jacket.

The illustrations are worthy of the text.
They are as a matter of fact more than mere
illustrations to a book: they amount to a selection of work, representative of the Hungarian fine arts of the last twenty years. The
same worn and grimly determined faces stare
up at us from the drawings of Gyula Derkovits, József Egry and Imre Ámos as those
which emerge from the printed page. The
compelling "Pipe Player" of Béni Ferenczy
pipes a bitter music to the harrowing sobbing
of the man in György Bálint's tale. There is
a strong dramatic element in all the drawings of the Nazi period. The drawings by
János Kass and Béla Kondor, though different in style, speak in the same passionate voice.
A poster-like quality which is a suitable
vehicle for their symbolical content is a common factor in the drawings of Gyula Hincz
and János Kass. True, some illustrations have
found their way into this volume which are
of little significance and reflect views that
are dated today; these illustrations are, however, likely to make a lasting impression on
the reader. It is pleasant to see in this volume
the peaceful coexistence of schools, of art,
represented by members of both the older
and younger generations of artists: the doyen
Professor Jenő Barcsay and the young Tibor
Csernus are both here, with a drawing each.

* An English translation of a chapter from
this novel appeared in No. 17 of *The N.H.Q.*

ANNA FÖLDES

170

A GUIDE TO THE ODYSSEY

The Translator's Introduction to the Hungarian Paperback Homer

I

In our garden on Szabadság Hill there are firs, poplars, chestnut-trees, walnut, lime and plane trees growing gently towards the sky; they have overtopped the house long since and whenever I see their crowns from the other side of the building, invariably and unfailingly the magic isle of the goddess Calypso comes to my mind where

Close to the cavern and clustered around it
was growing a coppice
Alder was there and poplar and cypress of
delicate perfume.*

And if a botanist should appear saying: "These are poplars, to be sure, but those are not alders—they are plane trees; not alders, I must insist, and still less cypresses"—well, I would simply shake my head. For me the verdant trees that promise tranquillity and a life of continuously unfolding beauty will always and everywhere evoke the garden of Calypso. And the hedge I see from my wife's window will always seem that "fence" of Laertes, the father of Odysseus, which the inhabitants of the farm made by

Gathering thorns to be used for the fence of
the garden enclosure.

Thus the arc of the Odyssey makes a great curve from the years of roaming and youthful fantasy down to quiet old age and cosy tranquillity; it has permeated life, just as life has become a part of its manifold story. And to use a phrase of Antal Szerb's, a Hungarian scholar of literature, whose war-time death was as premature as it was tragic, "all the centuries have been absorbed into it."

* This and subsequent quotations are taken from H. W. Cotterill's Odyssey-translation, London, 1911.

For so many centuries of poets, scholars and zealous readers, he reminds us, have joyfully absorbed the lines of this epic that our reading pleasure is enhanced by our knowledge of this fact. But the question of why human hearts have always been so irresistibly moved by Homer's epics, why poets have been so enriched by them and why scholars have always found the most thrilling adventure in them—it is for the reader to answer this. The translator's present attempt at a reply is that the Homeric epics, like every masterpiece, have from the very first comprehended life in all its fulness and everything that would be the quintessence of life in the millenia to come; and more than any other masterpiece they do this with a meticulous detail that covers every possible human situation with a confident, uniform simplicity. Their sentences and lines, like the reflections in a prism, resemble and repeat each other but with varying meaning and importance applied as they are to different situations. These thousand sparkling facets, suggesting a perpetuum mobile, reflect the myriad facets of human life; each single facet evoking all the others, flashing them unforgettably into our minds, each projecting the whole epic.
The first line of the Odyssey

Sing me, oh Muse, of the man so wary and
wise who in far lands
Wandered . . .

projects—and by no means accidentally— the contents of the whole poem. Its last line about the goddess appeasing the hosts in Ithaca, the isle of Odysseus

Once more likened to Mentor in voice and in
bodily semblance

contains its moral message less outspokenly but just as definitely, for it gives more importance to the appearance of the goddess (as ultimate Fate) in human shape than to her mere appearance as a goddess, in other words, it does no less than disclaim the miraculous character of reconciliation, or peace-making and harmony, for—lo!—they can be accomplished by man himself, he need only act in that spirit. While this line may appear to be merely a harmless termination of the poem, it is in reality gently insisting, as a good teacher does on the dramatic point playing a major part in the whole construction. The use of Mentor's figure here is like constructing a step for the stair leading to Athena.

It is certainly not the first time we encounter this step, but its position on the stair is essential. And its solidity increases the more we recognize it as a deliberately recurrent line. It is chiefly the musical and logical rhythm of the repetitions that points up the significance of a line or a series of lines.

And the many thousand lines between the first and the last? There is scarcely one line which is not a repetition in one way or another (at least in some degree) of a physical or spiritual situation already presented in relations to something else. When, at the height of the most fantastic part of the poem, Circe the enchantress says:

> Verily thou art Odysseus the wary and wise
> who was destined
>
> Hither to come...

then the attribute "wary and wise" nowhere else to be found but in the first line and here—endows the Circe story with major importance by lending it the emphasis of the initial line. On the other hand, when the Cyclops, the formidable one-eyed giant, says he was already told about the arrival of Odysseus (just as Circe was, who therefore suspects that she is confronting Odysseus), these two scenes mutually reflect their twin faces, victory won over the forces of nature, in different ways but with the same cleverness and boldness.

And when the Cyclops challenges Odysseus:

> Ha! Who are ye, good friends? Whence sail ye
> the paths of the waters?

and also asks him whether they are pirates, it is impossible not to recall the very same question asked Telemachus, the son of Odysseus, by old Nestor. Nestor's disposition, however, was essentially different. He was quite ready to entertain the most wicked people, provided they were willing to behave decently in Pylus, whereas the Cyclops intends to devour the newcomers in any case, even if they are honest men. All the same the question had to be asked—and precisely that question. In those days, when seafarers were usually either merchants or pirates, this question was a convention of mistrustful interrogation as much as it was a polite inquiry. Anyone coming from the sea was sooner or later bound to be asked it. Each of the seemingly identical situations differed in respect to the disposition of the questioner and preceded a different development, while the lines used for these situations coupled their verbatim identity with a quite different implication, either a suave promise or a menace, either exultation or rage, sorrow or belligerence. And just as in real life where situations recur in different circumstances, because of their apparent identity yet essential difference, or even antagonism, they evoke each other from afar, creating or suggesting the tension between them. Every masterpiece has a sort of circulatory system of its own. This Homeric epic has nerves that not only connect every line to the whole but to every other line as well; it almost seems at times as if a sensitive correlation had been created between the individual words.

This is what endows them so convincingly with vitality, this and other related qualities. For example, their solemn naturalness—or natural solemnity, if you like.

Homer even deliberately removes from the mythical heritage in his material all that is miraculous; at least he tries to represent it in such a way that it is no longer a miracle but simply a fine, important or reasonable human action. On the other hand he never ceases to call our attention to the *overall* miracle, the prodigious wonder of being, and this he does with inexhaustible enthusiasm. There is no person, landscape or object, there is scarcely an abstract quality that he would not declare beautiful. In doing so he either employs the adjective "beautiful" itself, which he always uses as a sort of synonym for appropriateness, i.e., to indicate the combination of a person's or object's innate qualities with his or its unquestionable fitness for a specific task, or he uses some other adjective implying the same thing. The ship is beautiful, because it is "swift" (even when it is at anchor in a harbour, this being its established quality); the town because it is "well built," the sky for being starlit (even if mentioned in the daytime), the cows for their "straight" or "crooked" horns, the horses because they are "swift as the wind," and the ships again because they "gallop," being "water steeds." For one reason or another—everything is beautiful. Nothing is a miracle, for everything is a miracle.

This accounts for that "natural solemnity" mentioned before. Homer is most humane when he is most solemn. He is understandable to everyone. And even at his most natural, no one could represent life more solemnly or loftily than he does. This all-embracing life seems to include the reader's also. Hence the immortal fluidity with which the emotion underlying the Iliad (and the Odyssey even more perhaps) is fused with the personal past of its readers and admirers, becoming one with their most intimate memories and with the world around them.

2

Seen from the standpoint of the Odyssey, the Iliad supplies the background for the story, although not the immediate back-

ground. The immediate background of the Odyssey is not the world of the Iliad, with the siege and capture of Troy, but what happened in the ten years between the destruction of Troy and the return of Odysseus. There were other fateful homecomings, first of all that of Agamemnon, chief of the Achaeans, and his bitter fate. The tragedy of Agamemnon shimmers ominously behind the story of Odysseus as if through a black gauze curtain on a stage. In front of it we see the sunlit figures of the Odyssey moving on the stage, bringing now a chronicle, now a myth to life. But that background is always present.

Agamemnon, the conquering hero of Troy, returns home. There he is awaited by his wife Clytemnestra ("the song shall be hateful telling her story on earth...") who murders him in complicity with her lover Aegisthus. A short time before Odysseus' return, Orestes, the now adult son of Agamemnon and Clytemnestra, returns secretly from exile and kills his mother and her lover.

Odysseus, the most ingenious of the Trojan war heroes, comes home the long way, roaming about the seas, after fabulous vicissitudes. Meanwhile his faithful wife Penelope is awaiting him at home, in despite of her truculent suitors who have made up their minds that if Odysseus should still return he will be killed, as will his son Telemachus. Unlike Agamemnon, Odysseus does not enter his home in state; disguised as an old beggar, he suffers one affront after the other in his own house. Finally he unmasks himself and with his son revenges himself on the suitors. In future,

*for earth-born man shall immortals fashion
the exquisite song of the true-souled Penelopeia.*

Having arrived in Ithaca, Odysseus sighs:

*Had I not heeded thy counsel, oh goddess,
I would have been sharing
The unlucky fate of the Atreides Agamem-
non...*

He addresses this to Athena, or common sense, that is, if you prefer, his own common sense. "Alas, I could also have shared the fate of Odysseus." This is what the sigh of Agamemnon's soul suggests at the end of the epic, and at the beginning, Telemachus is admonished by Athena and shortly afterwards by the old prince Nestor: "Be like Orestes."

Thus we see on this Homeric spectrum with its innumerable nuances of colour two extreme destinies, one bright, one dark, each continually recalling the other, each resembling the other in the manner of an object lesson. After starting out under similar conditions, two opposite fates are shown developing and lines of the poem vibrate with the current of their tension. The current runs both ways, but to stretch the metaphor—the beam of light it creates is projected in one direction only, onto Odysseus, the model to be followed.

Another paragon is presented by the Iliad, a brilliant one scarcely to be excelled; difficult to imitate—Achilles. And he is not the only one. The reader of the poem can identify himself with the hero of his choice: will it be Achilles, the demigod? Diomedes, the bravest of men? Perhaps it is the strength of Ajax he covets, the upright heroism of Hector or the beauty of Paris, who, guilty though he may be, refers proudly to the divine power of the love goddess, Aphrodite, and is, in spite of all, a fine warrior.

The reader of the Odyssey, on the other hand, identifies himself only with Odysseus. This was what Homer wanted. It was to this that he was trying to educate his audience, his compatriots, the world around him—and all of humanity. Odysseus is the central figure of his epic, far more than Achilles is of his. The personality of Odysseus radiates from it; he represents a step forward from Achilles to a new, more elaborate and more human ethos. The reader might conceive of a situation in which the reckless passion of Achilles would be the key, or where the the wisdom of Nestor,

the easy-going confidence in fate, or the good-natured laxity of Menelaus would be most useful, but none in which the self-preservation and humanitarianism of Odysseus' stratagem would not be the greatest and most fervently coveted asset. The inventiveness of Odysseus is called upon for the thoughtful and active solution of every problem, in a way that is at once sober and passionate. Careful and prompt, he saves himself from every unpleasant situation in which he has become involved; and in doing so he never forgets the "dear companions" for whose sake he risks his life, and not only does everything possible but attempts to do the impossible, as when he must steer between Scylla and Charybdis. As compared with Achilles, the man who chooses and accepts his fate, Odysseus is the man—the first!—who is able not only to accept his fate, but to take its measure, to change and to shape it. And not only his own fate.

Homer, in turn, has seen to it that Odysseus, capable of rising to the occasion no matter what happens, should actually be faced with every human and emotional situation. Between the battles of the Trojan war and the equally perilous years of peace that followed, he makes his hero roam across two seas—one was a real sea, and one was the sea of the tale. In this latter sea Homer submerged him still deeper; deep deep down to the most ancient times and through all that the layers of time could contribute. Sneezing and panting, Odysseus "spitting from his mouth the pungent brine of the billow," emerged from this sea when he landed on the shores of the Phaecians yet not completely, for the land of the Phaecians itself was still partly mythical; but he brought with him treasures that only a real hero—not a mythical one—could salvage from the depths. It is not for nothing that in this very, very old and well-known story of a husband returning from distant battlefields, the war is not just any war, but specifically the Trojan war, and the hero is not merely a returning husband who owes his importance only to this story and whose personality is not marked by characteristics other than those required by the story, but he is Odysseus, whose character is already well known from the Iliad; nor is Hades traversed by a mythical hero who would be unknown except for this voyage, but by Odysseus himself; and there he gets quite earthly information about his earthly home and has the opportunity of gaining earthly experiences from that symbolic world; the enchantress and the one-eyed giant are not overcome by a solitary mythical hero, but by a man whose conduct and capacity are known quantities, who avails himself of his famous ingenuity just as expected both for his own sake and for that of his companions. All this gives the poet plenty of scope to place his hero over and over again in situations, both expected and unexpected which shed a clearer light on him, which put him to the test and lead him to victory. For example, after Odysseus introduces himself to the Cyclops as "Nobody" (as a result of which the other giants merely make a bored gesture when the Cyclops, shouting for help, declares that "Nobody" has hurt him), this story is used to remind us again and again of the hero's mythical foresight as proven in a giant-shepherd fable as international as it is ancient, with variations from Africa to Hungary.

In the setting of the Odyssey, the Cyclops story presents this ruse without modifying it, not as a supernatural sort of clairvoyance but as the reasoning prudence which precedes bold action, after having imagined every possibility in advance—i.e., Odysseus' typical behaviour. In the setting of the Odyssey, the myth is simultaneously a demonstration of Odysseus' typical behaviour. Odysseus need not step out of himself in order to step into myth. On the contrary, because of its naturalness the Cyclops story unassumingly "moves into" the characterization of Odysseus. In just the same way, at the end of the poem the story-tale administration of justice, the revenge of the returning

husband, "moves into" a quite realistically represented Ithaca. And the story-tale administration of justice enforced by the poem in the real world, and not only in the epic, carries a great lesson, and was intended to do so. "You see—it could be done, and this is how it should be done in real life!" This is what the Odyssey seems to say about the judgments and deeds it has described, both in the final and in preceding scenes. The moral norms of the Iliad are extended to peace-time and raised a degree higher in humaneness. After vengeance has been done, Odysseus says to his nurse:

Woman, exult in thy heart, but in silence, subduing thy triumph.

Triumphing over the slain is a deed unseemly, unholy.

These hath the doom of the gods in the midst of their wickedness smitten.

This is something different and something more than what a myth or a fairy-tale could have said. This is a step towards the surrender of Hector's dead body, and beyond. As we have said, the figure of Athena Mentor is a step towards the acceptance of Athena's advice. Another such step is the figure of Odysseus himself, moving about in the world of myth and outstripping mythical heroes. He is a real man, realistically and painstakingly characterized, who can do anything that a mythical hero can, but his accomplishments stem from his character; his performances are as natural as they are self-evident, because that is the very thing he would be expected to do. Such an epic hero teaches us not to leave the ideal solution of problems to myths, since they can be solved in just the same way by a real man, provided he is like Odysseus—and why shouldn't he be? "Be like Orestes!" Athena and Nestor admonished Telemachus. Addressing his audience of centuries ago, the poet of the Odyssey guides them with a similar admonition, although not in so many words: "Be Odysseus yourself!"

In its time this admonition served a developing ideal of how a man should be. Just at that period the ideal was shifting from the figure of the victorious warrior to that of the sea-roaming, home-building, practical man who could turn his hand to anything who was eager to know and experience everything.

At all times it has served an eternal human evolution of ideals, especially the ideal of a man with creative curiosity, a man who can seize an opportunity and conjure up happiness, who can squeeze a humane "profit" out of nature for himself and his fellows, who knows compassion, aspires to justice, and attains "peace and plenitude."

3

And what sort of man was he, the poet who created in the Iliad first and then on a higher level in the Odyssey a world that condensed the experience and the poetic traditions of ages? How did he compose? For all we know, or rather infer, about his technique, we know practically nothing and can scarcely imagine the man himself. It is easy enough to evoke the image of the blind wayfaring singer that has come down to us from antiquity, improvising in the courts of kings his songs about the Trojan war and the adventures of Odysseus. It is not difficult to picture such a figure, but it is another matter to explain, how works of the quality and length of the Iliad and the Odyssey could have come about by extemporization. One may be able to imagine folk poets who created the separate epic poems born "on the lips of the people," one may even imagine an "editor" who gave them the final touch; but what is absolutely impossible to account for is the compilation of these masterpieces so that lines and words seem to converse with one another sparklingly across the distance of some twenty-odd cantos. For this cannot be the result of either an accidental miracle or of the work of some editor. It becomes more and more difficult to imagine the figure of the poet creating an *oeuvre* that is ultimately personal in its details yet collective in the process of its formation—and yet again an individual creation when taken as a whole. For the poet sums up centuries of folk recitation as well as the written works of poets who preceded him; debates with them in arguments that range from omission and minute alteration, through selection of the myths used, to personal comments which are implied rather than open, although always woven into the story; and thus consummates them all and makes them his own—and ours. This is what these epic poems do and this is the type of poet who confronts us.

We live in an age of archaeological excavations and the deciphering of ancient writings, when increasing light is being thrown on the background of these problems. Those legends connected with Homer which represent him as a wayfaring bard and improvisor or as the "synchronizer" of different poems are bound to be disproved—as are the theories that contest Homer's very existence. Even the hypothesis that two different poets wrote the Iliad and the Odyssey (although it is accepted by a number of highly qualified scholars) is inconsistent with the structure that these two poems have in common to the last detail—and only these two poems. This poet has held whole worlds in the palm of his hand. The "linear B" writing of the tables of Cnossus, Pylus and Mycenae, deciphered as Greek some ten years ago by Ventris and Chadwick, filled in the available background of the Homeric world in regard to time, while the documentary evidence presented in April, 1962 by Cyrus Gordon on the Semitic deciphering of the still older "linear A" writing is likely to extend the known dimensions of that world. The work of Ventris and his collaborators gave T. B. L. Webster an opportunity to outline the probable technique of the poetry that precedes Homer, which was a complex mixture of the literal and the literary. Carried out in the very places which provided the settings for Homer's epic poems, Cyrus Gordon's work may furnish evidence concerning manuscripts of Eastern poetry which we will definitely have to take into account, poetry, which pre-dates Homer and has an extensive inter-relationship in space and time. In the past few decades, Dornseiff, collating Homer and the Old Testament, as well as Károly Marót and Imre Trencsényi-Waldapfel in Hungary have been chiefly concerned with tracing and demonstrating the existence of this poetry.

As far as the person of Homer is concerned, there still remain far more questions than answers. The fanciful biographies that survive from antiquity tell us that the poet probably lived in the 8th century B.C. and was probably born in Asia Minor, but these cannot be regarded as anything but second-hand sources. The very first piece of information offered in the most ancient biography, according to which the profession of the poet's father was that of a river god, seems to be of questionable authenticity. All the other data are of a similar nature. For a long time to come, our only safe guide to the kind of man Homer was—and to the technique which makes it so hard to visualize him—will be the result of it all, the poems on which the world was suckled.

GÁBOR DEVECSERI

SHAKESPEARE THE REALIST*

I wonder if my English readers have ever guessed that Shakespeare wrote his plays in Hungarian and only later had them translated on into English. Yet this is, if not a historical fact or public belief, an everyday joke among Hungarian Shakespeare devotees; a joke that refers with some pride to the excellent Hungarian Shakespeare translations, which are regarded over here not as translations but as genuine masterpieces of our national literature. If you wish, however, to rebuke these boasting enthusiasts, just ask them about Hungarian Shakespeare criticism and the words will stick in their throats. For critics and scholars on both sides of the Danube have not distinguished themselves by epoch-making theories and revolu-

tionary discoveries. We cannot claim scholars of the stature of a Coleridge, A. W. Schlegel, Gervinus, Dowden or Bradley, and even our twentieth century Shakespeare criticism is comparatively poor in studies of international importance. Professor Kéry had to work in a more or less complete vacuum, and his success does him all the more credit.

Since László Országh's concise Shakespeare monograph (published in 1944), his is the first serious attempt in Hungary at treating one of the major issues of contemporary Shakespeare criticism. Kéry's study is comprehensive in two ways. It tries to sum up all the important problems relating to Shakespeare's comedies (giving a good survey of his fellow critics' views and opinions), including not only the comedies proper but also the so-called problem plays, the two parts of Henry IV and The Merry Wives of Windsor (on

* Kéry, László: "Shakespeare's Comedies" (*Shakespeare vígjátékai*), Budapest 1964, Gondolat Kiadó, 381 pp.

account of Falstaff), and, to conclude with, the four romances. The author presents with a new thoroughness Hegel's generally-accepted proposition that a certain tension is to be found at the core of every comedy as well as tragedy, a tension generated by the collision of some antagonistic forces. In the case of Shakespeare these forces are, as László Kéry puts it, the conflicting economic, social and ideological forces of decaying feudalism and emerging capitalism. In his early comedies the tension is still formal and its solution easy and playful; in the great comedies (A Midsummer Night's Dream, As You Like It, Twelfth Night) the conflict is already more penetrating, but it is still solved by the enormous vitality of some Renaissance men and women. In the critical years of the bitter or dark comedies the gap between reality and human effort has become too wide to be bridged any more by humanist optimism; and finally, when harmony is established once more in the late romances, it is achieved through self-deceiving fallacy and illusion.

Running parallel with this struggle of changing intensity and efficacy, Shakespeare's artistic development, distinguished by an ever growing richness and realism in the portrayal of human conditions and characters, culminates in the great comedies of the late nineties and then slowly decays, though still remaining superior to the melodramatic theatricalism of Beaumont, Fletcher and company.

More impressive than this general thesis itself is the author's meticulous analysis of the individual plays. He demonstrates how the mediaeval and early Tudor heritage affects Shakespeare's art, and he makes excellent use of historical, theatrical and literary evidence to account for the evolution of Shakespeare's peculiar way of seeing life and writing his plays. Trained in the Bradleyan tradition, he objects to the now fashionable pragmatic and symbolistic theories of an E. E. Stoll or G. Wilson Knight, and concentrates on plot and characters as the basic units of the Shakespearean plays, giving only occasional references to linguistic, stylistic and structural devices.

The author deserves credit for having laid special emphasis on the hitherto neglected universality of Shakespeare's comic world, as contrasted with the hackneyed universality of his tragedies. For him Shakespeare's comedies are not so much comic plays as serious dramas giving insight into the most important aspects of Elizabethan life. Shakespeare critics will certainly gain by reading his book, even if they do not agree with his conclusions. Brilliantly he reveals the hidden relations between Shakespeare's plays and the social and cultural trends of the age. If Bradleyan critics have been able to tell the "number of Lady Macbeth's children" he will outdo them by giving exact references concerning their social status, religious and philosophical views, and so on. He insists on the flesh-and-blood reality of the characters and claims for Shakespeare the merit of having assisted in shaping the new Renaissance type of man. He describes this type's distinguishing marks with such thoroughness that his book could have been used in those days instead of the manuals of a Castiglione, Della Casa or Thomas Elyot. There are few scholars who know so much about Elizabethan England as László Kéry does; this is an especially commendable fact considering his and any Hungarian critic's handicap in obtaining the necessary books and documents.

On the whole, László Kéry's work is a good introduction to Shakespeare's comedies. It suffers slightly, however, from the common disease of "introductions" meant for the general public. It is and cannot help being overburdened with facts well-known to experts (even plots are minutely narrated), so that little room is left for developing those ideas which represent the author's genuine contributions to recent Shakespeare investigations. This is the more regrettable considering that professor Kéry is rich in this sort of ideas. Here is, for instance, his proposition that the main source of Shakespearean realism is to be sought in the peculiar oscillation of his style and technique of characterization between sympathy and antipathy, satire and gentle humour, lyricism and matter-of-fact harshness, idealization and lashing criticism. Not less remarkable is his way of analysing the role of "error" in Shakespeare's comedies, tracing its development from a simple comic device to its becoming an expression of the sixteenth century's preoccupation with the epistomological questions of changing moral values, human identity, illusion versus reality, and so on. One would also willingly have heard more about the author's assertion that Shakespeare was more indulgent with characters representing the vanishing past than with types symbolizing the dangers and faults of the future. By pursuing this kind of analysis he could have helped even more than he does to locate Shakespeare in the intricate tangle of the conflicting political, social and spiritual trends of the Elizabethan age.

We hope that László Kéry will find times and occasion to take up these ideas and to delve deeply into all their implications.

ELEMÉR HANKISS

FROM OUR NEXT NUMBERS

(Continued from p. 103)

A REVOLUTIONARY PAINTER : DERKOVITS
Júlia Szabó

ART NOUVEAU AND "SEZESSION"
István Gál

CONGRESS OF FINNO-UGRIAN LINGUISTS IN HELSINKI
Gyula Ortutay

(Continued on p. 192)

ARTS

FERENC MARTYN'S ART

is of Irish origin. His great-grandfather, Robert de Martyn, emigrated to Hungary about 1800. His wife Antónia Gaál, was of Hungarian extraction. They made their home in Kazsok, a village in western Hungary. This is how it came about that the offspring of crusaders and sailors lost touch with his ancestors' way of life and his descendants absorbed the spirit of the new country.

Ferenc Martyn, the great-grandson, regards himself as a native of Somogy County in Transdanubia. No wonder this is so, since both his father and his grandfather were closely linked with the people and the soil of this County. But his romantic Irish background has left its traces. Family traditions, the fathers' stories and the sons' fantasy have kept alive the distant picture of the forsaken homeland, of kinsmen and landscapes never actually seen. But the peculiarly transmuted memories of seas, of fishermen and soldiers preserved through three generations again emerged in the paintings and drawings of the great-grandson. Inherited recollections of Ireland play a significant part in Ferenc Martyn's *oeuvre*, enriched by characters from Irish folk legends and literature and by their description of the countryside. The great-grandfather's past, the family stories heard in childhood and the reality of literature formed layers which

helped to shape Ferenc Martyn's art. Some of his works, unique in their substantial and formal elements, cannot be explained from the point of view of Hungarian artistic development; they are often incomprehensible in spite of their fascinating effect. Closer to Hungarian spectators and to the traditions of Hungarian fine arts are those of his works that depict the Transdanubian landscape, emerging as they do from the artist's immediate experience of the undulating Mecsek valleys, the gentle hills of Somogy County, the misty surface of Lake Balaton or the vineyards around it.

It was a lucky coincidence that an artist with such dual background became very early, the pupil of József Rippl-Rónai, who—recently returned from Paris—had been one of the pioneers of modern art in the French capital. As a member of *Les Nabis*, he was the friend of Maillol, Vuillard, Maurice Denis and Bonnard. The twenty years spent beside Rippl-Rónai deeply influenced the evolution of Ferenc Martyn's artistic career. Yet, Martyn refused to follow the well-trodden path. He was no more than 17 or 18 years old when his brush and lead pencil began to rid themselves of his master's manner and he took his first steps towards independent self-expression.

In 1926, Ferenc Martyn himself went to Paris, where, with unfailing sensitivity, he recognized even in the complex atmosphere of contemporary Paris, the best values of the art of his time. He was attracted by rationalism, by cubism and then by abstract painting. In 1934 he joined an international group of artists which called itself *Abstraction Création* and was under the spiritual leadership of Herbin, Vantongerloo, Delaunay, Béothy, Gleizes and Gorin. The works of Picasso, Kandinsky, Moholy Nagy (of Hungarian origin) and numerous other notable artists often appeared at their exhibitions and in their illustrated periodicals.

Martyn spent fifteen years in France, during which time his art came to full maturity. He not only went on shorter or longer journeys to the art centres of Europe, but remained in steady contact with Hungary, which he visited year after year. Prior to the Second World War a small group came into being in Budapest on Martyn's initiative and under the influence of his art. The activities of the group—whose motto was progress in art—was thwarted by the war. During his fifteen years' stay abroad Ferenc Martyn's art had become known to only a rather narrow circle in Hungary. Offical art policy was opposed to modern trends, of which Paris had become the centre. It even feared the revolutionary forces and "dangers" concealed in avantgardism. But the exhibitions of *Abstraction Création*—and within them the works of Ferenc Martyn—were well known to those who frequented French galleries as well as the galleries of Belgium, Holland, Germany and England, where the works of the group were shown. Nevertheless, Martyn continued to live in modest seclusion, devoting himself to his work. He disliked appearing in public and was even reluctant to display his pictures at exhibitions. This modesty is characteristic of him even today. He pursues his vocation with the strict discipline that prevails in a workshop.

In 1940, Ferenc Martyn returned from Paris on account of the war, in which, however, Hungary too became irretrievably involved. Inhumanity having penetrated all of society, Martyn opposed uncritical collaboration and servility by passive resistance. When called up for military service he failed to report and spent the whole war in hiding, although a warrant of arrest had been issued against him. He spent his years of concealment making drawings that expressed his hatred of fascism. Unfortunately, the end of the war did not open up the possibility for his talent to unfold. His abstract works or those expressing reality only indirectly could not arouse the interest of the vast number of working people hitherto unfamiliar with art. The increasingly isolated idiom of non-figurative art found itself excluded from the Hungarian art scene. This did not have a deep effect on the creative work of Ferenc Martyn, always inclined to a retired life. He continued to pursue his lonely path and to complete the *oeuvre* he had started in Paris. But in the past ten years—with the maturing of a new generation, aesthetically more cultured and more exacting in its demands—interest in abstract art has grown apace. The murals, frescoes and mosaics embellishing the many new buildings have contributed to creating a new artistic approach. Today Ferenc Martyn's paintings meet with greater understanding, crowning the success in recent years of his illustrations published in books or shown at exhibitions. In recognition of his work in this field the Government of the Hungarian People's Republic awarded him the Munkácsy Prize in 1962. The selected collection of his finest drawings was exhibited at the Biennale in Venice in 1962.

The Oeuvre

of Ferenc Martyn includes nearly all *genres* and media of the visual arts: oil paintings, pen-drawings and monotypes; sculptures made of wood or iron; plaster models for monuments and porcelain alike. Draughtsmanship, however, is always central to his work. "I do not really make a drawing, but evoke contents," he once explained, meaning

FERENC MARTYN: THE COCK (OIL)

FERENC MARTYN: COMPOSITION (OIL)

FERENC MARTYN: SHEPHERD WITH DOGS FACING STORM (OIL)

Ferenc Martyn: Souvenir

that he wishes to emphasize the interconnections of the contents, and that aesthetic and formal relations were subservient to this primary objective. It is in rich variations that this content, reality embodied in drawing, appears in his creations—now in representations that are true to nature and based on close observation of the world, then in an abstract transposition of reality. His approach is evinced in a unified and organic linking of content and form, the latter adjusting itself quite naturally and inseparably to the meaning of the former. It is always the given, concrete subject of artistic representation that determines the graphic solution. The subject determines the course the lines will follow, the rhythm and mutual relationship of the denser or looser hatching. Depending on the content the drawing becomes more detailed or more compact and finds itself more closely or more distantly linked with objective reality.

Ferenc Martyn does not aim at "depicting" but investigates, with a researcher's passion, the structure of objects, their compositional elements. In his abstract paintings and drawings he creates and builds a peculiar and new reality for himself.

Side by side with drawing the artist also methodically pursues painting. It takes a long time for an oil painting of his to get completed. Usually he will put the composition aside and take it up again after a time. The care he devotes to craftsmanship, to the elaboration of the surface, is reminiscent of the old masters. The logical order in which he arranges the different elements of his paintings, at the same time blending them into a unity, is a result of his French schooling; he thereby succeeds in creating a harmonious equilibrium among the different values and relations of the surface. The dynamism of his creations often asserts itself in intricate combinations. And yet his paintings can be traced back to the simplest basic formula in which dynamic movement is ordered in a closed, mostly elliptical form. He pays great attention to the equilibrium of positive and negative forms and to their pictorial qualities. At the same time, he emphasizes the constructive power of colours. In producing pictorial harmony the purity and relationship of colour values is of the same importance as the equilibrium of forms. He likes the variegated use of cadmium yellow and red, Paris blue, chrome-oxide green, umber and madder.

In the first part of this study we spoke of Ferenc Martyn's long association with French art. Our judgement would be far too one-sided, however, if we examined his works only from the point of view of the Paris school. If we did so we could not explain such odd figures appearing in his pictures as pirates, crusaders, knights fighting in front of a fantastic castle, or the frequent bird motif. The same applies to his still lifes with their representation of the tools of village craftsmen. Here the artist's imagination is enriched by traditional Irish legends and by the multicoloured reality of his motherland—the workaday life of Hungarian villages.

Ferenc Martyn observes the world with wide-open eyes, grasping the essence of our own time with an artist's sensitivity. Not only in his creations but in his everyday life as well he deals with the problems of society and tries to find answers to the great issues facing mankind. He is part and parcel of the world and of his motherland, of their joys and cares. At times he strikes a lyric note, at others a romantic one; now observing, measuring up and meditating, then again searching for the essence in the disguise of transposed reality. "However frail and pitiful the life, destiny and history of art—art has uttered the truths of mankind. Even in its fragments this utterance is a complete sentence, a declaration." These words of his apply to his life no less than to his *oeuvre*.

ÉVA HÁRS

AN EIGHTEENTH-CENTURY SWEDISH
TRAVELLER IN HUNGARY

Notes on an Ethnographic Exhibition

An exhibition opened this summer at the Budapest Ethnographic Museum is an interesting example of the wide international contacts of this institution. The nucleus of this exhibition consists of the ethnographic material collected by a Swedish traveller in Hungary in the 18th Century.

The traveller, Carl August Ehrenswärd, was a typical product of the European Enlightenment and 18th-century Sweden, where he is still considered a classic. A contemporary of Linnaeus and Swedenborg, and the scion of a famous family of soldiers, he was himself a high ranking officer and finished his life as Admiral of the Swedish Fleet. At the same time, he was a man of encyclopedic erudition and an enthusiastic admirer of Greco-Roman culture, an admiration that prompted him to travel at length in Italy in the 1780's. At the end of his last Italian trip he also visited Hungary. His journey resulted in two works that are held in high esteem to this day: a volume entitled "Travels in Italy, 1780, 1781, 1782," and a study in aesthetics entitled "Philosophy of the Free Arts." And what interests us most here, he prepared a number of sketches and notes partly included in his book—on contemporary Hungarian peasant costume, now temporarily in Budapest, at the Ethnographic Museum.

It will be of interest to summarize the events leading up to Ehrensvärd's visit to Hungary and to his interest in Hungarian culture, Hungarian peasant costume. After the revolution of 1772 the enlightened absolutist Swedish monarch, Gustav III, introduced a number of reforms that were of great importance to the Swedish people. (Subsequently he fell victim to the vengeance of the noblemen and was killed at an Opera ball in 1792.)

His fanatic passion for reform induced Gustav III to advocate a number of ideas which today strike us as somewhat capricious. These included his zeal for a reform of Swedish dress and the introduction of a new national attire based partly on the stylized forms of the period of Gustav Vasa and partly on foreign examples.

Already one year after the revolution the king, hiding behind the pseudonym of "An anonymous patriot", announced a competition for such a dress and devoted a series of writings to this topic. The contemporary Swedish press took a lively part in the discussion of this issue. On December 6, 1773, an unsigned article was published on the first page of "Dagligt Allehanda" (its author has never been ascertained) which set the dress of the Hungarian people as an example to be followed by the Swedes: "The Hungarian people are the closest and oldest relations of the Nordic peoples," the unknown author wrote inter alia. If this attire were to become general here, completed by the one that was worn in Sweden in the Middle Ages, could we rightly assume that we would have clothing that would not only protect us against the cold but also revive the memory of our famous ancestors."

This naive and romantic attempt at reform was bound to fail. But the king insisted stubbornly, and in 1778 he made a new attempt at popularizing his idea. Now he himself stepped forward as the author and wrote, in Swedish, his famous "Reflections," the French and Italian translations of which spread all over Europe. They were read by most of the great spirits of the period, and Voltaire himself praised them. In this work Gustav III again mentioned the Hungarian example and said: "The Hungarians are wearing their old attire to this day."

HEAD OF A WOODEN CRUCIFIX FROM A CALVARY
IN AN 18TH-CENTURY HUNGARIAN VILLAGE CHURCH

HEAD OF THE MOURNING VIRGIN MOTHER
(FROM THE SAME CRUCIFIX)

It was this background that induced Ehrensvärd to visit Hungary and study Hungarian folk dress. As can be seen from his "Travels in Italy," the clothing that most appealed to him was that worn by the women of Southern Italy and the men of Hungary. "In Hungary traces of ancient Roman military garb may be seen," he wrote. "It is remarkable that this can be found outside Italy. The clothing in question is solemn and resembles, in outline and somewhat idealized, the garb of the Dacians on the columns of Traian and Anthony. On working days they wear a sort of bussarong. The men have moustaches, the heads of the women are uncovered."

Ehrensvärd made a number of drawings of these male costumes, which—as ethnographic and historical comparisons have now shown—he must have seen in the south-western regions of Transdanubia, in County Zala. In line with his classicist tendency, the Hungarian peasant wear of the 18th century is noticeably stylized and adapted to antique traditions in his drawings. But perhaps those Swedish researchers are right who state that in this manner too he wanted to express his love and esteem for the Hungarians.

The present exhibition of the Budapest Ethnographic Museum, jointly organized by Swedes and Hungarians, is a worthy example of international cultural cooperation. It was initiated by Assistant Professor Holger Frykenstedt, a student of 18th century Sweden and, within this field, of the *oeuvre* of Ehrensvärd. The Ethnographic Museum received much encouragement from both the Hungarian and the Swedish authorities. The exhibition, as a result, includes unique exhibits, such as drawings coloured by Ehrensvärd himself, the first edition of his book, as well as manuscripts of his contributed by various Swedish museums, by the Royal Swedish Archives and by the private archives of the Ehrensvärd family. (Part of the latter material has never been exhibited before, not even in Sweden.)

Around the Ehrensvärd documents, a group of Hungarian ethnographers, making use also of the material of other Hungarian museums and collections, have arranged an attractive and instructive exhibition of Hungarian folk costumes, household utensils and 18th-century folk art. Among the surprises awaiting the visitor is a collection of contemporary wood carvings inadequately known both in Hungary and abroad, although their artistic and ethnographic value matches that of the deservedly world-famous Polish wood-carvings.

ZSUZSA KOROKNAI

MUSICAL LIFE

RECENT FINDINGS IN EIGHTEENTH
AND NINETEENTH CENTURY MUSIC

The musical "excavations" of the twentieth century are hardly likely to initiate a new style comparable in impact to romanticism. Their radius of activity takes in quite different ground, in the main that of historical research.

In the last twenty years Hungarian musicologists have turned up all sorts of finds, which range from the odd to the significant. The most interesting kind of discovery to be made is undoubtedly that of an unknown composition by a famous master, preferably in the original manuscript. The recovery of an unknown old composition in the form of a copy from the composer's period may also be considered a valuable find. In recent Hungarian music research there has also been a case where the original manuscript of a great master's composition was recognized through familiarity with the printed copy.

We hope the reader will share some of the excitement of exploration when, through the experiences described here, he watches the researcher open the door to a long-concealed scene of creative work, and gazes with him upon the materials their one-time owners used. Heavy, yellowed music sheets may bear traces of the sand used in the days before blotting-paper was invented, or dry hardened crumbs or faded grease stains witness to a lunch the composer had hastily consumed while working.

The scholar, of course, is more interested in the old handwriting, whose meanderings give clues to the development of the work itself, often through numerous erasures, deletions, paste-ups and even sewn-on patches. A copy or a page of printed sheet music betrays no sign of such episodes. It does not hint at the pace of the creative stride, it reveals neither an anxious laboriousness nor an elegant flow in setting down the notes, it shows neither youthful freshness nor the shaky hand of old age in the writing, it sheds no light on a decisiveness in the creative work or on a maturity gradually attained by struggles, as revealed by successive versions. A young pianist who visited Hungary recently declared that before beginning to study any piece of music he likes to make a pilgrimage to the manuscript, in order to derive inspiration and instruction from the master's own personal and characteristic handwriting.

It was in the summer of 1947 that Professor Bence Szabolcsi found a manuscript of Antonio Vivaldi's violin concerto "Il Ritiro" ("The Retreat," or "The Convent"), in the manuscript archives of the Conservatory of San Pietro Majella in Naples. A report on this find was published in Volume XV of the publication of the Accademia Chigiana (Siena, 1947). The score, dated 1727, was performed the next year at the Vivaldi concert of the Italian Cultural

Last part of the "18th Hungarian Rhapsody" in Liszt's recently discovered original manuscript.

Overleaf: The Kyrie from Mozart's Requiem in Süssmayr's handwriting. Süssmayr made use of the same fugue to finish the final part of the work beginning with the words "Cum sanctis tuis."

Institute in Budapest. Thus Hungary became the scene of the world premiere of a Vivaldi composition first published by a Hungarian musicologist and arranged by Hungarian musicians.

Bence Szabolcsi's discoveries in Italy, including the unearthing and first publication of Vivaldi's Concerto "Il Ritiro" and the Symphony in C major[1] were the first of a series of interesting postwar researches by Hungarian musicologists.

At the initiative and with the encouragement of Professor Dénes Bartha, the musicologist László Somfai made studies which led to his finding about forty original Haydn manuscripts which had been entirely unknown. He had gone through thousands of pages of opera manuscripts to find them. Professor Bartha reported on this research at the time in The New Hungarian Quarterly.[2] The details of his findings have been discussed extensively in a book published in German.[3]

---

[1] VIVALDI, Antonio: Violin Concerto E-flat major "Il Ritiro." Compiled for first publication from the parts preserved in the Library of the Conservatory S. Pietro a Majella in Neaples, by Bence Szabolcsi. Arranged and annotated by Angelo Ephrikian. Budapest, 1959, Editio Musica (Pocket Scores 48).
VIVALDI, Antonio: Sinfonia in a C a due violini, violetta e basso. Ed. by Bence Szabolcsi. Budapest 1961, Editio Musica. (Pocket Scores 95).

[2] BARTHA, Dénes: The Unknown Haydn. Haydn as an Opera Conductor at Eszterháza. The New Hungarian Quarterly, Vol. 2, No. 1, Budapest, 1960.

[3] BARTHA, Dénes–SOMFAI, László: Haydn als Opernkapellmeister. Die Haydn-Dokumente der Esterházy-Opernsammlung. (Musikbeil.: Haydn, Joseph: Scena die Pedrillo. ("Son due ore che giro...") 1789. Partitur. Budapest–Mainz 1960, Akadémiai Kiadó–Schott. 470 pp., 19 music plates. With a separate volume of 29 pp. with the score of "Scena di Pedrillo" and a record, Haydn, Joseph: Scena di Pedrillo, Aria for the opera "La Circe".—Cavatina der Nannina. Aria for the opera "La Metilde Ritrovata". 1779. Hungarian State Concert Orchestra conducted by Ervin Lukács. Soloists.: Judith Sándor, József Réti. Qualiton, Budapest.

Suffice it to state here that this extraordinarily valuable material, which was brought from the archives of the former Princes of Eszterházy for the music collection of the Hungarian National Széchényi Library, chiefly comprises the operas, by different composers, which Joseph Haydn taught the ducal opera company to sing and which he conducted during his stay at Eszterháza. Most of the manuscripts contain additional arias composed by Haydn to be sung in the operas by himself and others which he directed.

The material brought from the former Esterházy archives to the Hungarian National Széchényi Library has been found to contain manuscript compositions by a number of minor masters, in addition to those of Joseph Haydn. Johann Joseph Fux, Gregor Joseph Werner, Johann Georg Albrechtsberger, Johann Michael Haydn, Karl Ditters von Dittersdorf, and Franz Xaver Süssmayr deserve special mention. Actually almost none of them rose above the standard which German musicologists accord to a *Kleinmeister*. However, this sort of classification might mislead the reader who is not a specialist. The term *Kleinmeister*—to make it clear—does not refer to amateurs or people who make a business of superficial entertainment. It is applied to erudite composers who were respected or fashionable artists in their own time, but whose works were later overshadowed by the giants of music.

In the last few decades in Hungary the doors of inaccessible cabinets in aristocratic archives have been opened wide and all at once hitherto unknown compositions have unexpectedly been brought to light. Composers of the past whose names may have been unknown before or whose names and works were given only perfunctory mention in the history of music have now emerged from obscurity to become widely appreciated and often performed, as a result of their newly discovered works. It would seem that the concert-going public has reached a stage where it finds a little variation in the diet welcome and relaxing, and that both musicologists and audiences have reached the saturation point of steady doses of "nothing but masterpieces" and are tired of the music literature that re-hashes the great masters from every conceivable angle. The unexpected discovery of unknown compositions after the virtually exclusive concentration on works by famous composers has given impetus to a tendency to rescue the long neglected art of the minor masters from obscurity.

Johann Joseph Fux (1660–1741) is probably the strangest and most remarkable of the latter. For a long time he was remembered chiefly for his "Gradus ad Parnassum," a treatise on the art of composition, and was mentioned as the man who first summarized the rules of composition. Yet as early as 1772, Köchel, who acquired world fame for compiling a thematic catalogue of Mozart's works, published a similar index of Fux's compositions, listing about 400 of this Viennese master's works. Today Fux, who was born 25 years earlier than Bach, is recognized as the most illustrious composer of the Austrian baroque era, who, in addition to church music wrote several operas and instrumental music, as well. His "The Deum" for double choir and double orchestra recently discovered in Budapest is a particularly valuable manuscript, because it is the only known score that was written, signed, and dated in Fux's own hand. Indeed, scarcely more than ten manuscripts in Fux's handwriting are known to musicologists up to date. This monumental composition, dated 1706, is valuable not only as a manuscript, however, but as music. Although the "Te Deum" was published a few years ago in a critical edition of Fux's collected works[4], to the best of our knowledge it has not been performed publicly anywhere. It is to be hoped that this omission will soon be made good.

It is doubtful whether any of the compositions of Gregor Joseph Werner (1695–1766) would ever have been mentioned today, if it had not been for the recent discovery of over three hundred of his music manuscripts. This diligent and pedantic composer, who preceded Joseph Haydn in the post of conductor at Prince Esterházy's court, was also an adherent of the baroque style rather than of Viennese classicism. As a tribute to the memory of his predecessor, Haydn edited six of his twelve oratorio overtures as string quartets. All twelve overtures are being published now in their original form, with elaborated basso continuo, by Jenő Vécsey, head of the Music Collection at the Hungarian National Széchényi Library, in the series "Musica Rinata" which he himself has founded and edits, with the intention of introducing specimens from unknown old manuscripts in the Library's collection. Up to the spring of 1965, the scores and parts of two compositions by Albrechtsberger, two by Michael Haydn, one by Werner and one by Süssmayr appeared, comprising the first issue. Of the works now in preparation, the *Bassoon Concerto* of Johann (Jean) Fuchs, arranged by György Gábry, and Giovanni Paisiello's *Cantata Comica*, arranged by Dr. Zoltán Falvy, who assisted in discovering manuscripts by Fux and Süssmayr, should be especially mentioned.

The name of Johann Georg Albrechtsberger (1736–1809) has also survived chiefly on the basis of his activities as a musicmaster and as a theorist. Beethoven studied counterpoint with him. However the original manuscripts of a large number of his works have been brought to light in Budapest, showing that Albrechtsberger was also a

---

4 FUX, Johann Joseph: Te Deum, E.37. Vorgelegt von István Kecskeméti. Continuobearb., von István Kecskeméti. Kassel–Graz. 1963, Bärenreiter—Akademische Druck- u. Verlagsanstalt. IX. 118 pp., 2 music examples. (Fux, Johann Joseph: Sämtliche Werke. Serie II. Bd. 1.)

gifted composer. A thematic catalogue of his works is being published by László Somfai[5], while his compositions are also available in print and on records in Hungary. His concertos for harpsichord, trombone, and harp respectively have been performed on period instruments at matinées in the Hungarian National Museum. Several of his interesting string quartets have also been performed at these concerts.

Michael Haydn (1737–1806), the younger brother of Joseph Haydn, is another of the classical composers who were undeservedly relegated to obscurity. Both brothers were professionally active within the former territory of Hungary: Joseph at Eszterháza, Michael at Nagyvárad (now Oradea). Scores in their own handwriting now lie side by side on the shelves of strong-boxes in the Hungarian National Library. Thanks to the efforts of Jenő Vécsey, these unknown or long-forgotten compositions have been revived almost simultaneously. After nearly two centuries they have been presented to the public in printed form and are giving pleasure to new audiences in radio broadcasts and in concert halls. Editio Musica, Budapest, has issued two compositions by Michael Haydn in a series of pocket scores, edited by Jenő Vécsey, the flute concerto in D-major, 1766, and the Symphony in D-minor, 1784. The latter, ending with a Rondo composed around Hungarian and gipsy motifs has been performed with great success by Hungarian orchestras.

Karl Ditters von Dittersdorf (1739–1799) was one of the most outstanding of the Viennese classical minor masters yet a performance of any of his works is a rare event these days. Through the discovery of his seven compositions for the theatre in the opera manuscript collection of the Esterházy archives, now a part of the Hungarian National Library, a new impetus has been given to the appreciation of this master, who had been Michael Haydn's successor at Nagyvárad. The beginnings of a revival of Dittersdorf's popularity have been signalized by the publication and radio rendition of a few arias from his operas[6].

Among the most fascinating and exciting finds have been those in connection with Franz Xaver Süssmayr (1766–1803). Research has produced documentary proof that it was really Süssmayr who completed the Mozart "Requiem". Furthermore recently discovered manuscripts have thrown light on Süssmayr's quite extensive and prolific efforts as a composer. Although the author of this article has already given an account of Süssmayr's work on the "Requiem"[7], a brief recapitulation will render the picture more complete here.

The fact that after Mozart's early death his unfinished "Requiem" was completed by his friend and pupil Süssmayr, although widely known, was not universally accepted. Süssmayr's own confirmation of the fact is on record and has often been quoted in literature on music. Incontrovertible objective evidence was obtained only a few years ago, however, when a four-page music manuscript was found containing exactly the eighty bars in Süssmayr's own handwriting which he took from the opening of the "Requiem" to complete and round out the unfinished composition.[8]

---

[5] SOMFAI, László: Albrechstberger-Eigenschriften in der Nationalbibliothek Széchényi, Budapest. In: Studia Musicologica Academiae Scientiarum Hungaricae. Mitteilung I: Tomus I. fasc. 1–2. 1961; Mitteilung II: Tomus IV. fasc. 1–2. 1963; to be completed.

[6] Serate d'opere di Eszterháza.—Opera Evenings at Eszterháza. Arias for voice and piano with Italian text. According to manuscripts of operas performed in Haydn's time, published by Jenő Vécsey–László Somfai. Soprano–Mezzosoprano / Tenore / Baritono–Basso. Vol. 1–3. Budapest 1962, Editio Musica.

[7] The Man Who Completed Mozart's Requiem. Unknown Finds in Süssmayr's Autograph Legacy. The New Hungarian Quarterly. Vol. 2, No. 4. Budapest 1961

[8] For details see the paper "Beiträge zur Geschichte von Mozart Requiem" by the author of the present study (Studia Musicologica Academiae Scientiarum Hungaricae, Tomus I, fasc. 1–2, 1961).

The seventy manuscript compositions preserved at the Hungarian National Széchényi Library in Budapest, forty-nine of which were written in Süssmayr's hand provide a revealing picture of his work as a composer on his own. The variety of these works may be indicated by the fact that they include more than ten operas, numerous opera fragments, cantatas, songs and sacred music, as well as compositions for orchestra. On closer inspection we find them to be the works of an often original composer with a light touch and an engaging manner, apparently inspired by the art of Mozart, Haydn and Cimarosa. One can scarcely wonder at the wide popularity enjoyed by Süssmayr which culminated in the years around 1800. This popularity soon waned, however; before long Süssmayr shared the fate of the other minor masters who had slipped into oblivion. The recent recovery of his manuscripts has revived interest in him. The writer of this article has started editiog a thematic catalogue of his works,[9] and publishing some of them in the "Musica Rinata" series ("Overture in C-major"; "Das Namensfest," a cantata for children's choir; Symphony in C-major. Preparation of the latter two is in progress). The Cantata had its world premiere on May 20, 1961, performed by the ensemble and soloists of the Hungarian Radio and Television Children's Choir, with chamber orchestra, before an audience which filled the concert hall of the Budapest Academy of Music.

The treasures in the former Esterházy archives were not the only source of the series of discoveries. In Otto Erich Deutsch's fundamental catalogue of Franz Schubert's works, the original manuscript of the song "Die Nacht" ("Die Nacht is dumpfig und finster...") is referred to as lost (No. 534). It was found among the old music manuscripts in the collection of the National Széchényi Library.

Important finds have been made in the field of Liszt research. The composer István Szelényi has discovered a whole series of Liszt compositions in manuscript and has published them in separate volumes at Editio Musica, Budapest. These compositions edited by Szelényi are *Csárdás macabre, Bagatelle sans tonalité, Portraits hongrois historiques, Hungaria 1848, Le forgeron*.

Another find in the Hungarian National Széchényi Library may be added here to István Szelényi's Liszt discoveries.

Liszt's "18th Hungarian Rhapsody" appeared in print the year it was composed, 1885, as the first item in an ornate volume published in Budapest on the occasion of a national exhibition.[10] After that it was reprinted in an annotated collected edition of Liszt. The original manuscript of this "Rhapsody" was unknown however. It was only quite recently that the music written in Liszt's own hand was accidentally discovered pasted between picture postcards and jottings in an album, part of a collection of letters, pictures, and autographs that had been offered for sale.[11] Unfortunately the entire manuscript has not been recovered, only the second *Friss* ("lively") section of the "Rhapsody." A deeply evocative manuscript by the old master nearing the end of his life has thus been restored to us, a composition of peculiar, bleak atmosphere that points the way to the music of Bartók.

István Kecskeméti

[9] Süssmayr-Handschriften in der Nationalbibliothek Széchényi, Budapest. (Mitteilung I) Studia Musicologica, Tomus II. fasc. 1–4. Budapest 1962; to be completed.

[10] Magyar zeneköltők kiállítási albuma. Budapest 1885, Rózsavölgyi.

[11] Cf. from the same author "Unbekannte Eigenschrift der XVIII Rhapsodie von Franz Liszt." Studia Musicologica, Tomus III. fasc. 1–4, Budapest 1962.

THEATRE

THE SUMMER SEASON

During the summer months, when the regular theatres in Hungary are closed, performances can only be seen on special, open-air stages. For long there has not been so rich a summer season as that of 1965. Of the many productions, three have been selected for review in the pages that follow.

Gyula is the name of a small town near the south-eastern border of the country. At the town limits, beyond a wooded strip, there stands a castle. Although it is fairly big, one should not connect it with any image of the austere bastions of the Tower of London or the lovely turrets of Windsor Castle; nor is it reminiscent of French chateaux or of the lofty, fairy-tale castles of Germany. Hungarian castles are simple and solid, and Gyula Castle is a typical example, but it has a significant history of its own. When, in the early 1500's, King Ulászló began mustering his army of crusaders against the Turks he appointed György Dózsa —who later became one of the greatest figures of Hungarian history—commander of the army. Born in serfdom, but raised to the nobility, Dózsa continued to side with the peasantry and became a resolute rebel who turned his army against the despotic lords with a view to vanquishing them, rallying the Hungarian people around him and thus, after having got rid of traitors, fighting the Moslems with the support of a loyal rearguard. He was defeated, tortured and burn-ed to death on a red-hot throne. He became the hero of several legends, and the greatest Hungarian poets, from Sándor Petőfi and Endre Ady to Gyula Illyés, paid tribute to his memory in their verses. When György Dózsa set out against the Turks he camped at Gyula Castle with his army. And now, more than four hundred years later, it was on a stage erected in the court of this castle that György Sárközi's drama, György Dózsa, was performed.

Sárközi, a poet, novelist, translator and editor, was a member of the important literary circle which, between the two world wars, opposed the spread of fascism and became the torch-bearer of the European spirit and of progressive western culture. A deep humanism and a sure sense of form were as characteristic of him as of the other members of the circle. Ultimately he shared the martyr's fate of the hero whose tragedy he described in his play. Along with many other outstanding representatives of Hungarian literature he fell victim to fascist cruelty in the last months of the war.*

His drama is centred around the idea of how a man becomes a hero. The plot begins at the moment when Dózsa takes over supreme command of the army. In the course of lyrical scenes and gorgeous historical ta-

* See Iván Boldizsár's "A Lost Generation" in The New Hungarian Quarterly, Vol. VI, No. 18, Summer, 1965.

bleaux the fight waged by Dózsa against the royal court is brought to life on the stage, and we are shown the spiritual and emotional aspects of this struggle. With poetic force and the dramatist's sure touch Sárközi leads his hero to his tragic fate. György Dózsa is bound to fail and be defeated by the forces he has opposed: the rebel, having come too soon historically, was—for this very reason—forsaken by all.

The stage, felicitously set in the axis of the castle building, offered a *milieu* that was in full keeping with Sárközi's drama. The plot, which conjured up the past, became convincingly blended with the ancient bricks, the quaint walls and embrasures, which similarly evoked bygone days. A particular genre of the drama, that of castle plays, was thus revived. The talented young director, István Miszlay, chose the actors from among the ensembles of several theatres, both in Budapest and in the provinces. Outstanding among them were Ádám Szirtes, Gyula Szabó and Imre F. Nagy.

Another interesting experiment in adapting a play to the surrounding open-air scenary took place during the theatre festival at Szeged, also in the south of Hungary. On the stage erected before the twentieth-century cathedral built in Romanesque style, the gem of Hungarian dramatic literature, Imre Madách's *The Tragedy of Man*, was performed.* This Faustian dramatic poem, which investigates the essence and meaning of human destiny with great philosophical power, was analysed in our review on the occasion of its recent performance at the National Theatre in Budapest. The director of the Szeged production, László Vámos, has become internationally known in theatrical circles, particularly through his *Hamlet* production at the Budapest Madách Theatre.

The intellectual depths of *The Tragedy of Man* can be genuinely explored only in a

* See: Vol. VI, No. 19, of *The New Hungarian Quarterly.*

small theatre. True, great masses of people make their appearance in the Tragedy, because the representative of Madách's ideas, Lucifer, lets the two protagonists of the play, Adam and Eve, travel through many a historical era. Vámos aimed at producing a spectacular performance in which Madách's gigantic visions are realized—but always centred around the struggle of thinking man.

No doubt, the stage presented a fascinating sight. Imagine a vast space with numerous flights of stairs, bridges and platforms, and with the massive Cathedral standing in the axis of this space. Imagine several hundreds of extras, grandiose lighting effects and technical devices—all in an artistically homogeneous composition. Nor was the beauty of the sight merely superficial. It expressed life itself and life's crowded turbulence, as expressed by Madách in the visionary words of the London scene: "Ever roars life's boundless ocean, With each wave new worlds arise."

No sooner had the Szeged *première* taken place than a sharp debate broke lose about the performance and the director's conception. The problem exceeds local bounds—it is being heatedly discussed in the European theatre world.

One camp of critics rejected Vámos's conception on the grounds that in applying so vast a technical apparatus he was giving predominance to mere trappings and that emphasis on the spectacular was inappropriate in the contemporary theatre because it spelled a lack of content. Others, while inclined to accept the presence of spectacular qualities in general, felt that a philosophical work as profound as *The Tragedy of Man* does not tolerate such an inordinate amount of externalities.

An open-air performance of a dramatic work is in any case a compromise. The director has to approach the drama in a different way from the one he would pursue in an ordinary theatre. But this difference in approach not only refers to the director but to the audience too. Although there are plenty of spectacular plays in world literature, they were not written for open-air performances. Even among Shakespeare's works only *A Midsummer-Night's Dream* is perfectly suited to being performed under the starry vault of heaven. An exception is the Greek drama, which was really meant to be performed in the open air, as well as the medieval mysteries, whose world, beyond and above the world of man, really suits the surroundings offered by nature. All other dramatic works can be performed in the open air only in an unnatural manner, and as a result the conception of the director producing them may justly conflict with the conception governing their performance on the traditional stage. Vámos thus pursued the right course. In such cases everything depends on whether the visual elements composing the spectacle succeed in expressing the contents and ideas of the drama. In a number of scenes László Vámos left nothing to be desired in this respect. Whenever the visual characteristics of the stage allowed him to explore the deepest intellectual regions of Madách's drama, he suceeded brilliantly. Where he was unable to achieve this, his production remained superficial, leaving the more profound problems of the play unsolved. The performance thus became an interesting experiment in the open-air staging of a philosophical drama and thus deserved international interest. Miklós Gábor, who had played Hamlet at the Madách Theatre, gave a valuable, thought-provoking interpretation of the role of Lucifer, Éva Ruttkai fully deserved the great success she scored in the part of Eve, and Adam was played by the young and talented Attila Nagy

After the much debated performance of *The Tragedy of Man* the third significant production of the summer season was a double-bill of Thomas Mann's works at the Budapest Theatre in the Round. *Fiorenza* is Mann's own play, while *Mario and the Magician* was adapted for the stage by the Polish Skuszanka and the Hungarian Károly Kazimir.

Theatre lovers at first had some qualms about meeting Thomas Mann on the stage.

In the stream of Mann's novels the youthful play *Fiorenza* is almost lost. And what can become of *Mario and the Magician* on the stage? Yet, the performance of the two plays resulted in a real encounter. Károly Kazimir's production of the two works—akin in spite of all their differences—succeeded in conveying to the audience the writer's painful realization of the collapse of his ideal—in the ruins of which a new and ruthless force was emerging which the man of elusive reveries was no longer able to stem. The production also suggested that only a new defiance, the "Marionesque attitude," could rescue the threatened values.

Fiorenza, a play aglow with the rich colours of the quattrocento, introduced the evening. Its air is not permeated with the gentle breeze of northern harbours, no "dull and milky fog" descends on the town—and yet the environment of the play is familiar to those who have read *Tonio Kröger*, which Thomas Mann had finished a few months before he wrote the first lines of *Fiorenza*. The same enchanting mood that quivers around Tonio Kröger's figure embraces Lorenzo de Medici, the other great representative of Thomas Mann's ideal of beauty. The production enhances this mood by giving expression to Thomas Mann's attitude: his devotion to this ideal of beauty and, at the same time, his awareness of its inevitable destruction. Lorenzo and Savonarola are presented as antagonists worthy of each other. The audience is made to feel that Lorenzo, at death's door, rising against his great opponent striving for power, is aware of the failure of his own ideal as well as of the danger involved in Savonarola's appearance, yet he cannot prevent the latter from raising high the torch of destruction.

The ominous atmosphere introduced by Savonarola's appearance had settled heavily on the stage when the second play, *Mario and the Magician*, started. The dramatized form exposed Cipolla more rapidly than in the original story, but after that everything followed in the footsteps of the original. Director and actors guided us along the path carved in our memory and letting us participate in the demon's birth and fall.

The performance was both beautiful and significant. Kazimir, the director, seated the actors playing the audience to be enchanted by Cipolla around the circular stage. This was a bold venture, because Cipolla had to subdue not only the audience in the play but also the genuine theatre audience. Unless he cast a spell upon both audiences, his acting would not serve its purpose. Zoltán Latinovits succeeded in holding everybody spellbound. His Cipolla was formidable, compelling and demoniac; at the same time he could be airily playful. Moving in dance steps and cracking his whip, he could kindle the fire underneath the globe.

The other significant piece of acting was that of Rudolf Somogyvári as Lorenzo de Medici. Masculine even in his feebleness, he was the very Medici Thomas Mann must have seen in his nostalgic dreams. The sorrow of the cathedral-builders glowed throughout his performance—the sorrow of those who know that soon everything they have created is bound to collapse, because they are unaware of the means by which these treasures could be saved from destruction.

IVÁN SÁNDOR

FROM OUR NEXT NUMBERS

(Continued from p. 178)

ECONOMIC LIFE

GETTING ACQUAINTED WITH ACQUAINTANCES

Exchange of Ideas Between Hungarian and Austrian Economic Experts

The growing participation of Hungarian scientists and research workers in the international exchange of experiences and ideas with the countries of the West is both a sign of, and a factor in, the improved international atmosphere.

Contacts with Austria have of late become particularly lively as a natural result of geographical and historical circumstances. Normalization of inter-state relations, expansion of trade and rapid growth of tourist traffic in both directions have been followed by an intensification of scientific and cultural contacts between the two countries.

It is particularly encouraging that these steadily broadening relations now also extend to the social and historical sciences. In a certain sense, this may indeed be considered a standard by which to measure the improvement in good neighbourly relations. Experience teaches us that economic ties (no matter how limited), exchanges of thought in the field of the natural sciences, and perhaps even a mutual interest in each other's literary and artistic achievements tend to persist even in a period of otherwise cool or strained relations between two countries (not to mention the wholesome effects of football matches and other sporting events). In the sphere of social and historical sciences, on the other hand, contacts are rarely established—even at a time of *rapprochement*—before the atmosphere has reached a certain warmth. The reason for this may be that in these domains the greatest number of controversial issues between the different social systems is likely to arise. Between the representatives of different social systems, a discussion of socio-historical subjects may easily deteriorate into an ideological controversy. This inevitably involves the risk that objectivity and scientific reasoning will give way to passion and impulse, and the exchange of scientific ideas degenerate into a "theological" dispute.

With this in mind, it is a favourable symptom that neighbourly relations between Hungary and Austria now seem to have reached the stage of friendly dialogue in the sphere of social and historical sciences as well. It is evidence of the development of an atmosphere free of prejudice, in which a sincere wish for mutual understanding and an exchange of ideas based on facts rather than opinions will render cooperation fruitful in this field too.

An example of cooperation of this type was provided by the International Congress of Historians which was held in Budapest in May 1964 under the auspices of the Hungarian Academy of Sciences and was attended—among research workers from several countries—also by Austrial historians.[1] A similar spirit of objectivity was evident at two other conferences—this time

[1] For details see Zoltán Horváth, "Afterthoughts on the Hapsburg Monarchy". *The New Hungarian Quarterly*, Vol. 5, No. 16, pp. 171–174.

13

on economic subjects—organized last winter by Austrian institutions. The writer of the present article had the honour of participating in both meetings and of delivering a lecture at each of them on various questions of Hungarian economic life.

The first of these was a two-day conference held in Linz on October 15 and 16, 1964, under the joint auspices of the *Gesellschaft für Ost- und Südostkunde*, Linz, and the *Österreichisches Ost- und Südosteurope-Institut*, Vienna. In addition to the Austrian delegates and audience it was attended by guests from Poland, Rumania, the U.S.A., the U.S.S.R., West-Germany and Hungary. Under the chairmanship of Professor Rudolf Jagoditsch of Vienna University and the competent management of Dr. Georg Dox, director of the *Gesellschaft für Ost- und Südostkunde*, the conference heard two lectures and a number of reports which became the subjects of discussion.

Mr. L. Martinides, editor of the periodical *Internationale Wirtschaft*, gave a survey in his lecture of the present-day economic situation in the socialist countries and in Austria, as well as of the prospects of their economic development, from the point of view of increasing economic cooperation between these countries. With complete objectivity and basing himself on a wealth of carefully prepared data, he pointed out that economic progress in Hungary and in other socialist countries had now reached a new phase, characterized by the emergence of a varied and discriminating demand. Investments concomitant with dynamic growth and with the modernization of the economic structure afforded numerous opportunities for furthering economic relations.

In his thoroughgoing analysis Mr. Martinides showed why it was both necessary and advantageous for Austria to expand her trade with the socialist countries. Among possibilities of economic cooperation Mr. Martinides pointed to joint ventures in third markets and mentioned the participation of Hungary and Austria in a project of this

type, involving the joint delivery of power stations to India and Lebanon by the Komplex Company of Budapest and the Austrian Simmering-Graz-Paucker Works.

It was only at the conference that I made the acquaintance of Mr. Martinides; there was thus no prior agreement between the two of us concerning the subject of our respective lectures. Yet it was probably for this very reason that our lectures fitted so well together in structure and that each served as a complement to the other as if there had been some previous understanding between us.

In my lecture on "The Market in Hungary" I dealt primarily with market elements in Hungarian economic life. As a matter of fact, the current practice of labelling the two great economic systems of the era as "market economy" and "planned economy" is an over-simplification of these concepts to the point where the two terms no longer serve as exact definitions. At present, the "free market economies" of Western countries are already characterized by attempts at economic planning, while socialist planned economy cannot simply be regarded as a marketless system. Consumption—which in 1963 was valued at some 70 per cent of Hungary's national income—depends entirely on the market. Foreign trade, which plays such an important role in Hungarian economic life, is to a considerable extent carried on with capitalist countries. The volume of Hungary's total external trade (exports plus imports) is equivalent to two-thirds of the national income, and nearly one-third of it is dependent on capitalist markets.

Although the market plays a different role in the Hungarian planned economy from what it does in the capitalist countries, the free choice of the consumer asserts itself in the Hungarian market in the same manner as under capitalist conditions. Here too the consumer's principal means of influencing the market is his money, which he is free to spend wherever, whenever and however he wishes—or to save if he so choses. It is the consumer's money for which in the Hungarian market of today the commercial and servicing enterprises as well as the travel agencies and savings-bank branches compete.

All this is a consequence of the process of broadening and differentiation that has been evident in the Hungarian market in recent years as a result of economic development. Reality thus greatly differs from the picture which, based as it is on the more difficult and contradictory pre-1956 phase in the development of the Hungarian economy, may still survive in the imagination of most Western newspaper readers. No socialist economist would suppose that present-day capitalism was the same as the social and economic order described in the novels of Charles Dickens. Nor does the Hungarian society of the sixties show any similarity to what George Orwell in his *1984* presented as socialism.

In the debate which followed the two lectures and the reports, several Polish and West-German guests—in addition to the Austrian economists and experts—took the floor. Conversations naturally were also carried on throughout the social gatherings that accompanied the conference. The talks touched on many aspects of Hungarian economic life, from market-research methods through the price system to the supply of commodities. This also goes to show that the analytical objectivity which had marked the proceedings of the conference found a response in those present, and that theoretical economists and men of practice alike are able to carry on fruitful discussions even if they happen to repesent different or opposite views.

                              *

At the second conference held in Vienna on February 25, 1965, under the auspices of the *Donaueuropäisches Institut*, the writer had the opportunity of speaking to an audience composed of Austrian specialists on the subject of the discussions now taking place in Hungary regarding the system of economic planning and management as well as on the background and trend of the changes now taking place.

The conference, under the chairmanship of Dr. Dollberg, director of the institute, revealed considerable interest on the part of Austrian economic and financial experts in the economic system of Hungary and its management methods. Interest in the "neighbour's affairs" is proving stronger than the comprehensible hesitations caused by confrontation with a different economic system and its unfamiliar concepts.

In my lecture I endeavoured to give a survey of the economic development determining the present economic situation. The Hungarian economy is at present in a phase which Professor József Bognár describes as intensive growth type. This phase calls for enlarged productivity and greater economic efficiency. Consumption has reached a high level and increased in variety; the degree of participation in the international division of labour is also increasing. The economy is now more complex, is more liable to change and requires more elastic methods of administration. Accordingly, the purpose of the debates on and experiments in planning now going on in Hungary is to render economic administration (primarily on the level of the management of firms) more capable of quickly reacting to market impulses and utilizing the existing opportunities for raising productivity. All this goes with an increased independence and scope for manoeuvre for the individual firm.

Though comparisons are odious, I nevertheless ventured to illustrate the background of the changes through an analogy taken from the history of the capitalist economic system.

In the course of the 19th century the organization of capitalist enterprises reached a stage where actual management tended to become separated from ownership, and the role of the paid employee acting as manager steadily grew. The owners themselves became increasingly incapable of personally coping with the ever more intricate technical and market problems requiring daily decisions.

At present, an interesting process is taking place in Hungarian economic life: there is no longer any reason for the State to manage its enterprises directly as it did when the foundations of planned economy were being laid. With the growing scope and complexity of economic life, more and more decisions will be left to the firms themselves, while the State, through the instruments of economic policy at its disposal, will ensure that the decisions taken by the individual firm are in harmony with the interests of society as a whole, expressed in its economic aspects by the national economic plan.

The representatives of Austrian economic and financial life who constituted the major part of the audience advanced a number of questions concerning the structure of the Hungarian economy and the methods of economic planning and management. A lively debate arose also on various questions of principle. All this goes to show that the more liberal possibilities of contact have thrown open the door to an objective knowledge of one another's affairs. The years of isolation gave rise to many opinions and assumptions regarding the socialist economic system; their refutation will not only serve the interests of science but also encourage an intensification of practical economic contacts.

The main lesson to be drawn from the conference may be summed up in two statements. The first is that even in the neighbouring country of Austria the ideas held by many a financial and economic expert on the actual economic situation of Hungary and on her economic system correspond to a state of affairs existing ten years ago. And for this we are to a certain extent responsible ourselves. Because (and this is the second statement) the realism of Austrian scientific and economic experts and their desire for objectivity are stronger than the aversion and obsolete views formed during the years of isolation. Scientific curiosity and readiness to learn are proving stronger than adherence to preconceived ideas. The promotion of tourism, the acquisition of factual information, the widening of scientific contacts will all play their part in making our neighbours—and other foreign countries as well—familiar with the Hungary of the sixties, as contrasted with a situation that no longer exists.

EGON KEMENES

REGIONAL PLANNING

THE SYSTEM AND PRINCIPAL TASKS OF REGIONAL ECONOMIC PLANNING IN HUNGARY*

With an area of 93,000 square kilometres Hungary is a very small country; indeed, it occupies only the sixteenth place in Europe as regards size. Its population on the other hand is somewhat over 10 million, making it one of the more densely populated countries of the Continent (approximately 110 heads per square kilometre).

The country has remarkably varied natural endowments which, however, are concentrated in well-defined regions. All of its mineral wealth (coal, oil, bauxite, manganese ore, industrial minerals, etc.) is to be found in the region of the Hungarian Central Highland Belt and the environs of the Mecsek range, while the Great Plain and the Small Plain offer the most favourable climatic conditions and soil for farming (Central and Northwestern Hungary). Owing partly to the territorial differentiation of natural conditions, partly to the dissimilar economic character of various regions of the country, productive forces in Hungary are very unevenly distributed.

Before the liberation in 1945 over 80 per cent of industry was situated in Budapest,

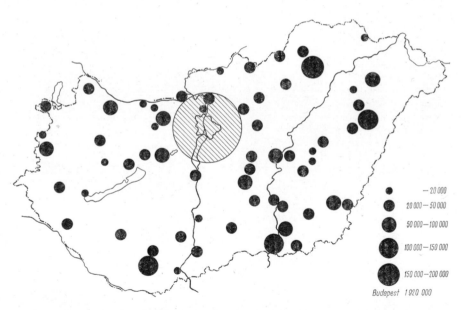

- —20 000
- 20 000 — 50 000
- 50 000 — 100 000
- 100 000 — 150 000
- 150 000 — 200 000

Budapest 1 920 000

The present urban network of Hungary
(Size of black disks indicates size of population)

* The term "regional economic planning" should not be confused with "regional planning" which, in Hungarian, corresponds to "physical planning," the term applied in western countries to the planned regulation of building and of land utilization. The present paper is intended to give a survey of the points raised by regional economic planning.

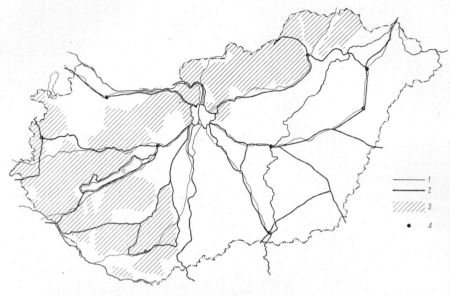

Hungary's rail and highway network

1. Principal highways   3. Hilly regions
2. Principal railroads   4. Main traffic junctions

the Transdanubian Hills, the Mecsek range in Southern Hungary, and the area of the Small Plain bordering Czechoslovakia (60 per cent of industry was concentrated in Budapest and its outskirts). At the same time the vast expanses of the Great Plain and of Transdanubia (Western Hungary), which include over half of the country's population, were almost exclusively devoted to agriculture. The inability of the densely populated agrarian districts to give satisfactory employment to the great majority of the population led to grave political, social and economic consequences. Regional economic problems were aggravated by the centralized, radial lines of communication (every main railway line starting from Budapest) and lack of transversal lines, by the backwardness and uneven location of the towns and by the system of widely scattered villages and homesteads. According to the national census of 1938, 13 per cent of the population lived on isolated homesteads;

at the time of the 1960 census the figure was 8 per cent.*

For these reasons regional economic development became an acute problem in Hungary already before the Second World War, but no comprehensive plans were devised for its solution.

It was not until after the end of the war that this unfortunate heritage could be tackled. Besides the conditions above described, economic planning with its large-scale construction projects and the consequent change in the regional division of labour directed the attention of planners and research workers towards regional economic development.

* The *tanya* system of homesteads is a special Hungarian form of agricultural settlement, evolved several centuries ago. After the Turkish occupation a part of the population massed in the towns and big villages went to live in the surrounding agricultural districts and brought into existence their peculiar system of scattered homesteads. For an account of the *tanya* system, see *The New Hungarian Quarterly*, Vol. III, No. 8, pp. 61–81.

The System of Regional Economic Planning

Many a debate took place in the past as to whether regional economic planning was at all necessary in Hungary in view of the country's small size and whether it was expedient to devise such plans for the whole country or only for those areas labouring under the gravest economic problems. Without attempting to answer these and numerous other questions that were debated, let us proceed to a presentation of the developed system of planning as it functions at present.

The aim of regional economic planning is a rational siting of industry, agriculture, communications, commerce and other branches, a planned, proportional (*i.e.*, economically balanced) advance in every part of the country to achieve a maximum increase of the population's material welfare and cultural standards.

Regional economic plans are drawn up parallel and closely interwoven with planning by branches of the economy. Regional planning is consequently not confined to marking out for every region the tasks and objectives laid down in the national plan and in the branch projects; its principal aim is to set up the most expedient regional structure on a country-wide basis and with due regard to the targets of the various branches.

Regional planning involves the following chief tasks:

Prior to formulating ideas as to siting and regional development the first stage of planning involves an analysis of natural-geographic (raw material sources, climate, soil, water supply, etc.), demographic and economic conditions in different regions, revealing prevailing disproportions in the distribution of productive forces, deficiencies in the regional division of labour, etc. The conclusions drawn from this analysis are taken into consideration in setting up the targets for future development.

To insure regional coordination and maxi-

mum economic efficiency, location plans are drawn up on the basis of the new projects previously decided on in the plans for the development of industry, farming, transport and communications, as well as of the planned enlargement of existing projects. *

In devising proposals for resettlement and regional development planners strive to secure a gradual elimination of incongruities that have come down to us from earlier periods.

Commercial undertakings and warehouses, the construction of apartment houses and public buildings, hygienic, educational and cultural institutions are planned to correspond in various regions and districts of the country with the development of production and communications as well as with the anticipated territorial distribution of the population (sources of manpower). This is an exceedingly intricate process, demanding a vast number of calculations.

All these tasks are solved not at one stroke but in several stages.

It is a special task of regional planning, closely connected with the above requirements, to plan the complete network of sites as well as the development of important individual sites with due regard to the need that they should function economically, provide favourable living and working conditions for the population, and utilize available means to the best advantage.

The units of regional planning are the economic districts formed by regional division of labour within the country. From the aspect of economic development these economic districts are interlinked units which are formed for the given period of planning (five to ten years) after scientific

---

* Since—as is well known—the bulk of industry and of transport is owned by the Hungarian State, since in farming the socialist sector is predominant and since investments are centrally allocated, there are favourable preconditions for a rational regional deployment of productive forces.

analysis of the position and state of development of regional economic correlations, particularly of regional specialization and complex development.

Despite research work and debates carried on over several years, we still lack a clear and generally acceptable delimitation of economic districts. The government has therefore divided the country into six districts, set up by a suitable grouping of the 19 administrative territorial units (counties). Owing to their hypothetical character, these districts are referred to as "planning districts."

Two main types of regional economic plan are distinguished in Hungary:

regional planning by branches (siting);

regional planning of complex development.

The former provides for proportional and economical locating of economic branches (in various fields within industry) and their regional development. They furthermore deal with the location of new factories (paying special attention to the site requirements of various branches of industry and of individual factories and to the divergent industrial conditions in various parts of the country), and with the estimates and other important indices of industrial and agricultural production per planning district (and, within it, per county).

Regional planning of complex development provides for coordinating the development of the various branches with one another and with local conditions; for rational production-and-supply connections between the planning districts; for furthering unpaid voluntary labour; for planned development of communications and of the network of sites. The regional plans for complex development are elaborated for each planning district and, within it, for each county and important site.

In elaborating regional economic plans numerous regional balance sheets are prepared relating to manpower, water supply, energy, production and utilization of important industrial and agricultural goods, building requirements and capacity of the building trade, transport and delivery. These and other regional balance sheets play a highly important role in the regional adjustment of production to consumption, or sources of manpower to available working places, as a foundation for realizing national aims.

The two types of planning are closely related. The elaboration of plans for the regional siting of branches is closely connected with the complex development of planning districts; on the one hand, the profile of a district (as determined by its natural conditions), its economic structure, the size of its population, etc., have to be taken into consideration in drawing up projects for the siting of branches; on the other hand, complex development projects depend on the targets set up in the various regional plans for the location of branches.

In the past few years several alternate projects have been drafted both as regards regional economic plans and branch plans, so that the most desirable variant from the economic viewpoint may be selected.

Regional economic plans are drawn up for long terms (15 to 20 years) and short terms (3 to 5 years).

Planning is controlled by the National Planning Office, which, with the government's authorization, fixes the order, method and deadlines of regional planning, and the initial planning data and concepts; it undertakes the indispensable analyses, calculations and studies; finally it organizes and directs the planning on the part of ministries, county planning organs, etc., and submits the proposed regional economic plans to the government for approval as part of the national economic plan.

The research work connected with regional planning and development is directed by a committee* organized by the Hungarian Academy of Sciences on the basis of

* The Presidential Committee for the Coordination of Regional Research.

a five-year research plan. During the past five years this work has yielded important results in the following spheres:

Hungary's physical and economic geography by regions has been mapped;

mathematical methods and models have been devised for research relating to industrial and agricultural siting;

useful studies have been made on regional specialization and rational dimensions of large-scale farming;

model variants of the network of sites have been prepared, representing a hypothetical development of towns and villages;

ideas have been formulated for the better management of water supplies and the improvement of transport facilities.

Principal Tasks of Regional Economic Planning

The main task of regional economic planning is the gradual liquidation of the imbalance in the regional distribution of industry and of the adverse consequences flowing from this situation.

One of the most difficult economic problems is how to reduce the excessive concentration of industry in Budapest. Long-term plans envisage a decrease of the capital's share in total factory employment from the present 43 per cent to 28 per cent. This means that there is to be scarcely any absolute increase in the number of industrial wage-earnes in Budapest. To achieve this the following steps are envisaged:

Regional plans are to avoid the creation of new industrial plants within the area of the capital, save in exceptional cases when they are necessary to complete existing industry or to improve the supply of goods and services for the inhabitants.

In developing existing factories preference is to be given to technical advances that do not call for any increase of working force. Meantime, Budapest factories have been divided into categories as regards suitability for improvement. Factories which

The industries of Budapest and vicinity

can be developed further at their present site are placed in the first category. Those which can carry on with their present capacity at their present site, but whose production cannot be expanded by the construction of new buildings, are in the second category. The third category comprises those factories, about 100 in number, which are to be removed to the provinces or gradually scaled down. *

To curb further industrialization of the capital and, at the same time, promote industrialization of several rural districts, it is planned to limit the number of the city's industrial wage-earners and to give the factories and their working staffs re-

---

* Shifting of factories to the provinces has been going on ever since 1958, chiefly into the industrially less advanced parts of the country. Workers from factories that are being closed down are in any case assured of transfer to Budapest plants undergoing enlargement.

moved to the provinces a financial stake in their factory, etc.

Owing to the excessive concentration of industry—notably of the processing industry—in the capital, and particularly since the adoption of restrictive measures against further industrial development within the city limits, factories have been established at a rapid rate inside a 25 to 30 kilometres belt in the precincts. Prohibitive measures have therefore been extended by the government to this area too.

It is an important task of regional economic planning in Hungary to draft schemes for the industrialization of densely populated but industrially backward or poorly developed areas in the Great Plain and in Transdanubia with large manpower reserves. Formerly planning was confined to the rational selection of sites for new industrial works. Today we know that optimal siting of industrial plants can be realized only within the framework of regional economic planning which gives due consideration to all the consequences of the new location and to changes of the infrastructure.

What are the concrete factors to be taken into account in connection with the industrialization of poorly developed areas?

First of all the prevailing conditions and characteristics of various parts of the country have to be considered. Mineral resources (coal, oil, natural gas, bauxite),

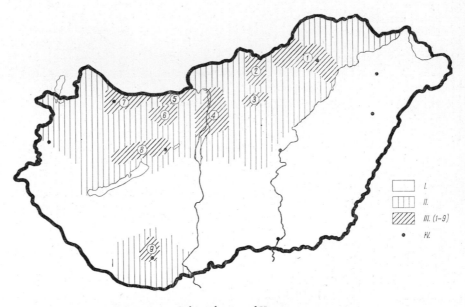

Industrial regions of Hungary

I. Industrially underdeveloped or undeveloped regions
II. Industrially developed regions
III. Principal industrial areas
IV. Other industrial centers

1. Borsod industrial area
2. Salgótarján industrial area
3. Gyöngyös industrial area
4. Budapest industrial area
5. Dorog–Tokod industrial area
6. Tatabánya–Oroszlány industrial area
7. Győr–Komárom industrial area
8. Székesfehérvár–Várpalota–Veszprém industrial area
9. Pécs–Komló industrial area

the geographical situation, water supplies, demographic factors, settlement conditions, natural and economic circumstances of farming, transport bases and network, questions of employment, and, last but not least, the geographical position of local industry are of decisive importance in the selection of sites for new factories.

The question of whether rural industrialization should follow a more centralized or a more decentralized pattern has aroused considerable controversy. Calculations show that concentrated siting is advantageous for the industrial branches concerned; on the other hand, in several cases it has had an unfavourable effect on the rational development of the provincial areas as a whole.

Hungarian planners have come to the conclusion that the industrialization of backward districts cannot be accomplished without creating large industrial centres and founding major concerns. From the aspect of national economy it is, at the same time, advantageous to establish rationally scattered minor factories in places where manpower is readily available.

In Hungary the development of areas engaged in one-sided production of raw materials for heavy industry constitutes a special problem. In order to reduce transport costs and improve openings for female employment, the industrial structure of these areas must inevitably be changed. A typical example is provided by the industrial district of Borsod, where the branches producing basic raw materials account for 90 per cent of total production. Whereas the country-wide average of female employment is 40 per cent, in Borsod the figure amounts only to 18 to 20 per cent, owing to the excessive preponderance of heavy industry. The employment of women has therefore become a serious problem in this district.

Another task awaiting solution by regional economic planning is the reconstruction of the transport network with its rapidly increasing demand for conveyance of goods and passengers. The first requirement here is an alteration of the geometrical pattern of railways and highroads to render them more serviceable. * The development and reconstruction of the railway and road network, of repair and filling stations at busy junctions, and of the water-ways and ports of the Danube and Tisza will lead towards a rational solution of specific transport problems.

Particular attention is being devoted to the improvement of suburban communications. Thousands of people now travel daily or periodically between their homes and their jobs. To bring working places and homes nearer to each other is another task of regional development in the future. But for some time to come several hundred thousand workers will continue to travel daily to and from their jobs.

It is therefore of utmost importance to improve suburban communications, especially in the outskirts of Budapest.

The undeveloped state of Hungary's network of settlements, their irrational distribution and out-of-date conditions are a further problem faced by regional planning.

Budapest is a city of nearly two million inhabitants, a figure which rises to over 2.2 million in the day-time. Hungary has no other city of comparable size, the four largest towns after Budapest being Miskolc (164,000), Debrecen (142,000), Pécs (131,000) and Szeged (111,000), which together have fewer than 600,000 inhabitants. There are, in addition, 57 towns and over 3,200 villages. It will take a long time to change the structure of this network of settlements. All regional economic planning has the common objective of insuring that the transformation should be carried out in accordance with a well-considered strategy, based on certain fundamental concepts. The ideas thus far advanced may be outlined as follows:

* It requires a long time to rennconstruct a radially centred communications system.

It is expedient to confine the further development of Budapest within definite limits, mostly through concentrating on programmes for the economic development of the provinces. Even so an increase of the capital's population to 2.3 million cannot be avoided in the long run.

To counterbalance the dominant role of the capital it is intended to hasten the development of the above-mentioned four provincial towns, so that by 1980 they will have from 200,000 to 300,000 inhabitants each.

It has also been suggested that, following the examples of London, Paris, Moscow and other metropolises, six to eight so-called satellite towns should be created around the capital, within a belt of 25 to 30 miles. The decisive difference—apart from size—is that in England, France and the Soviet Union the capital is not the only large city, such as is the case with Hungary. Though the creation of satellite towns in 35 to 40 years cannot be ruled out, in the next 20 years it is the counter-balancing towns that are to be primarily developed.

The rapid socio-economic transformation taking place in Hungary has led to accelerated urbanization. At present the towns account for 45 per cent of the total population. In another fifteen years this figure is expected to increase to from 55 to 56 per cent, calculated for the same number of settlements.

Modernization and further development of the villages is a no less complicated matter. As a long-term solution it has been suggested that Hungary should concentrate on the development of about 1,000 villages as the most economical measure and allow the remaining 2,200 villages to shrink gradually and planfully. *

A related exceedingly complicated social, economic and technical problem is that of gradually transforming and ultimately eliminating the system of isolated homesteads (*tanya*). Calculations show that it will take from 20 to 25 years for the greater part of the homestead population to migrate to towns and for the smaller part to settle in existing villages. In addition, new villages will have to be founded.

An optimal network of villages will emerge in close correlation with the planned large-scale farming units. Although planners are fully aware of the tremendous obstacles to the emergence of a new, modern network of towns and villages throughout the country, its realization cannot be abandoned or left to chance.

Regional economic planning is thus a many-sided task, requiring both scientific and practical efforts. The complex nature of planning calls for close cooperation between central and local organizations, between scientific and planning institutes. Experience to date in Hungary and study of the methods applied in other countries have greatly enriched our still far from perfect planning practice with many new ideas.

JÓZSEF KÓRÓDI

* This would mean that apartment houses, primary and—especially—secondary schools, hygienic and other institutions should be built first of all in these 1,000 villages enjoying the most favourable conditions. Investments could thus be made to the best advantage and at reduced maintenance costs, while the living standard could be raised, at the same time, to a high level in every part of the country.

NEW TOWNS IN SCOTLAND

New towns are dear to the British town planner's heart. He has an opportunity to start from scratch, to put into practice his ideas, from socio-economic experiments to avant-garde architecture—and to do it all uncluttered by the traditions and sins of the past and with a population half the average age of a normal town. In short, this is his chance to make his dream a reality within his own lifetime.

In fact, it is not as simple as all that. New towns are inhabited by real-life people not all of whom are naturally adventurous. Their shape and character is influenced by the local authority in whose area they are situated; and not all councillors are adventurous by nature either. So most new towns are a compromise between the planner's dream and the timidity of 'locals'—although, it sometimes happens the other way round.

Scotland, the northern third of Great Britain, has four new towns in various stages of development. A fifth one is being planned by extending an existing town and there are suggestions for still more. Scottish new towns are somewhat different from English ones, just as the Scot prides himself on being different from the English, or Welsh, or Irish. For one thing, Scottish new towns, like Dunaújváros in Hungary, have generally started with an industrial base—a large new factory or coal-mine—which left its mark on the first housing developments. Like other new towns in Britain, Scottish ones have Development Corporations responsible for building and letting houses and offices, providing schools, shops, churches and hotels. But one of their major functions is to attract industry to expand that first industrial base. In this respect, new towns are no different from Scottish local authorities, virtually all of which are trying to attract expanding companies and enterprises from other parts of the country and from abroad, to stave off unemployment and to ensure industrial growth in their areas. New towns have the advantage of good housing, youthful populations and pleasant surroundings: that is why they play a major part in Government efforts to expand industry in Scotland with its comparatively narrow economic base.

Once a new town achieves a certain size, some of the functions of the Development Corporation are transferred to a newly-constituted town council: as it happened last year in the case of East Kilbride, oldest of Scotland's new towns. Self-government does not come automatically and the people of East Kilbride had to fight by presenting petition after petition to the Government. Now it not only has *its own council* but a civic committee—a group of leading individuals in the town who act as a "brain's trust" to the council. It also shot ahead of other, older towns in that it was the first to let older schoolchildren watch the proceedings and after the meetings question the Provost, engineering worker Mr John Gordon, about the issues discussed.

The population of East Kilbride, once a small village, has grown to over 40,000 in fifteen years. The majority of families have come from the great industrial metropolis of Glasgow, only 20 kilometres away: part of a massive drive to "overspill" 70,000 families in an effort to reduce congestion and replace entire slum districts by modern skyscraper blocks of flats and houses. But the Development Corporation is still there to carry on building at East Kilbride until the population reaches about 100,000. Then it may "wither away," leaving the town council in full control.

Development Corporations in Britain consist of a chairman and about half a dozen members (usually local notables), all part-time. In Scotland the chairmen have ranged from a Socialist firebrand of pre-war days to the former commander of British troops in

Palestine at the time of the troubles just after the war. One ex-chairman is now a Scottish Minister in the Labour Government.

Chairmen and members are appointed by the Secretary of State for Scotland, a Minister of Cabinet rank with extensive nominal powers which include education, legal matters, agriculture, forestry, fishing, roads, town planning, electricity power suplies, housing and local government among other things. If he is a strong man, with a high standing in his party, these powers are exercised with considerable force; if he is not, Scottish issues receive scant attention in the Parliament of Westminster.

But Development Corporations also have fair-size full time staffs headed by a general manager. It is he and the chief architect whose personalities are apt to leave their mark on the physical appearance and social character of new towns in their formative years. East Kilbride is no exception, though the first districts of the town show every sign of haste to provide homes for returning soldiers and newly-wed couples in the immediate post-war years of acute housing shortage. But more recent developments have attracted a great deal of attention from all over the world: the ultra-modern, starkly simple Roman Catholic church with its oblong red-brick tower dominating the landscape as much as the bright and airy secondary school with its broad mural in the entrance hall.

It might be assumed that the new surroundings have transformed the lives of former city slum dwellers; but this is not always so, for with all their squalor and agony, slums did breed a certain crude fellowship. So many people were in trouble so often—about food, jobs, money and frequently the police—that a strong bond developed which was broken with a move to new towns such as East Kilbride. Yet at no time is there more need for some kind of a bond than when a family moves into a street without a pavement and with the bull-dozers still in full cry, with on shops and schools within walking distance, only a dark, forbidding night and a few blinking street lamps to keep you company.

There will be many more streets like this in East Kilbride as the town grows full size; even its town centre is only one-third completed. But there already are plenty of parks and tree-lined avenues to please the eye; a sports stadium; and soon an olympic-size covered swimming pool will add to the attractions.

East Kilbride's original industrial base was the Rolls-Royce factory which makes aircraft engines and employs around 2,500 workers (including Provost Gordon). But there are now over 60 other factories of all types and sizes, making everything from cranes to cans. More people come to East Kilbride to work than are residents of the new town working elsewhere. It also houses the National Engineering Laboratory, one of the foremost institutes of engineering research and development in the world, with a staff of 700, including over 200 qualified scientists and technologists.

Glenrothes, in the County of Fife, was the second new town. It, too, has grown from a small village to a population of 17,000; and it has perhaps the closest resemblance to Dunaújváros in that it was planned to house miners working at what was then believed to be the richest and most modern coal mine in Scotland. But Rothes Colliery, which took 11 years to sink, soon ran into trouble, from geological faults to huge underground lakes; and after five years of frustrating existence it was finally abandoned in 1962.

This was a bitter blow to all Fife, a county of strong mining traditions and the scene of hard struggles between the coal owners and the miners in the years before nationalisation. (Abe Moffat, the well-known miners' leader and president of the Scottish Mineworkers' Union until two years ago, is a "Fiter"). It was a setback all the more because so many of Fife's pits have been closed in recent years as "uneconomic." But Glenrothes New Town has survived nevertheless, and while the majority of people earn their living in factories making anything from intricate electronic instruments, components and gadgets to mining machinery, the strong community spirit so characteristic of miners is very much in evidence. So is the sturdy independence for which Fifers are generally known.

Glenrothes, too, has a town centre, one-third completed. It has a glass roof and will one day become as fine a shopping centre as any in Scotland. The town also has an airstrip, the first of any new town in Britain to provide this kind of facility to busy industrialists. Moreover, it is only about 20 kilometers from the new Fort Road Bridge which is along one of the main arteries of road traffic between Scotland and the South. Before the bridge opened in September, 1964, the passage of goods and people had often been delayed by the ferry crossing the mile-wide tidal River Forth; the opening of the road bridge has removed one major obstacle to trade between Fife and the mass-population areas of England and Wales.

Cumbernauld is about the same distance from Glasgow to the east as East Kilbride is to the south-east. It, too, houses a large number of Glasgow families and has many of the social problems experienced in the oldest new town. But here resemblance stops: for while East Kilbride spreads over a wide area, Cumbernauld promises to be the most compact of all towns of its size (ultimate target 70,000 people) in the British Isles.

Cumbernauld when finished will only measure about $3^1/_2$ kilometers by $1^3/_4$ kilometers. It is the first town ever to be designed for the Car Age, with a garage to every house; yet it is a town where children can run around in safety, which can be crossed entirely along footpaths in 40 minutes from end to end, without ever meeting a motor vehicle; and which can only be approached

on wheels along the ring roads and access roads criss-crossing the town.

Its town centre will be perhaps the most spectacular one of all; a huge ten-storey block, with shops, cafés, restaurants, banks, offices occupying the first half-a-dozen floors and luxury flats the rest. There will be a bus station and huge car park at ground level, with moving escalators taking people to the upper floors flanked by galleries. The town centre will be at the bottom of a natural bowl on the slopes of which the new town is being built; a natural advantage rarely enjoyed by other towns. Cumbernauld only has 12,000 inhabitants at the moment but there are signs of a distinct character evolving; a freedom of movement which starts at the earliest childhood and an absence of fear from cars and buses. It has many industries, too, including one of the biggest factories making accounting machines in Scotland.

The fourth new town, Livingston, is at its early stages, with only a few houses built, but it promises to be equally if not more remarkable than the other new towns. Livingston, although destined to house many thousands of Glasgow "overspill" families, will be nearly 50 kilometers from the city and only about half that distance from Edinburgh, capital of Scotland. Livingston itself, with an eventual population of about 120,000, will be a "capital" of an area of 250 square kilometers, now disfigured by straggling mining villages, slagheaps of coal and shale and unkempt roads. It is all going to change in the next 15 to 20 years; and a master plan is being evolved to regenerate the whole area.

The coal mines and shale mines are worked out or deemed "uneconomic" and closed; new industries have not come fast enough to absorb all the workers, many of whom have had to leave the district in search of jobs. But Livingston, too, has its firm industrial base: the new British Motor Corporation factory at Bathgate, about eight kilometers from the planned town centre, which already employs nearly 5,000 workers making tractors and commercial vehicles. It is still in the expansion stage; many more jobs will also be provided by a new factory making motor components, but obviously Livingston will need even more to keep its big population fully employed.

It is going to be a town unique for another reason: a very large proportion of it will be factory-produced on the spot—erected at a rate of about six houses a week, with windows, doors, floors, roofs and other components manufactured indoors so that even the hardest winter cannot interfere.

The fifth new town is planned to be Irvine, in Ayrshire, about 40 kilometers south-west of Glasgow. Until a few years ago it was a sleepy market town with barely 15,000 inhabitants, with little industry and few prospects. But it had an energetic town council which, five years ago, set up an industrial estate that has by now grown to 15 factories covering a large range of industries. Irvine, too, has now many Glasgow families and is expecting even more; and in the autumn of 1964 it was scheduled to be developed as another new town, with a population of 55,000.

The surroundings of Irvine are among the pleasantest in Scotland: rolling countryside with prosperous farms, interspersed with towns, most of which (whith the exception of Kilmarnock) escaped the squalor and overcrowding of the industrial revolution. The sea is there, too, with the holiday resorts of Ayr and Troon within a few kilometers of Irvine. The future inhabitants of the New Town of Irvine will have a great deal to enjoy.

Scotland's new towns are too young —even East Kilbride—to have become a part of social history, although they undoubtedly will. Because by their very nature new towns develop fresh attitudes, climates and outlook that may eventually exert a powerful influence on the shape and direction of the future. We live in a fast-moving technological age: and all its features are displayed in a somewhat exaggerated fashion in these man-made communities, growing prematurely like an outsize child. Yet, like children, they also react more sharply to the winds of change and so become the socially most significant barometer we know to change itself.

ANDREW HARGRAVE

THREE HUMOROUS WRITINGS

(From the Hungarian Press and TV)

THE CURSE

Heaven has blessed me with a materialist philosophy of life, thank God, so I take no stock in miracles, charms, ghosts or other rubbish of that sort. Knowing this, you can imagine how reluctantly and after what inner torments I voice a realization that seems to conflict with my progressive point of view. But what can I do if there just happens to be a curse on the graduating class of Barcsay Street Grammar School? Yes, you heard me, there is a curse on class 8B, the graduating class my humble self was in, at Barcsay Street Grammar School in Budapest in 1928. I have no idea who laid this curse on our class, or when, or why; we were neither better nor worse than any other class.

Now take a fellow walking down the street and casually eyeing the people coming towards him. All sorts of people come along, men and women, young and old, ugly, beautiful, gorgeous. He glances at the passersby and sees that this girl, for example, is about twenty, that old boy must be well over seventy, this woman might be fifty, that one over there thirtyish. Every age has its own demeanour, its own gait, its own expression. But what do I find when I occasionally meet somebody or other from class 8B? That they seem to be at least twenty years older than they really are. I've been noticing this for a long time. What I mean is, everybody else looks the age he must be, but those who were in that particular class 8B have gone completely to pot.

It must have been a few weeks ago that I ran into Soponyai in Rákóczi Street. At first I simply refused to believe it was he. No, I said to myself, this can't be Soponyai, Soponyai was in my class in 8B, so he can't be any older than me; this is probably Soponyai's oldest brother or his father, which would explain the strong resemblance. And what do you know, it was Soponyai! My God! That corpulent, gray-whiskered, bald-headed, dilapidated figure—fantastic!—was Soponyai! We looked at each other, we stopped short for a moment, and then without a word we passed each other by. The reason I didn't speak to him was because I would only have stammered with dismay at the sight of him. Why he didn't speak to me, I have no idea. But among others I also met Rudi Speck not long ago. Heavens, what that man had turned into! Snow-white hair, one foot dragging behind him—the curse had got him too, poor devil.

I won't go on listing them; believe me, it hurts too much. It stabs a man in the heart, so help me, to see that everybody looks his proper age and only 8B has gone to pot before its time. Bercsényi was standing next to me in the bus the other day. Swollen bags under the eyes, the skin gray and slack, a double chin dangling—8B. Who was the filthy viper that laid the curse on our class? Why did he do it? I don't know. We were neither better nor worse than any other. When I got off the bus I looked at myself in the glass of a display window. Curious, the curse had not fallen on me.

I think I must have been absent on that particular day. I was lucky. *(From: Népszabadság, June 1965).*

László Tabi

ON NEW YEAR'S EVE

I'm supposed to wish you a happy new year. But what for? I've wished so often, this and that... And people have wished me this and that... And what was the result? I don't say we aren't happy, but somehow it isn't the real thing... Because happiness in itself doesn't make you happy. When other peoples are happy, they're happy. In Hungary nothing is that simple. Lately I've been asking one friend after another:

"How are you?"

"Fine. Just great. Happy. Only—I'm sort of fed up."

"What are you fed up about?"

"Ugh."

"Has anything changed?"

"No."

"Is anything going to become worse?"

"No. It's been made quite clear that nothing's going to change."

"Then why are you fed up?"

"Ugh."

What is this "ugh"? I decided to investigate. But first I sat down in a restaurant, and I was very glad I could sit down in a restaurant. There was a time when I couldn't sit down in a restaurant because I had no money. Then there was a time when I couldn't sit down in a restaurant because I did have money. Only there were no restaurants.

Now, however, I ordered stuffed goose as a first course. I was glad I could, because there was a time when I never would eat the goose that might lay the golden egg next day... which the day after that would have to be handed in...

Now, however, they duly brought me my meal. When it comes to eating you can really do yourself magnificently in this country. You couldn't before, but now ?!—I accidentally catch sight of a newspaper: "Hungarians' Diet Deadly. Results in Hardening of Arteries, Apoplexy, Thrombosis. . ." So this was just the meal I shouldn't have been eating. What should I have been eating? Cheese-curd.

What do you do in a case like that? Send back the goose and ask for cheese-curd? Don't be silly. No man would do that. You eat your way through the meal, only your mind is on apoplexy. And somehow this isn't the real thing.

After the meal I rummage in my pockets for my lighter. Now for a smoke, I think; our cigarettes have finally improved. They used to positively stink, but now ?!—I accidentally catch sight of a tabloid weekly: "Cigarettes Shorten Life."

What do you do now? Not light up? Don't be silly. No man would do that. You light up and smoke your cigarette to a butt, only your mind is on. . . And somehow it isn't the real thing.

In the afternoon I have a date. I sit in an expresso bar waiting for her, and I think what a joy it is to be a man in this country. It didn't use to be. Women used to ruin their looks in the belief that they would win equality with us if they became just as repulsive. But now? All of a sudden I catch sight of a tremendous article in the literary weekly: "We Must Vindicate Our Moral Principles Once and for All."

What do you do in a case like that? Walk out on your beloved and rush off to vindicate? Don't be silly. No man would do that. You kiss your beloved, but meanwhile you struggle with morals. And somehow it isn't the real thing.

In a little Buda tavern we sit down to supper in a wonderful mood, and a—a man approaches our table. . . a—what are they called?. . . Not a gipsy. . . Because when is a gipsy a gipsy? When he plays in a documentary. But when he plays in a tavern? Then he is a *folk musician*. . . I burst into song: "Broken is my violin. Cannot now be sounded. . ." when all of a sudden I am struck by something I read the other day: This is one of those trashy coffeehouse hits, decadent products of the declining feudal class. You mustn't sing this sort of thing, you must sing genuine folk songs such as "The gipsy boy is eating curd. . ." Curd again!

What do I do now? Carouse with. . . curd? You can't have much of a time with that. So I continue wailing "Broken is my violin" and think to myself what a rotter I am, what a feudal degenerate. . . And at this point the carousing somehow isn't the real thing.

And in general young people in this country are well off today—but at the same time there's this debate in the press constantly preying on their minds: Am I a hooligan or am I not a hooligan? And old people in this country today are well off—but the discussion in the magazines about the tainted generation keeps them in continuous anxiety: Am I or am I not tainted? And somehow this isn't the real thing.

And altogether we're living quite tolerably—but it isn't good form to say so or write it, because in this country lately one just doesn't enthuse or enjoy or appreciate. It's good form to criticize and expose and pick holes and view with alarm and shrug eloquently and lecture pedantically and agonize over right and wrong... We always find some way of making each other feel slightly fed up.

So I say: Wishing each other hapiness in the new year is not enough. It's no use at all. What we want is happiness without the "ugh"! In this spirit I join you in raising my glass!

But don't forget: Alcohol destroys, brutalizes, and reduces man to destitution! Cheers!

From the New Year's Eve Programme
of Hungarian TV.

JÁNOS KOMLÓS

FROM A JOURNALIST'S NOTEBOOK

Think twice before starting to think.

Most women have a great love of animals—sables, blue foxes, minxes.

The divorce suit had a happy ending. The grandmother was awarded the custody of the child.

Essential requirements for a good critic: a clear head and an obscure pen.

Argument is the best way to confirm people in their fallacies.

Mrs. X—an intelligent woman. Falls for no gossip; only passes it on.

He keeps his flag flying—to prevent your reading the device on it.

It wouldn't be a bad idea to be able to foresee the past.

Many a person will spend hours before the mirror studying his ideal of a human being.

He has the kind of mind that makes him think of four not as twice two but as the square root of sixteen.

Some people are proud when told that their views are changeable like the weather. They are the meteorologists.

People will believe anything said in a whisper.

X sees his doctor frequently because of the opportunity it gives him to talk about himself.

It's important to choose one's enemies with care.

It's not difficult to know ourselves well; it's only disagreeable.

Before I married my wife I had had three theories about the way to raise children. Now I have three children and no theory.

It's said to be a play with a present-day theme, and yet there isn't a single four-letter word in it.

When putting in a word for anyone, take a good look round to make sure he doesn't hear your.

The chap who is voted down is not always right.

There's something he is very puritanical about. He looks askance at the naked truth.

Wire-pulling won't get you anywhere—unless the wires reach high enough.

The words most difficult to pronounce in any language: "I was wrong."

He could tell you a great deal if only he would talk less.

Remarkable personality, X. Since 1945 he's had the same address, same job, same wife, and stuck to the same football club, same make of car, and same views.

The annoying thing about telephoning is that the wrong number is never engaged.

The boss knows nothing about anything, but knows everything better than you.

That young man knows his own mind perfectly well. He is well aware he is just a plain, common, run-of-the-mill genius.

The conference was a success. Each of us now sees perfectly well what the other fellow has to do.

Every girl ought to know all about housekeeping—in case she fails to net a husband.

Some people believe they have a clean conscience when all they have is a bad memory.

There are no new jokes, only old vices.

People would not get divorced for ridiculous reasons if they didn't get married on the same grounds.

The money is the same; only the pockets change.

The danger in our time is not in machines beginning to think, but in people beginning to think like machines.

It's true he'll stab you in the back whenever he gets a chance, but he says it's no pleasure to him, either.

Free time is the time spent at home, engaged in work one is not paid for.

It's not true that you can't make the modern girl blush. She just needs to be told when.

That fellow loves to boast. I prophesy a fine past for him.

He is a bigamist; he doesn't believe in divorce.

X has made a signal contribution toward a solution of the traffic problem: he has sold his car.

Motorist's mentality: It's better to be held up before a railway barrier for half an hour than endure the humiliation of being beaten by another car by half an inch.

It's dangerous to hanker after the past unless you're sure it can't return.

Boss, making bedside call in hospital: "To be frank, I believed you were just shamming. I'm glad to see you really *are* sick."

Luckily for him he has so many enemies they trip one another up in their urgency to get at him.

An opinion of one's own is always more dearly paid for than one that is shared.

Debtors sometimes hate their creditors more than the fellow who refused to grant them a loan.

The shortest way between two points is the straight one. It isn't always the easiest.

That young man has an inferiority complex: He believes he is no better than anyone else.

You never can tell when you will discover America. Columbus couldn't either.

(From various issues of Népszabadság)

JÓZSEF VETŐ

216

CORRESPONDENCE

April, 1965

Sir,

I consider that the range of topics covered, and the expert manner they are dealt with, are truly splendid. I have learnt much, not only about the life and literature of your country, but about many other subjects, from your magazine.

A. GODSELL
Bedminster
Bristol, England

May, 1965

Sir,

I have been receiving this excellent magazine for some time. I find it one of the most informative journals of contemporary literature, from any socialist country.

As you know, the government of India does not allow foreign exchange for the import of books and magazines from abroad, on account of the shortage of foreign credit of our country. Could you therefore send me a copy of *The New Hungarian Quarterly* as a gift to me in my capacity as Secretary General of the Afro-Asian Writers' Solidarity Committee.

MULK RAJ ANAND
Bombay, India

July, 1965

Sir,

May I say how much I appreciate the *Quarterly*, which is truly an international review with a Hungarian flavour. Last year we reprinted your article on Music and Modern Society and this was quoted in discussions at the Executive Committee of our Musicians' Union.

I hope to visit Hungary next year and hope to have the pleasure of calling on you.

ALFRED CORUM
Music and Life
London, England

July, 1965

Sir,

For your information I may tell you that I am myself a writer in Bengali and already I have translated two stories picked up from *The New Hungarian Quarterly*. These two stories have also been published in Bengali periodicals. I find your journal very interesting and thought-provoking containing as it does articles on different aspects of Hungarian life and letters.

GOPEL BHAUMIK
Calcutta, India

July, 1965

Sir,

I am in receipt of your letter regarding subscription arrears for the *Hungarian Quarterly*.

It is true that I asked my bank to discontinue my subscription and thought that this decision had been communicated to the Trading Company. I can only presume that this has not been done, in which case I must officially terminate the subscription. (I was surprised to get a new copy of the *Quarterly*.)

It is only fair to say that the termination of the *Quarterly* is in no sense due to any feeling of dissatisfaction with either the quality of the contents or the arrangements for receiving it. I must, in fact, compliment you on an excellent production and wish you every success. One cannot always afford to take all the magazine subscriptions one would like and I try to "ring the changes" from time to time.

I've taken *The New Hungarian Quarterly* since I spent my first holiday in Hungary—four years ago: I love your country and have very good friends there, so please don't imagine anything but L. s. d. would make me cancel the H. Q.

RACHEL MOORHOUSE
Keswick,
Cumberland, England

OUR CONTRIBUTORS

BOGNÁR, József (b. 1917). Economist, MP, Professor of Economics at Karl Marx University in Budapest, President of the Institute for Cultural Relations. Has held various high official posts since 1946, was Mayor of Budapest, Cabinet Minister, etc. In his work as an economist he has turned from problems of demand analysis to questions of general economic planning. His Planned Economy in Hungary has been published in English and four other languages. At present he is working on theoretical problems in the development of economically backward areas. He is a member of the Editorial Board of this review as well as a frequent contributor. See his Economic Planning in Ghana, Vol. III, No. 7; Science and its Application in Developing Countries, Vol. IV, No. 11; The Structure of Hungarian Economy, Vol. V, No. 14; Coexistence and the World Trade Conference, Vol. V, No. 16, of the N.H.Q.

CSIKÓS NAGY, Béla (b. 1915). Economist, D.C.L., President of the National Price Board. Has published numerous studies on price policy in Hungarian and foreign periodicals.

VARGA, Gyula (b. 1938). Agrarian economist, research worker at the Agrarian Research Institute of the Hungarian Academy of Sciences in Budapest. Has written a book in collaboration with fellow scientists on long-range production planning in agriculture and contributed to several publications in this field. See A Hungarian Cooperative Farm, in Vol. VI, No. 19, of the N.H.Q.

ILLYÉS, Gyula (b. 1902). Poet, writer, dramatist, essayist and translator, an outstanding personality in contemporary Hungarian letters. His Rácegres Notebook appeared in No. 1, Switch-Over in No. 5,

Ode to Bartók in No. 11, The Favourite, a historical tragedy, recently performed at the theatre Vieux-Colombier in Paris, in Nos. 12 and 13, of the N.H.Q.

DÉRY, Tibor (b. 1894). Novelist, an internationally known figure in contemporary Hungarian literature. His most important novels are the trilogy Befejezetlen mondat ("The Unfinished Sentence"), written between 1934 and 1938 but published only in 1945 (also German, Italian and American editions); the two-volume Felelet ("Answer," 1950 and 1952, also in German and Italian); G. A. úr X-ben ("Mr. G. A. in X," from which we published two chapters in Vol. IV, No. 10), also in French and German; and the recent A kiközösítő ("The Excommunicator"), written in 1964, from which we took the chapter printed here. He has also written plays and a number of short stories; the latter and his short novel Niki (1956) have been published in a dozen languages.

CHARAIRE, Georges (b. 1914). Writer; studied at the Sorbonne; was a friend of Valéry and Éluard; took an active part in the Resistance and after the war founded the Théâtre du Tertre of which he is the present manager. Works: La lettre sur la liberté; Le livre aux pages blanches; Daphné I, II; Les veines ouvertes; Aventure; Parallèles.

PERNECZKY, Géza (b. 1936). Critic and art historian. Studied music and art history in Budapest. See his Two Exhibitions, in Vol. IV, No. 12, and Béla Kondor, the Painter, in Vol. VI, No. 17, of the N.H.Q.

TAKÁCS, Imre (b. 1926). Poet; published three volumes of poems. At present devotes himself besides his poetry to fiction and essays.

SZABOLCSI, Bence (b. 1899). Musicologist, Professor of Music History at the Budapest Academy of Music, member of the Hungarian Academy of Sciences. He is a member of the editorial staff preparing the *Corpus Musicae Hungaricae* for publication, a series originally begun by Bartók and Kodály and now directed by Kodály. His most important works: *Mozart; A 17. század magyar főúri zenéje* ("Seventeenth Century Music of the Hungarian Nobility"); *Tinódi zenéje* ("Tinódi's Music," a critical edition of the songs of the Hungarian "Minnesänger"); *A melódia története* ("A History of Melody," also in German and English); *Liszt Ferenc estéje* ("The Twilight of Ferenc Liszt"); *A zene története* ("A History of Music"); *A magyar zenetörténet kézikönyve* ("A Handbook of the History of Hungarian Music," also in German); *A magyar zene századai* ("The Centuries of Hungarian Music"); *Beethoven*. He is a member of the Editorial Board of this review. His Previous contributions include: Liszt and Bartók, Vol. II, No. 1; Man and Nature in Bartók's World, Vol. II, No. 4; Zoltán Kodály's Youth, Vol. III, No. 8; Daybreak over Europe, Vol. IV, No. 10; Two Letters of Béla Bartók, Vol. IV, No. 11; Folk Music, Written Music and the History of Music, Vol. VI, No. 17, of the N.H.Q.

MARÓTI, Lajos (b. 1930). Physicist, poet and essayist, working at present as publisher's reader in the science department of Gondolat Publishing House in Budapest. Besides his poems he mainly devotes himself to the writing of essays and to translation (Yevtushenko). He has published two collections of poems and two volumes of essays. See his The Limits of Parnassus, in Vol. IV, No. 12, and A Panorama of Contemporary Ideas, in Vol. VI, No. 17, of the N.H.Q.

YOUNG, Percy Marshall (b. 1912). M. A., D. Mus. Musicologist and composer, educated at Selwyn College, Cambridge. One of his latest works was a monograph entitled Zoltán Kodály, a Hungarian Musician, Benn, London 1964, reviewed in Vol. VI, No. 17, of the N.H.Q. See also his Hungarian Music in England, Vol. IV, No. 10, of the N.H.Q.

KLINGER, András (b. 1930). Statistician, D.C.L., on the staff of the National Statistical Office in Budapest. Has published numerous studies on demography and statistics in Hungarian and foreign periodicals, attended several conferences in these fields in America, Asia and Africa.

MÁRKUS, László (b. 1920). Historian, research worker at the Hungarian Academy of Sciences, Institute for Historical Studies. Wrote monographs on Richard Guillon and on "The Hungarian Social Democratic Concept of History" and a number of essays on the Hungarian history of the inter-war period.

JEMNITZ, János (b. 1930). Historian specializing in the history of the international labour movement. Published a study, *Az 1926-os angol általános sztrájk előzményei* ("The Background of the 1926 General Strike in England"), and a number of articles in historical reviews. See also Keir Hardie in Hungary, Vol. IV, No. 10, ot the N.H.Q.

SZILÁGYI, György János (b. 1918). Archeologist, art historian, curator of the Greek-Roman collection at the Budapest Museum of Fine Arts. Specializes in the early history of the Greek and Roman arts and literature. Main publications: *Görög művészet* ("Greek Art"), 1954; *A görög művészet írott forrásai* ("Written Sources of Greek Art"), 1960; *A görög művészet világa* ("The World of Greek Art"), 1962. See also his The New Hungarian "Complete Homer," in Vol, II, No. 2, of the N.H.Q.

RADNÓT, Magda (b. 1911). M. D., Professor of ophthalmology at the Budapest

University of Medicine. Specializes in research on glaucoma and trachoma.

FÖLDES, Anna (b. 1928). Journalist and literary historian, at present on the staff of *Nők Lapja*, an illustrated weekly for women. Besides studies in literary history, she has published a book on the problems raised by low-standard popular literature. See also her Mr. G. A. in X., Tibor Déry's New Novel, in Vol. VI, No. 17, of the N.H.Q.

DEVECSERI, Gábor (b. 1917). Poet, essayist, dramatist, classical scholar. Has translated many Greek and Latin poets (including the complete Homer) as well as tragedies and comedies. Published his first volume of poems at the age of 15. Wrote his Ph.D. thesis in 1941 on Callimachos. His collected essays on classical poetry appeared in a volume entitled *Műhely és varázs* ("Workshop and Magic") in 1959. He has made important contributions to the theory of verse-translation; at present he is engaged in writing a book on Homer's Poetic Craft. Other works: ten volumes of poetry, several verse-plays, a travelogue on Greece. Also translated Shakespeare's *The Merry Wives of Windsor* as well as a number of English lyric poets.

HANKISS, Elemér (b. 1928). Literary historian. Worked for ten years at the National Széchényi Library's Department of Theatrical History, now heads the department of English and American literature at Európa Publishing House in Budapest. Has published several studies in various periodicals at home and abroad. See The Hamlet Experience, Vol. V, No. 13, of the N.H.Q.

HÁRS, Éva. Art historian specializing in modern Hungarian art. Heads the department of art and applied arts in the Janus Pannonius Museum in Pécs.

KOROKNAI, Zsuzsa. Journalist and critic on the staff of the Budapest literary and cultural weekly, *Élet és Irodalom*.

KECSKEMÉTI, István (b. 1920). Musicologist, research worker at the Music Division of the National Széchényi Library in Budapest. Studied piano and musicology at the Academy of Music in Budapest. Publications: *Süssmayr-Handschriften d.r Nationalbibliothek Széchényi in Budapest* (Mozart-Jahrbuch, 1959); *Beiträge zur Geschichte von Mozarts Requiem* (Studia Musicologica, 1961); *Unbekannte Eigenschrift der XVIII. Rhapsodie von Franz Liszt* (Studia Musicologica, 1962); "Debussy's Last Sonatas," in *Revue Belge de Musicologie*, 1962; ed.: Te Deum by J. J. Fux (1706) in Vol. 1 of the Critical Edition of J. J. Fux's Complete Works (Kassel, Graz, 1963).

SÁNDOR, Iván (b. 1930). Playwright and drama critic, on the staff of *Film, Színház, Muzsika*, an illustrated Budapest weekly for film, theatre and music. Has written several plays for the stage as well as for radio and television.

KEMENES, Egon (b. 1924). Economist, author of several essays on market research. At present with the African Institute of the Karl Marx University of Economics in Budapest. See his Comparison of National Income, in Vol. IV, No. 9; Experimental Micro-Economics in Vol. V, No. 14; The Firm as a Functional Model in the Planned Economy, 1: Economic Analysis, in Vol. VI, No. 18, of The N.H.Q.

KÓRÓDI, József (b. 1930). Economist, head of the department for the location of industrial plants in the National Planning Bureau, Budapest. Published several studies in the field of regional industrial and agricultural planning.

HARGRAVE, Andrew (b. 1912). Freelance journalist in Glasgow specializing in industrial questions.

TABI, László (b. 1910). Humorist and playwright, editor of the satirical Budapest weekly *Ludas Matyi*. For years has been writing a weekly column entitled *Pardon egy percre* ("Just a Moment Please") in *Népszabadság*, on the absurdities of everyday life. His plays and volumes of satirical sketches have also won him great popularity.

KOMLÓS, JÁNOS (b. 1922). Journalist and author, has published several volumes of humourous sketches and a collection of journalistic writings on various historical topics. Works on the staff of *Népszabadság*, the daily of the Hungarian Socialist Workers' Party. Jerome K. Jerome's Three Men on the Bummel and Kingsley Amis' Lucky Jim appeared in Hungarian in his translation. He writes a permanent satirical feature entitled "The Third Side of the Medal" for Hungarian TV.

VETŐ, József (b. 1910). Journalist, member of the Editorial Board of *Népszabadság*. For several years he worked as a sports journalist and published a number of books in this field. His *Sport in Hungary* was published in English by Corvina Press, Budapest.